API Testing and Development with Postman

A practical guide to creating, testing, and managing APIs for automated software testing

Dave Westerveld

BIRMINGHAM—MUMBAI

API Testing and Development with Postman

Associate Group Product Manager: Pavan Ramchandani
Publishing Product Manager: Bhavya Rao
Senior Editor: Sofi Rogers
Content Development Editor: Rakhi Patel
Technical Editor: Saurabh Kadave
Copy Editor: Safis Editing
Project Coordinator: Manthan Patel
Proofreader: Safis Editing
Indexer: Priyanka Dhadke
Production Designer: Aparna Bhagat

First published: April 2021

Production reference: 2020921

Published by Packt Publishing Ltd.
Livery Place
35 Livery Street
Birmingham
B3 2PB, UK.

ISBN 978-1-80056-920-1

www.packt.com

To my wonderful wife, Charlene, the one who always believes in me and celebrates my accomplishments. As a musician, you aren't always interested in "all that technical stuff," but you never doubt that I can do it and you make my life better with your unwavering love and loyalty.

– Dave Westerveld

Contributors

About the author

Dave Westerveld is a senior software test developer. He has worked for several years as a software tester and has been involved in numerous projects involving test automation. He is an API testing expert. He was part of a team that developed new APIs and worked on automation projects for API tests as well. He has published various well-received video courses. He is passionate about sharing his knowledge and expertise to help testers stay relevant in the changing world of software testing.

I wish to thank my wife, Charlene, for supporting me in this. You were excited for me to do this and never once complained about the time spent on it. I also want to thank my employer, D2L, for working with me to give me the time to write this book.

About the reviewer

Deepak Pathania is a full-stack developer based out of India, with a proven record of building scalable products and leading high-performing teams. He currently works as a senior software engineer at Gojek, where he spends his time building ad tech products for merchants. He is passionate about developer experience and frequently shares his learnings with the community by speaking at conferences. In his spare time, Deepak enjoys reading about start-ups, technology, and manga.

Table of Contents

3

OpenAPI and API Specifications

4

Considerations for Good API Test Automation

Section 2: Using Postman When Working with an Existing API

5

Understanding Authorization Options

6

Creating Test Validation Scripts

7

Data-Driven Testing

8
Running API Tests in CI with Newman

9
Monitoring APIs with Postman

10
Testing an Existing API

Section 3: Using Postman to Develop an API

11
Designing an API Specification

12
Creating and Using a Mock Server in Postman

13
Using Contract Testing to Verify an API

14

Design and Create an API

Other Books You May Enjoy

Index

Preface

Welcome! I think quality is an underrated characteristic of modern software. In some ways, we have made huge strides as an industry. The average modern web app probably has far fewer bugs than the average software application from 30 years ago. However, as the world of software becomes more and more complex, there are whole new areas that require a quality-first approach as regards design and development. I believe that APIs need this. APIs are becoming the backbone of the internet. They serve external clients for my companies and are increasingly becoming the glue that holds the different internal pieces of modern software systems together.

On the surface, this book is primarily about using the API testing tool Postman, and you will certainly have an in-depth knowledge of it by the end of the book. However, while explaining how to use Postman, I have also sought to provide principles that apply no matter what tool is used. I want you to have more than just the ability to manipulate the tool to do what you want it to. I also want you to be able to know when and how to use the tool so that you can be part of creating high-quality APIs.

Who this book is for

The first person I write for is myself. A lot of the stuff I talk about in this book is stuff I was learning myself a few years ago. API testing is a huge topic, and it can be intimidating to get started with, so I wrote this book primarily for those software testers who find themselves needing to test an API and not really knowing where to start. Throughout the book, I try not to assume too much in-depth programming knowledge, although an understanding of some of the most basic aspects of programming will certainly help with some sections of this book.

If you are working as a software tester and you are interested in expanding your skills into the API testing realm, this book is certainly for you. If you are a developer who is looking to enhance their skills in terms of understanding quality and testing, congratulations, you are setting yourself up for a successful career! You may be able to skim through some parts of this book, but you will certainly find a lot of helpful advice in here on how to design and write a test in a way that leads to good-quality APIs.

What this book covers

Chapter 1, API Terminology and Types, covers some of the basic terminology used in API testing and development, along with providing an explanation of the different types of APIs.

Chapter 2, Principles of API Design, covers the design principles that apply to API creation and testing.

Chapter 3, OpenAPI and API Specification, explains what API specifications are and enables you to get started using them in Postman.

Chapter 4, Considerations for Good API Test Automation, explains how to execute long-lasting and useful API test automation in Postman.

Chapter 5, Understanding Authorization Options, explains how to use many of the common API authorization options in Postman.

Chapter 6, Creating Test Validation Scripts, explains how to create and use test scripts in Postman.

Chapter 7, Data-Driven Testing, explains how to use data-driven testing in Postman to create scalable API tests.

Chapter 8, Running API Tests in CI with Newman, explains how to run API tests at the command line with the Newman application.

Chapter 9, Monitoring APIs with Postman, explains how to monitor the production usage of APIs with Postman Monitoring.

Chapter 10, Testing an Existing API, goes through an existing API and explains what kinds of tests to add and how to add them.

Chapter 11, Designing an API Specification, goes in-depth in terms of how to create an OpenAPI specification that can be used in Postman.

Chapter 12, Creating and Using a Mock Server in Postman, explains how to set up and use mock servers.

Chapter 13, Using Contract Testing to Verify an API, explains what contract testing is and how you can create and use contract tests in Postman.

Chapter 14, Design and Create an API, covers all the steps involved in creating an API, from design through to specification and testing.

To get the most out of this book

This book does not assume a lot of prior knowledge in either the realm of API development or in testing principles. As long as you have a basic grasp of web technology and what software development looks like in general, you should be able to follow along with this book and pick up everything that you need. Some of the testing in Postman uses JavaScript, but you don't need to know much about how that works in order to follow along, although a basic understanding would be helpful. There are examples and challenges throughout the book. These are an important part of the book and in order to get the most that you can from them, you should take the time to work through them.

Software/hardware covered in the book	OS requirements
Postman v8.0.7	Windows, macOS X, or Linux
Burp Suite Community Edition v2021.2.1	
JavaScript ES6 and above	

This book only uses the free features of Postman and Burp Suite, so you should be able to follow along with all the examples without needing to buy anything.

If you are using the digital version of this book, we advise you to type the code yourself or access the code via the GitHub repository (link available in the next section). Doing so will help you avoid any potential errors related to the copying and pasting of code.

This book is intended to equip you with skills that you can use immediately in your work as a tester or developer. The best way to get the most out of it is to do all the hands-on challenges and try to expand them into the work that you are doing. Don't hesitate to start using what you learn right away!

Download the example code files

You can download the example code files for this book from your account at www.packt.com. If you purchased this book elsewhere, you can visit www.packtpub.com/support and register to have the files emailed directly to you.

You can download the code files by following these steps:

1. Log in or register at www.packt.com.
2. Select the **Support** tab.
3. Click on **Code Downloads**.
4. Enter the name of the book in the **Search** box and follow the onscreen instructions.

Once the file is downloaded, please make sure that you unzip or extract the folder using the latest version of:

- WinRAR/7-Zip for Windows
- Zipeg/iZip/UnRarX for Mac
- 7-Zip/PeaZip for Linux

The code bundle for the book is also hosted on GitHub at `https://github.com/PacktPublishing/API-Testing-and-Development-with-Postman`. In case there's an update to the code, it will be updated on the existing GitHub repository.

We also have other code bundles from our rich catalog of books and videos available at `https://github.com/PacktPublishing/`. Check them out!

Download the color images

We also provide a PDF file that has color images of the screenshots/diagrams used in this book. You can download it here: `https://static.packt-cdn.com/downloads/9781800569201_ColorImages.pdf`.

Conventions used

There are a number of text conventions used throughout this book.

`Code in text`: Indicates code words in text, database table names, folder names, filenames, file extensions, pathnames, dummy URLs, user input, and Twitter handles. Here is an example: "Frontend developers will probably require a `/products` endpoint to enable product information to be displayed."

A block of code is set as follows:

```
openapi: 3.0.1
info:
  title: ToDo List API
  description: Manages ToDo list tasks
  version: '1.0'
servers:
  - url: http://localhost:5000/todolist/api
```

When we wish to draw your attention to a particular part of a code block, the relevant lines or items are set in bold:

```
/carts:
    post:
    get:
        queryParameter:
            username:
    /{cartId}:
        get:
        put:
```

Any command-line input or output is written as follows:

```
npm install -g newman
```

Bold: Indicates a new term, an important word, or words that you see on screen. For example, words in menus or dialog boxes appear in the text like this. Here is an example: "Click on the **Import** button and choose the **OpenAPI** option."

> **Tips or important notes**
> Appear like this.

Get in touch

Feedback from our readers is always welcome.

General feedback: If you have questions about any aspect of this book, mention the book title in the subject of your message and email us at customercare@packtpub.com.

Errata: Although we have taken every care to ensure the accuracy of our content, mistakes do happen. If you have found a mistake in this book, we would be grateful if you would report this to us. Please visit www.packtpub.com/support/errata, selecting your book, clicking on the Errata Submission Form link, and entering the details.

Piracy: If you come across any illegal copies of our works in any form on the internet, we would be grateful if you would provide us with the location address or website name. Please contact us at copyright@packt.com with a link to the material.

If you are interested in becoming an author: If there is a topic that you have expertise in, and you are interested in either writing or contributing to a book, please visit authors.packtpub.com.

Reviews

Please leave a review. Once you have read and used this book, why not leave a review on the site that you purchased it from? Potential readers can then see and use your unbiased opinion to make purchase decisions, we at Packt can understand what you think about our products, and our authors can see your feedback on their book. Thank you!

For more information about Packt, please visit packt.com.

Section 1: API Testing Theory and Terminology

This section will show you how to approach testing an API and teach you the terminology that you will need in order to speak intelligibly and think carefully about API testing and design.

This section includes the following chapters:

- *Chapter 1, API Terminology and Types*
- *Chapter 2, Principles of API Design*
- *Chapter 3, OpenAPI and API Specifications*
- *Chapter 4, Considerations for Good API Test Automation*

1
API Terminology and Types

Learning something new can feel a little like falling over the side of a ship. Everything is moving and you can barely keep your head above water. You are just starting to feel like you understand how something works and then a new piece of knowledge comes out of nowhere and your whole world feels topsy turvy again. Having something solid to hold on to gives you the chance to look around and figure out where you are going. This can make all the difference in the world when learning something new.

In this chapter, I want to give you that piece of land to stand on. As with almost any specialty, API testing and development has its own terminology. There are many terms that have specialized meanings when you are working with APIs. I will be using some of those terms throughout this book and I want to make sure that you and I share a common understanding of what they mean. This will allow me to more clearly communicate the concepts and skills in this book and will give you that piece of solid ground to stand on as you try to learn how to do effective API testing and development.

As much as possible, I will use standard definitions for these terms, but language is a byproduct of humans and human interactions and so there is some degree of messiness that comes into play. Some terms do not have clearly agreed-on definitions. For those terms, I'll share how I intend to use and talk about them in this book, but be aware that as you read or listen to things on the internet (or even just interact with teammates), you may come across others that use the terms in slightly different ways. Pay attention to how others are using a term and you will be able to communicate well.

This book is not a dictionary, and so I don't intend to just write down a list of terms and their definitions. That would be boring and probably not all that instructive. Instead, I'll spend a bit of time on the theory of what an API is and how you test it. I will fit in some terminology explanations as we go.

This chapter will cover the following main topics:

- What is an API?

- Types of API calls

- Installing Postman

- The structure of an API request

- Considerations for API testing

- Different types of APIs

By the end of this chapter, you will be able to use Postman to make API requests and have a good grasp of basic API terminology. You will also have the opportunity to work through an exercise that will help you cement what you are learning so that you can start to use these skills in your day-to-day work.

What is an API?

A 1969 NASA publication entitled *Computer Program Abstracts* (which can be found at the following link: `https://tinyurl.com/y52x4aqy`) contains a summary of a real-time display control program sold by IBM (only $310! Plus $36 if you want the documentation). This program is said to have been designed as an operator-application programming interface, in other words, an API.

Application Programming Interfaces, or **APIs**, have been around for about as long as computer code has. Conceptually, it is just a way for two different pieces of code (or a human and some code) to interface with each other. A class that provides certain public methods that other code can call has an API. A script that accepts certain kinds of inputs has an API. A driver on your computer that requires programs to call it in a certain way has an API.

However, as the internet grew, the term *API* narrowed in focus. Almost always now, when someone is talking about an API, they are talking about a web API. That is the context I will use in this book. A web API takes the concept of an interface between two things and applies it to the client/server relationship that the internet is built on. In a web API, a client is on one side of the interface and sends requests, while a server (or servers) is on the other side of the interface and responds to the request.

Over time, the internet has changed and evolved, and web APIs have changed and evolved along with it. Many early web APIs were built for corporate use cases with strict rules in place as to how the two sides of the interface could interact with each other. The SOAP protocol was developed for this purpose. However, in the early 2000s, the web started to shift toward becoming a more consumer-based place. Some of the e-commerce sites, such as eBay and Amazon, started to publish APIs that were more public and flexible. This was followed by many of the social sites, including Twitter, Facebook and others. Many of these APIs were built using the REST protocol, which was more flexible and is built directly on the underlying protocols of the internet.

The internet continued to change though, and as mobile applications and sites grew in popularity, so did the importance of APIs. Some companies faced challenges with the amount of data they wanted to transfer on mobile devices, and so Facebook created GraphQL. This query language helps to reduce the amount of data that gets transferred while introducing a slightly more rigid structure to the API. Each of the different API types work well in some scenarios, and I will explain more about what they are later in the chapter. However, before I get into the differences between them, I want to talk about some common terms that all web APIs share.

Types of API calls

Some calls to APIs can change things on the server, while others return data without changing anything. It is important to distinguish between these different types of calls when testing or designing an API. There are a few different terms that are used to describe these differences. In order to help you understand these terms, I will use an analogy using Lego pieces.

Imagine that there is a table with a couple of Lego pieces on it. Now imagine that the guy on the right in the following diagram is me. I represent an API, while the Lego pieces represent a server:

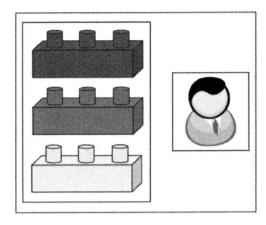

Figure 1.1 – Representation of a server and a client

You are going to be the client in this imaginary relationship. This means you can ask me to do things. You ask me to tell you what color the top Lego piece is. I reply that it is blue. This is an example of an API request and response that is **safe**. A safe request is one that does not change anything on the server. By asking me for information about what is going on in the server, you have not changed anything on the server itself.

There are other kinds of API calls that can happen though. Imagine that you gave me a green brick and asked me to replace the top brick on the stack with the green one. I do that, and in doing so I have changed the server state. The brick stack is now made up of a yellow, red, and green brick, as shown in the following diagram:

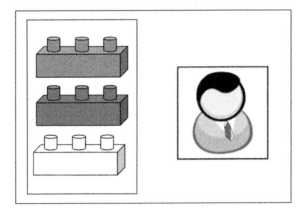

Figure 1.2 – New server state

Since the server has changed, this is not a safe request. However, if you give me another green brick and ask me to once again replace the top brick with the green brick, nothing will change on the server. The stack will still be made up of a yellow, red, and green brick. This is an example of an **idempotent** call. API calls that return the same result no matter how many times you call them are known as idempotent.

Let's imagine one more type of call. In this case, you give me a green brick and ask me to add it to the top of the stack. I do that and so now we have a stack of four bricks. This is clearly not a safe call since the server has changed, but is it idempotent?

The answer is no, but take a second to think about it and make sure you understand why this call would not be idempotent.

If you are struggling to see why it is not idempotent, think of what happens if you repeat the same request again. You give me another green brick and you ask me to add it to the top of the stack. If I do that a second time, is the brick stack still the same as it was after the first time you added it? No, of course not! It now has five bricks and every additional brick you give to me to add to the stack will change it. An idempotent call is one that only changes things the first time you execute it and does not make any changes on subsequent calls. Since this call changes something every time, it is not idempotent.

Safety and idempotency are important concepts to grasp, especially when it comes to testing APIs. For example, if you are testing calls that are safe, you can run tests in parallel without needing to worry about them interfering with each other. But if you are testing calls that are not safe or idempotent, you may need to be a little more careful about what kinds of tests you run and when you run them.

Now that you have an understanding of some of this basic terminology, I want to talk about the structure of an API. However, it will be a lot easier to do that if we have something concrete to look at, so at this point let's take a brief pause to install Postman.

Installing Postman

Installing Postman is the same as pretty much any other program you've ever installed. Go to `https://postman.com` and click on the download button. From the **downloads** page, choose the download for your operating system and then install it as you would any program on your computer. I will be using the Windows version of Postman, but other than the occasional screenshot looking a bit different, everything should be the same regardless of which platform you are running Postman on.

Starting Postman

Once you have Postman installed, open the application. The first time you open Postman, it will ask you to sign in. If you do not yet have a Postman account, I would highly recommend that you sign up for one. You can skip signing in, but creating an account is totally free and this makes it a lot easier to manage and share your work. Everything in this book will work with the free features of Postman. However, some of the things that I will cover will assume that you have a Postman account, so I would strongly recommend that you register for one.

Once you've signed in, you will see the main screen with a bunch of different options for things that you can do with Postman. Don't worry about all these options. We will cover all of them (and more) as we go through this book. For now, just note that they are there and that you can do a lot of cool stuff with Postman. Maybe even get a little bit excited about how much you are going to learn as you go through this book!

Setting up a request in Postman

It's time to set up an API call so that we can dissect it and see how it all works. You can do that with the following steps:

1. Start by clicking on the **New** button and then choose the **Request** building block:

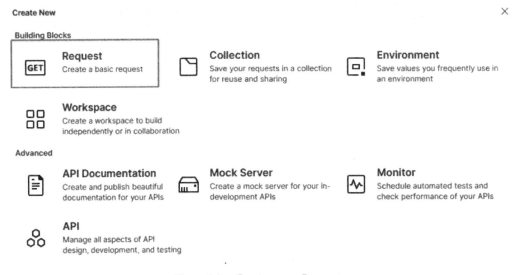

Figure 1.3 – Create a new Request

2. For this first example, I will use the GitHub API, so name it something like **Get User Repos**.

3. Postman organizes requests into collections, so you will also need to create a collection that you can store the request in. Scroll down on the dialog and click on the **+ Create Collection** link:

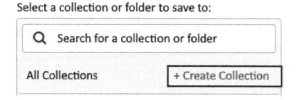

Figure 1.4 – Creating a collection to store the saved request

4. Name the collection something like `Github API Requests` and click on the checkmark to choose that collection as the place where you will store the request you are making.

5. Now, click the **Save** button on the dialog.

You will be taken to a tab where you can fill out the details of the request. There are a few different pieces that come together to make an API request and, in the next section, I will walk you through those different pieces and help you understand the structure of an API request.

The structure of an API request

The request tab in Postman provides a lot of information about the various pieces that make up an API request. Each of these pieces plays an important part in sending and receiving data with an API, and so I will walk you through each one in turn. Some parts of an API request are optional depending on what kind of request it is and what you are trying to do with it, but there are two pieces that are required for every API request. Every API request needs an endpoint and an action.

API endpoints

Every web-based API request must specify an **endpoint**. In the **Postman requests** tab, you are prompted to enter the request URL. Postman is asking you to put in a URL because an API endpoint is just a URL. We use the term *URL* so much that we can sometimes forget what it stands for. URL is an acronym for **Uniform Resource Locator**. The endpoint of an API call specifies the resource, or the "R" of the URL. In other words, an API endpoint is the uniform locator for a particular resource that you want to interact with on the server. URLs help you to locate resources on a server, and so they are used as the endpoints in an API call.

Fill in this field in the requests tab by typing in the following URL: `https://api.github.com/users/djwester/repos`. This endpoint will give you information about my repositories on GitHub. If you have a GitHub account of your own, you can put in your username in the part of the URL where it says **djwester** and get back data for your own repositories.

You will often see an API endpoint specified without the base part of this API. So, for example, if you look at the GitHub API documentation, it will report the endpoint for this as `/users/:username/repos`. All the GitHub API calls start with the same base URL (in other words, `https://api.github.com`), and so this part of the endpoint is often left out when talking about an endpoint. If you see API endpoints listed that start with a / instead of with **http** or **www**, just remember that you need to go and find the base API URL for the endpoint in order to call it.

API actions

Every API call needs to specify a resource that we are working with. This is the endpoint, but there is a second thing that every API call needs. An API needs to do something with the specified resource. We specify what we want an API to do with API **actions**. These actions are sometimes called **verbs**, and they tell the API call what we expect it to do with the resource that we have given it. For some resources, only certain actions are valid, while for others there can be multiple different valid API actions.

In Postman, you can select the desired action using the drop-down menu beside the textbox where you entered the URL. By default, Postman sets the action to **GET**, but if you click on the dropdown, you can see that there are many other actions available for API calls. Some of these actions are specialized for particular applications, and so you won't run into them very often. In this book, I will only use **GET**, **POST**, **PUT**, and **DELETE**. Many APIs also use **PATCH**, **OPTIONS**, and **HEAD**, but using these is very similar to using the four that I will use, and so you will be able to easily pick up on how to use them if you run into them. The rest of the actions in this list are not often used and you will probably not encounter them much in the applications that you test and create.

The four actions (**GET**, **POST**, **PUT**, and **DELETE**) are sometimes summarized with the acronym **CRUD**. This stands for **C**reate, **R**ead, **U**pdate, and **D**elete. In an API, the **POST** action is used to create new objects, the **GET** action is used to read information about objects, the **PUT** action is used to modify existing objects, and (surprise, surprise) the **DELETE** action is used to delete objects. In practice, having an API that supports all aspects of CRUD gives you the flexibility to do almost anything you might need to, which is why these four actions are the most common ones you will see.

API actions and endpoints are required for web APIs, but there are several other important pieces to API requests that we will consider.

API parameters

API parameters are used to create structure and order in an API. They organize similar things together. For example, in the API call we are looking at, we are getting the repositories for a particular user in GitHub. There are many users in GitHub, and we can use the exact same API endpoint to get the repository list for any of them with the change of username in the endpoint. That part of the endpoint where it accepts different usernames is a **parameter**.

Request parameters

The username parameter in the GitHub repositories API endpoint is known as a **request parameter**. You can think of a request parameter as a replace string in the API endpoint. They are very common in web APIs. You will see them represented in different ways in the documentation of different APIs. For example, the GitHub documentation uses a colon in front of the request parameter to indicate that it is a request parameter and not just another part of the endpoint. You will see endpoints specified like this in the GitHub documentation: `/users/:username/repos`.

In other APIs you will see request parameters enclosed in curly braces instead. In that case, the endpoint would look like `/users/{{username}}/repos`. Whatever the format used, the point of request parameters is to get particular information about different objects that are all the same type. We have already seen how you can do that with this endpoint by replacing my username with your username (or any other GitHub user's name).

Query parameters

There is another kind of parameter that you can have in an API endpoint. This kind of parameter is known as a **query parameter** and it is a little bit trickier to deal with. A query parameter often acts like a kind of filter or additional action that you can apply to an endpoint. They are represented by a question mark in the API endpoint and are specified with a key that is the item you are querying for, and a value, which is what you want the query to return.

That's all very abstract, so let's take a look at it with the GitHub request we have open. This endpoint supports a couple of different query parameters. One of them is the **type** parameter. In order to add parameters to an API endpoint in Postman, make sure you have the **Params** tab selected and then put the name of the query parameter into the **Key** field and the value into the **Value** field. In this case, we will use the **type** parameter, so enter that word into the **Key** field.

this endpoint, the type parameter allows us to filter based on whether you are the
ner of a repository or just a member. By default, the endpoint will return only those
positories that you are the owner of, but if I want to see all the repositories that I am a
member of, I can put **member** in the **Value** field for this. At this point, the request should
look something like this:

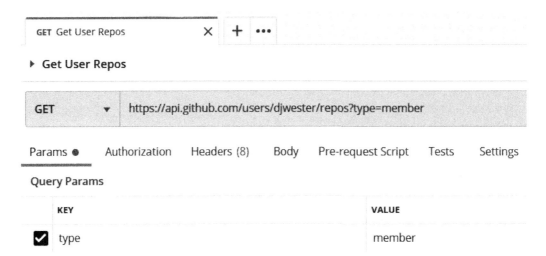

Figure 1.5 – Query parameter type in an API call

If I send this request, I get back all the repositories that I am a member of, as opposed
to the ones that I own. Parameters are a powerful API paradigm, but there are still a few
more fundamental pieces of the API structure that I haven't talked about yet. The next
thing we will look at are API headers.

API headers

Every API request needs to include some **headers**. Headers include some of the
background information that is often not that important to human users, but they help
the server have some information about the client that is sending the request. Sometimes,
we will need to modify or add certain headers in order to get an API to do what we want,
but often we can just let the tool that we are using send the default headers that it needs to
send without worrying about it.

In Postman, you can see what headers will be sent with your request by using the **Headers**
tab. You can also modify the headers and add additional ones here as needed. I will get
into more details on how headers work and how to use them in future chapters, but for
now, you don't need to worry about them too much. The point of mentioning them here is
just to make sure you know the terminology. Let's turn our attention instead to the body
of an API request.

API body

If you want to create or modify resources with an API, you will need to give the server some information about what kind of properties you want the resource to have. This kind of information is usually specified in the **body** of a request.

The request body can take on many forms. If you click on the **Body** tab in the Postman request, you can see some of the different kinds of data that you can send. You can send from-data, encoded form data, raw data, binary data, and even GraphQL data. As you can imagine, there are a lot of details that go into sending data in the body of a request. Most of the time, **GET** requests do not require you to specify a body. Other types of requests, such as **POST** and **PUT**, which do require you to specify a body, often require some form of authorization since they allow you to modify data. We will learn more about authorization in *Chapter 5, Understanding Authorization Options*. Once you can authorize requests, there will be a lot more examples of the kinds of things you might want to specify in the body of an API request.

API response

So far, we have spent a lot of time talking about the various pieces that make up an API request, but there is one very important thing that we have been kind of ignoring. An API is a two-way street. It sends data to the server in the request, but then the server processes that request and sends back a response.

The default view that Postman uses displays the response at the bottom of the request page. You can also modify the view to see the request and the response in side-by-side panels. You can change to this view if you so wish by clicking on the **Two pane view** icon at the bottom of the application, as shown in the following screenshot:

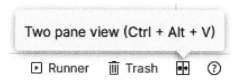

Figure 1.6 – Switching views

There are a few different aspects to the response. The most obvious one is the body of the response. This is usually where most of the information that you are looking for will be included. In the GitHub repositories requests that you have made, the lists of repositories will show up in the body of the response, and Postman will display them in that tab.

An API response can also include a few other things such as cookies and headers. These kinds of things can be very important hints as to what is going on when testing or creating APIs, and I will talk about them more as we go through the book

We have covered a lot of ground when it comes to how APIs request work. We have seen how an API request can have a lot of different pieces to it. These simple pieces all come together to create a powerful tool. You now have a grasp of the basic pieces that make up an API call and how to use them in Postman. It's almost time to talk about how to use this to test APIs, but before we get into that, I want to pause for a minute so that you can put into practice all this theory I've just gone over.

Learning by doing – making API calls

Books are a great way to grow and learn. You are reading this book, so I don't think I need to convince you of that! However, reading a book (or even three or four books) on a topic does not mean you understand that topic. There is theory and there is practice. There is knowing something that you've *read* and knowing something that you've *done*. These are two very different things, and if all you do is read about a topic, you will feel like you know that topic, but that will be more of a feeling than a reality. This book is a hands-on guide, and my purpose in writing this is to help you improve your skills around API testing and to give you a deep knowledge of how Postman can help you understand API quality.

If you want that to be a reality and you don't just want this book to be another piece of theoretical knowledge bouncing around inside your head, you need to put into practice the things that you are learning. I know it's hard when you are reading a book. I personally find it difficult to interrupt the flow of a book that I am reading in order to do exercises. I get it. It feels like you are slowing down your learning. This isn't a book on the theory of how we learn, but please believe me when I say that you will learn a lot more if you pause along the way and work through practical examples related to what you have just been learning. I will include those throughout this book and encourage you to work through them. As with any learning project, you will get out of it what you put into it. Take that time to do the exercises.

OK. With that out of the way, let's look at an exercise that you can do to help make all this theory about the structure of an API request stick. I will call this exercise "Map the app" – a nice catchy title, right?

Map the app exercise

The purpose of this is to help you cement what you have learned about APIs and to make sure you know how to call them. For this exercise I want you to map out the API of an application. If you have one that you are currently testing – great, use that! If not, you can find a simple public API on the internet. You can find a list of some of the public APIs here: `https://github.com/public-apis/public-apis`. Pick a simple API from that list (the Cat Facts API, for example). Make sure that you pick one that does not require authorization.

When I say map your application, I'm not talking about a cartographic map. I am talking about something like a line diagram linking different parts of the application together, or even a mind map or a list of different parts of the application. What I want you to do with this exercise is this:

1. Try calling some of the different endpoints of the application and write down some observations about what they do and how they relate to each other.

2. See whether you can map out what the API lets you do and how the different parts relate to each other. You can do this by creating a list of the different endpoints.

3. Create a collection in Postman and see whether you can organize the different endpoints within that collection.

4. Explore the different options in the API and get some practice calling API endpoints!

As you complete this exercise, take a bit of time to reflect on what you have learned and what you are already able to do. You can make API calls and do some investigation to dig in and understand how an API is put together. This is a great start and I will continue to expand on what you know as I walk you through some considerations for API testing.

Considerations for API testing

This is a book about how to use Postman to make better APIs. Part of making a better API is testing it. There is a lot to API testing, and I will walk you through many aspects of it as we go through this book, but now that you know some of the basics of how an API request works, what are some of the things to consider when you test an API?

Beginning with exploration

I can still clearly remember the first time I saw a modern web API in action. The company I was working at was building a centralized reporting platform for all the automated tests and I was assigned to help test the reporting platform. One of the key aspects of this platform was the ability to read and manipulate data through a web API. As I started testing this system, I quickly realized how powerful this paradigm was.

Another part of my job at that time was to work with a custom-built test automation system. This system was quite different from the more standard test automation framework that many others in the company were using. However, the fact that the new reporting platform had an API meant that my custom test automation system could put data into this reporting platform, even though it worked very differently to the other test automation systems. The test reporting application did not need to know anything about how my system, or any other one, worked. This was a major paradigm shift for me and was probably instrumental in leading me down the path to where I am writing this book. However, something else I noticed as I tested this was that there were flaws and shortcomings in the API.

It can be tempting to think that all API testing needs to be done programmatically, but I would argue that the place to start is with exploration. When I tested the API for that test reporting platform, I barely knew how to use an API, let alone how to automate tests for it, and yet I found many issues that we were able to correct. If you want to improve the quality of an API, you need to understand what it does and how it works. You need to explore it.

But how do you do that?

Thankfully, Postman is one of the best tools out there for exploring APIs. With Postman, you can easily try out many different endpoints and queries and you can get instant feedback on what is going on in the API. Postman makes it easy to play around with an API·and to go from one place to another. Exploring involves following the clues that are right in front of you. As you get results back from a request, you want to think of questions that those results bring to mind and try to answer them with further calls. This is all straightforward with Postman. To Illustrate, I will walk you through a case study of a short exploratory session using Postman.

For this session, I will use the `https://swapi.dev/` API. This is a fun little API that exposes data about the Star Wars movies. Don't worry if you aren't into Star Wars. No specialized knowledge is needed!

Exploratory testing case study

Let's try this out. First of all, create a new collection called *Star Wars API* and add a request to it called *Get People*. Put `https://swapi.dev/api/people/1/` into the URL field and send that request. You should get back a response with some data for the character *Luke Skywalker*:

Figure 1.7 – Response for the Star Wars API request

In the response, there are links to other parts of the API. A response that includes links to other relevant resources is known as a **Hypermedia** API. The first link in the films list will give us information about the film with ID 1. Since we are exploring, let's go ahead and look at that link and see what it does. You can just click on it and Postman will open a new requests tab with it already loaded. At this point, you know what to do: just click on **Send** and Postman will give you data about that first film. Under the characters in that film, you can see that there are several different characters, including, of course, a link to / people/1.

Seeing this triggers a thought that there might be more things to check in the `/people` API, so let's go back and explore that part of the API a bit more. Click on the **Get People** tab to go back to that request and change the URL to remove the **/1** from the end of it. You can now click **Send** to send a request to the endpoint, `https://swapi.dev/api/people`. This response gives back a list of the different people in the database. You can see at the top of the response that it says there is a count of **82**.

We are in exploration mode, so we ask the question, "I wonder what would happen if I tried to request person number 83?" This API response seems to indicate that there are only 82 people, so perhaps something will go wrong if we try to get a person that is past the end of this dataset. In order to check this, add `/83` to the end of the URL and click **Send** again. Interestingly (if the API hasn't changed since I wrote this), we get back data for a Star Wars character. It seems like either the count is wrong, or perhaps a character has been removed somewhere along the way. Probably we have just stumbled across a bug!

Whatever the case may be, this illustrates just how powerful a little bit of exploration can be. We will get to some powerful ways to use Postman for test automation later in this book, but don't rush right past the obvious. API testing is testing. When we are testing, we are trying to find out new information or problems that we might have missed. If we rush straight to test automation, we might miss some important things. Take the time to explore and understand APIs early in the process.

Exploration is a key part of any testing, but it takes more than just trying things out in an application. Good testing also requires the ability to connect the work you are doing to business value.

Looking for business problems

When considering API testing and design, it is important to consider the business problem that the API is solving. An API does not exist in a vacuum. It is there to help the company meet some kind of business need. Understanding what that need is will help to guide the testing approaches and strategies that you take. For example, if an API is only going to be used by internal consumers, the kinds of things that it needs to do and support are very different to those needed if it is going to be a public API that external clients can access.

When testing an API, look for business problems. If you can find problems that prevent the API from doing what the business needs it to do, you will be finding valuable problems and enhancing the quality of the application. Not all bugs are created equal.

Trying weird things

Not every user of an API is going to use it in the way that those who wrote the API thought they would. We are all limited by our own perspectives on life and it is hard to get into someone else's mind and see things through their perspective. We can't know every possible thing that users of our system will do, but there are strategies that can help you get better at seeing things in a different light. Try doing some things that are just weird or strange. Try different inputs and see what happens. Mess around with things that seem like they shouldn't be messed with. Do things that seem weird to you. Often, when you do this, nothing will happen, but occasionally it will trigger something interesting that you might never have thought of otherwise.

Testing does not need to be mindless repetition of the same test cases. Use your imagination. Try strange and interesting things. See what you can learn. The whole point of this book is for you to learn how to use a new tool. The fact that you have picked up this book shows that you are interested in learning. Take that learning attitude into your testing. Try something weird and see what happens.

There is obviously a lot more to testing than just these few considerations that I have gone over here. However, these are some important foundational principles for testing. I will cover a lot of different ways to use Postman for testing in this book, but most of the things that I talk about will be examples of how to put these strategies into practice. Before moving on to more details on using Postman though, I want to give you a brief survey of some of the different types of APIs that you might encounter.

Different types of APIs

There are several types of APIs commonly used on the internet. Before you dive too deep into the details of using Postman, it is worth knowing a bit about the different kinds of APIs and how to recognize and test them. In the following sections, I will provide brief explanations of the three most common types of APIs that you will see on the internet.

REST APIs

We'll start with what is probably the most common type of API you'll come across on the modern web, the **RESTful API**. REST stands for **Re**presentational **S**tate **T**ransfer, and refers to an architectural style that guides how in terms of how you should create APIs. I won't go into the details of the properties that a RESTful API should have (you can look them up on Wikipedia if you want, at `https://en.wikipedia.org/wiki/Representational_state_transfer`), but there are a few clues that can let you know that you are probably testing a RESTful API.

Since RESTful APIs are based on a set of guidelines, they do not all look the same. There is no official standard that defines the exact specifications that a response must conform to. This means that many APIs that are considered to be RESTful do not strictly follow all the REST guidelines. REST in general has more flexibility than a standards-based protocol such as **SOAP** (covered in the next section), but this means that there can be a lot of diversity in the way REST APIs are defined and used.

So how do you know whether the API that you are looking at is RESTful?

Well, in the first place, what kind of requests are typically defined? Most REST APIs have **GET**, **POST**, **PUT**, and **DELETE** calls, with perhaps a few others. Depending on the needs of the API, it may not use all these actions, but those are the common ones that you will be likely to see if the API you are looking at is RESTful.

Another clue is in the types of requests or responses that are allowed by the API. Often, REST APIs will use JSON data in their responses (although they could use text or even XML). Generally speaking, if the data in the responses and requests of the API is not XML, there is a good chance you are dealing with a REST-based API of some sort. There are many examples of REST APIs on the web and, in fact, all the APIs that we have looked at so far in this book have all been RESTful.

SOAP APIs

Before REST, there was **SOAP**. SOAP stands for **S**imple **O**bject **A**ccess **P**rotocol. SOAP has been around since long before Roy Fielding came up with the concept of REST APIs. It is not as widely used on the web now (especially for smaller applications), but for many years it was the default way to make APIs and so there are still many SOAP APIs around.

SOAP is an actual protocol with a **W3C** standards definition. This means that its usage is much more strictly defined than REST, which is an architectural guideline as opposed to a strictly defined protocol.

If you want a little light reading, check out the w3 primer on the SOAP protocol (`https://www.w3.org/TR/soap12-part0/`). It claims to be a "non-normative document intended to provide an easily understandable tutorial on the features of SOAP Version 1.2.

I'll be honest, I'm not sure how well it delivers on the "easily understandable tutorial" part of that statement, but looking at some of the examples in there may help you understand why REST APIs have become so popular. SOAP APIs require a highly structured XML message to be sent with the request. Being built in XML, these requests are not that easy to read for humans and require a lot of complexity to build up. There are, of course, many tools (an example is SoapUI) that can help with this, but in general, SOAP APIs tend to be a bit more complex to get started with. You need to know more information (such as the envelope structure) in order to get started.

But how do you know whether the API you are looking at is a SOAP API?

The most important rule of thumb here is: does it require you to specify structured XML in order to work? If it does, it's a SOAP API. Since these kinds of APIs are required to follow the W3C specification, they must use XML, and they must specify things such as `env:Envelope` nodes inside the XML. If the API you are looking at requires XML to be specified, and that XML includes the `Envelope` node, you are almost certainly dealing with a SOAP API.

SOAP API example

Let's look at an example of what it would look like to call a SOAP API. This is a little bit harder than just sending a **GET** request to an endpoint, but Postman can still help us out with this. For this example, I will use the country info service to get a list of continents by name. The base page for that service is here: `http://webservices.oorsprong.org/websamples.countryinfo/CountryInfoService.wso`. In order to call this API in Postman, we will need to set up a few things. You will, of course, need to create a request in Postman. In this case though, instead of having the request method as a **GET** request, you will need to set the request method to **POST** and then put in the URL specified above. SOAP requests are usually sent with the **POST** method rather than the **GET** method because they have to send so much XML data. It is more difficult to send that data via a **GET** request, and so most SOAP services require the requests to be sent using the **POST** protocol.

Don't click **Send** yet though. Since this is a SOAP API, we need to send some XML information as well. We want to get the list of continents by name, so if you go to the **CountryInfoServices** web page, you can click on that first link in the list, which will show you the XML definitions for that operation. Use the SOAP 1.2 example on that page and copy the XML for it.

In Postman, you will need to set the input body type to **raw** and choose **XML** from the dropdown and then paste in the **Envelope** data that you copied from the documentation page. It should look something like this:

Figure 1.8 – SOAP API information

For this particular API, we would also need to modify the Content-Type header (by adding a new one) at the bottom, so that it is set to application/soap+xml:

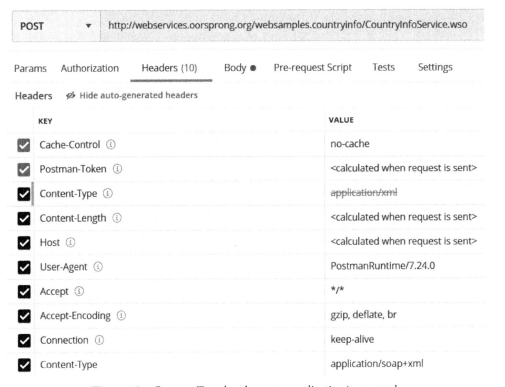

Figure 1.9 – Content-Type header set to application/soap+xml

Now you are finally ready to click on **Send**. You should get back a list of the continents, but as you can see, there is a lot more complexity to calling SOAP APIs. REST APIs can, of course, have complex bodies specified as well, but the requirement to do this in XML and the existence of the `Envelope` node in this indicates that this API is indeed a SOAP API.

GraphQL APIs

SOAP came before REST and, in many ways, REST was designed to deal with some of the shortcomings of SOAP. Of course, in software we are never done making things better, and so we now have a type of API known as GraphQL. GraphQL is a query language and it was designed to deal with some of the situations where REST APIs have shortcomings. RESTful APIs don't know what specific information you might be looking for, and so when you call a REST API endpoint, it gives back all the information it has. This can mean that we are sending extra information that you don't need, or it can mean that we aren't sending all the information you need and that you must call multiple endpoints to get what you want. Either of these cases can slow things down, and for big applications with many users, that can become problematic. GraphQL was designed by Facebook to deal with these issues.

GraphQL is a query language for APIs, and so it requires you to specify in a query what you are looking for. With REST APIs, you will usually only need to know what the different endpoints are in order to find the information you are looking for, but with a GraphQL API, a single endpoint will contain most or all of the information you need and you will use queries to filter down that information to only the bits that you are interested in. This means that with GraphQL APIs, you will need to know the schema or structure of the data so that you know how to properly query it, instead of needing to know what all the endpoints are.

How do you know whether the API you are looking at is a GraphQL API?

Well, if the documentation is telling you about what kinds of queries you need to write, you are almost certainly looking at a GraphQL API. In some ways, a GraphQL API is similar to a SOAP API in that you need to tell the service some information about what you are interested in. However, a SOAP API will always use XML and follow a strict definition in the calls, whereas GraphQL APIs will usually be a bit simpler and are not defined in XML. Also, with GraphQL, the way the schema is defined can vary from one API to another as it does not need to follow a strictly set standard.

GraphQL API example

Let's take a look at a real-life example of calling a GraphQL API to understand it a bit better. This example will use a version of the countries API that you can find hosted at `https://countries.trevorblades.com/`. You can find information about the schema for it on GitHub: `https://github.com/trevorblades/countries`. Now, you could just create queries in the playground provided, but for this example, let's look at setting it up in Postman.

Similar to calling a SOAP API, we will need to specify the service we want and do a **POST** request rather than a **GET** request. GraphQL queries can be done with **GET**, but it much easier to specify the query in the body of a **POST** request, so most GraphQL API calls are sent with the **POST** method. You will need to choose the **GraphQL** option on the **Body** tab and put in the query that you want:

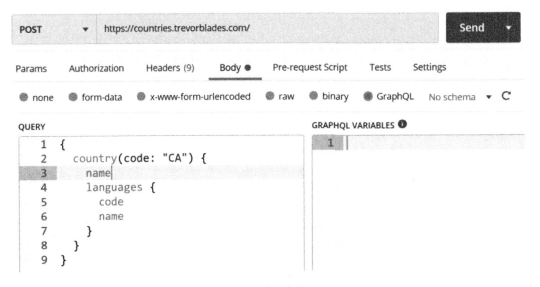

Figure 1.10 – GraphQL query

As you can see, in this example, I have requested the name and languages of Canada. Once I have specified this information, I can click **Send** and I get back some JSON with the country name and a list of the official languages. If I wanted additional information (say the name of the capital city), I could just modify the query to include a request for that information and send it off again using the same endpoint, and I would get back the new set of information that I requested.

At this point, I have obviously only been able to give a very quick introduction to each of these types of APIs. If you are working with a GraphQL or SOAP API, you may need to spend a bit of time at this point making sure you understand a little more about how they work before proceeding on with this book. Most of the examples through the rest of this book will use RESTful APIs. The concepts of API testing will largely stay the same though, regardless of the type of API testing that you need to do. You should be able to take the things that you will learn in this book and put them to use regardless of the type of API you are working with in your day job.

Summary

Let's pause for a minute to consider everything we have gone over in this chapter. You've installed Postman and already made several API requests. You have learned how API requests work and how to call them. I explained some basic testing considerations and gave you strategies that you can start to use right now in your day-to-day work. You also got to make calls to GraphQL, SOAP, and REST APIs and learned a ton of API terminology.

You now have some firm ground that you can stand on as we proceed through the rest of this book. I will take you deep into a lot of API testing and design topics and help you get the most out of Postman, but in order to get the most out of it and not feel frustrated, it would be good to make sure you understand the topics covered in this chapter.

Take a minute to ask yourself the following questions:

- Would I feel comfortable reading an article on API testing? Could I follow along with the terminology used?

- What are some basic strategies and approaches that I can use in API testing?

- If I was given an API endpoint, could I send a request to it in Postman? What things would I need to do to send that request?

- If I was given some API documentation, could I figure out what kind of API it was and send requests to it?

If you can answer these questions, you certainly have the grounding that you need for moving on in this book. If you are not totally sure about some of them, you might want to review some of the relevant sections in this chapter and make sure you have that solid ground under your feet.

You've learned a lot already! In the next chapter, we will dive into some of the principles of API design and look at how to use Postman to help put those principles into practice when creating an API.

2
Principles of API Design

You might be surprised that there is a chapter on API design in a book about API testing and development. Don't designers work on making things look good? An API doesn't really have much to look at, so why would I spend a whole chapter talking to you about API design?

I believe that design, testing, and documentation are just as much a part of creating a quality product as development is. Perhaps they are even more important. Good design can make the life of a developer or tester much easier. Designing something isn't so much about making it look good as it is about ensuring that it brings satisfaction. We humans enjoy things that look nice and so designs can sometimes be focused on the look and feel of something, but even in the realm of APIs where there isn't much to "see," good design can make it much more enjoyable to use and thus improve the quality.

This chapter will go over the principles of API design and cover the following main topics:

- Figuring out the purpose of an API
- Design principles for structuring an API so that it is easy to use
- Creating documentation in Postman
- Using specification languages to design an API before writing any code

The material in this chapter can feel a bit abstract and theoretical, but I have included a few exercises to help you figure out how to use these concepts. I would encourage you to spend the time to work through those exercises and by the end of this chapter, you will be able to use these design principles to come up with great insights for APIs that you are currently working on, as well as having a strong foundation that you can use if you need to create a new API. This chapter will also help you get started with API documentation in Postman. You will also be able to use the RAML specification language to design and model an API and to automatically add requests into Postman.

Technical requirements

The code used in this chapter can be found at `https://github.com/PacktPublishing/API-Testing-and-Development-with-Postman/tree/master/Chapter02`.

Start with the purpose

We don't just build an API because it is a fun thing to do. We build APIs to achieve a purpose. They help us or our users do something that we want to do more efficiently. This might seem obvious, but let's be honest: we forget to do this far too often.

Design is a difficult domain. Perhaps your company has designers (as mine does). Technical people such as testers and developers can sometimes dismiss what designers do as "just making things look pretty," but the reality is that good design is very hard. Good design makes something that is suited for its purpose. This book is not a book on designs (if you want to read more about the theory of design, check out books such as *The Design of Everyday Things* by Don Norman). However, if you are interested in good-quality APIs, you need to think for a few minutes about the purpose of your API and how you will design it to meet that purpose.

Knowing that you need to do something is an important first step. Unfortunately, many talks, articles and books stop there. But what good does that do you? You are convinced that it makes sense to design an API with the purpose in mind, but what is the purpose? What do you do if you don't know? How do you figure out the purpose of your API?

Figuring out the purpose

You want to figure out the purpose of your API, but how do you do that? There are a few simple strategies that you can use for this. The first thing is to ask questions. If you or your team is writing an API, you were probably asked to do it by someone. Perhaps your manager or the product manager or one of the clients. Someone asked you to create the API. Talk to that person! Why do they want the API? What do they want to do with it? What problems do they think it will solve? Ask them these questions and see if you can figure out some of what the purpose of the API is.

Personas

Another simple strategy that you can use to think of personas. A persona is simply a made-up person that you use to help you think through who might be using your API. For example, you might have a persona representing a user in your company who will be using the API to develop user interfaces, or you might have a persona of a software engineer who works for one of your clients and is using the API to develop a custom application. Thinking through different kinds of users and considering how they might interact with your API will help you with understanding the purpose that it serves.

When creating a persona, think about things that go beyond just the technology that the person might use or understand. Think about things like the goals and motivations they might have and the things that might frustrate them. It's also helpful to think of some personal details that might make them a bit more relatable to you. For example, you could think about whether they are a dog person, or whether they have kids. Is there some other thing that makes them unique? In other words, what kind of person are they? Writing down details like this can seem a bit silly at times, but it helps you to better empathize with this persona and as you are able to do that you will be more able to put yourself in their shoes and understand the kinds of things that are important to them. The more you understand this, the better you will be able to understand the purpose of your API.

The why

At the heart of figuring out the purpose is the question why. Why are we making this API? The why is almost always about solving a problem. A great way to figure out the purpose of an API is to figure out what problem it solves. Does it make it easier to write UI elements? Does it enable clients to customize the application? Does it enable third-party developers to use your platform? Does it simplify integrations with other applications? What problem is your API solving? Answer these questions and you will be well on your way to knowing the purpose of your API.

> **Important note**
>
> This exercise of figuring out the purpose of an API doesn't just apply to new APIs. If you are working with an existing API, there is a lot of value in understanding the purpose. It may be too late to radically alter the design of the API, but there is no more important threat to quality than not actually helping people solve the problems they need to solve. If nothing else, understanding the purpose of an existing API that you are testing will help you figure out which bugs are important and which ones might not matter as much. It takes some skill to figure out which bugs are urgent, and which are not, and understanding the purpose of the API helps with that.

Try it out

I have just given some practical advice, but it won't do you much good if you don't use it. This book isn't just about filling your head with some theory. It is about helping you immediately get better at testing APIs. A little later in this book, I will show you some of the tools that Postman has for helping with API design, but right now I want you to pause and try out what we have just been talking about.

Take an existing API that you have been working on and see if you can write down the purpose in two or three sentences. Use the following steps to work through the process:

1. Identify at least two key stakeholders for the API. Do this by asking the question "who wants (or wanted) this API built?" Write down these stakeholder names.

2. If possible, talk to those stakeholders and ask them what they think the purpose of this API should be and why they want to build it. Write down their answers.

3. Create preferably two (but at least one) personas that list out the kinds of people that you think will be using the API. What skill level do they have? What work are they trying to accomplish? How will your API help them?

4. Write down what problem(s) you think the API will solve.

5. Now, take all the information that you have gathered and look through it. Distill it down into two or three sentences that explain the purpose of the API.

Creating usable APIs

Usability is about the balance between exposing too many controls and too few. This is a very tricky thing to get right. On the extremes, it is obvious when things are out of balance. For example, the Metropolitan Museum of Art has an API that gives you information about various art objects in their possession. If all the API did was provide one call that gave you back all that data, it would be providing too few controls. You would need to do so much work after getting the information that you might as well not use the API at all. However, if on the other hand, the API gave you a separate endpoint for every piece of meta data in the system, you would have trouble finding the endpoint that gave you the particular information you wanted. You would need to comprehend too much in order to use the system.

You need to think carefully about this if you want to get the balance right. Make sure your API is providing users with specific enough data for the things they need (this is where knowing the purpose comes in handy) without overwhelming them. In other words, keep it as simple as possible.

Usable API structure

One thing that can help create a usable API is to use only **nouns** as endpoints. If you want users to be able to understand your API, structure it according to the objects in your system. For example, if you want to let API users get information about the students in a learning system, don't create an endpoint called `/getAllStudents`. Create one called `/students` and call it with the `GET` method.

Creating endpoints based on nouns will help you better structure your data. For example, if you have `/students` as an endpoint, you can easily add an endpoint for each student at `/students/studentId`. This kind of categorization structure is another helpful API design principle to keep in mind. Creating a structure like this maps the layout of the API onto the kinds of things that the API user needs information about. This makes it much easier to know where to find the relevant information.

A structure like this works nicely, but does it really match up with how users will interact with the API? If I am looking for information about a student, am I going to know what their ID is in the API? Perhaps, but more likely I will know something like their name. So, should we modify the structure to have an additional endpoint like `/students/name`? But what if we are looking at all the students of a certain age? Should we add another endpoint `/students/age`? You can see where I am going with this. It can get messy pretty quickly.

This is where **query parameters** are helpful. A query parameter is a way of getting some subset of the category based on a property that it has. So, in the examples that I gave earlier, instead of making "name" and "age" be endpoints under the "students" category, we could just create query parameters. We would call `/students?name='JimJones'` or `/students?age=25`. Query parameters help keep the endpoints simple and logical but still give the users the flexibility to get the information they are interested in in an effective way.

Good error messages

A usable API helps the users when they make mistakes. This means that you give them the correct **HTTP codes** when responding to a call. If the request is badly formatted the API should return a 400 error code. I won't list all the HTTP codes here as they are easily searchable online but ensuring that your API is returning codes that make sense for the kind of response you are getting is an important quality consideration.

In addition to the HTTP codes, some APIs may return messages that let you know what possible steps you can take to correct this issue. This can be very helpful, although you will want to be careful that you don't reveal too much information to those who might be bad actors.

Document your API

One often-overlooked yet vitally important aspect of a good-quality API is proper documentation. Sometimes testers and developers can overlook documentation as something that is outside of their area of expertise. If you have a team that writes documentation for your API, it is certainly fine to have them write it, but don't treat documentation as a second-class citizen! Documentation is often the first exposure people have to your API and if it does not point people in the direction they need to go, they will get confused and frustrated. No matter how well you have designed your API, users will need some documentation to help them know what it can do and how to use it.

Documenting with Postman

Postman allows you to create documentation directly in the application. In *Chapter 1*, *API Terminology and Types*, I showed you how to create a request to the GitHub API. Of course, GitHub has its own API documentation, but let's look at how you can create documentation in Postman using that API request. If you did not create the GitHub collection, you can import the collection from the GitHub repo for this course:

1. Download the `GitHub API Requests.postman_collection.json` collection file from `https://github.com/PacktPublishing/API-Testing-and-Development-with-Postman/tree/master/Chapter02`.

2. In Postman, click on the **Import** button.

3. On the resulting dialog, click on the **Upload Files** button and browse to where you downloaded the collection file and select it.

4. Click on the **Import** button and Postman will import the collection for you.

Once you have the collection set up, you can create some documentation with the following steps:

1. The first thing to do is to navigate to the **GitHub API Requests** collection and click on it.

2. To the right of the application, you will see a few icons. Click on the **Documentation** icon as shown in the following figure:

Figure 2.1 – Open the Documentation panel

This brings up the **Documentation** panel.

At this point, you can edit the documentation for the collection itself, if you want. There might be times when you want to do this, but in this case, you only have one request so there probably isn't too much documentation to put in here. Instead, go to the **Get User Repos** request as shown in the following figure:

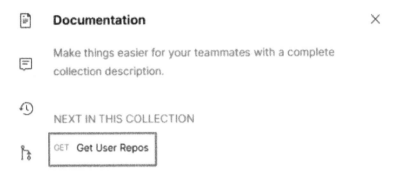

Figure 2.2 – Go to the request documentation

If you click on it, you will be taken to that request and you can once again use the documentation icon on the right of the page to open the documentation panel for the request. Click on the edit icon and you can start typing your documentation for this request directly into the provided text box.

> **Important note**
>
> Postman API descriptions support Markdown. If you are not familiar with Markdown, it is a simple set of rules that can be used to format text. A great resource showing the kinds of commands available is the Markdown cheat sheet, which you can find at `https://github.com/adam-p/markdown-here/wiki/Markdown-Cheatsheet`.

Let's write down some documentation for this endpoint:

1. At this point, just type something simple in here so that you can try it out. Type in something like this: `This Endpoint will get information about the given user.`

2. Click **Save** and now you are ready to publish this.

3. In order to publish, click on the **View complete collection documentation** link at the bottom of the panel, as shown in the following figure:

Figure 2.3 – The view collection documentation link

4. Click on the **Publish** icon, as shown in the following figure:

Figure 2.4 – Publish documentation

5. This opens a web page where you can choose various formatting options for your documentation. Once you have set up the options that you want on this page, you can scroll down and click on the **Publish Collection** button to make this documentation available to others.

6. The published page tells you the URL from which you can see the documentation that you made. Click on that and you can see a nice documentation page.

When looking at this documentation, I think it could be improved if the example request showed a response. You can easily add examples in Postman with the following steps:

1. Return to Postman and once again go to the **Get User Repos** request.

2. Click on the **Send** button for the request to send it off. Now go down to the response and Click on **Save Response**, and choose the **Save as example** option.

Figure 2.5 – Adding examples

3. Postman will automatically add an example to this request. Give it a meaningful name and click on the **Save** button. Return to your API documentation page and refresh it. You will now see an example request and response:

Figure 2.6 – Example API request and response in documentation

It is worth spending more time exploring how to document your API well, but these features make it straightforward to do in Postman. Whether you are a tester or developer and whether you are working on a new API or one that has been around for some time, I would encourage you to take the time to properly document your API. Good documentation will make a world of difference to your users and will also lead to you and your team having a better understanding of how it works. It is well worth the time that it takes, especially when working with a tool like Postman that makes it so easy to do. In fact, although this is not a book on API documentation, I think it is worth spending a few minutes on some of the theory of how to write good API documentation.

Good practices for API documentation

One key practice to keep in mind when writing API documentation is **consistency**. In this chapter and the previous one, I have been giving you a lot of API-related terminology. There is always going to be some variation in how terms are used, but as much as possible try to use terms in a way that is consistent with how other APIs use them. You should also try to have as much internal consistency as possible in your documentation. This means things like using the same terms to mean the same thing throughout the documentation. It also means that as much as possible you want your API structure to be consistent so that you don't have to explain similar things in different ways throughout your documentation.

Sometimes, in reading or creating documentation, things will jump out to you. You might see how two things that are quite similar are laid out in very different ways. I think this is another benefit of good API documentation. It lets you see where there might be flaws in the API layout.

Another very important thing to keep in mind when it comes to API documentation is the importance of examples. We already saw how easy it is to make examples in Postman documentation. Take advantage of that! It has been said that a picture is worth a thousand words. I think that an example in an API doc is worth nearly as many. Some things are difficult to explain well in words and it takes seeing it done in an example for people to grasp how it works. Do not underestimate the power of a well-crafted example.

One final thing to keep in mind with API documentation is a problem that happens with all documentation. It gets out of date. Code changes, and that applies to API code as well. Over time, what your API does and the exact ways that it does it will change. If you don't keep your documentation up to date to match those changes, the documentation will soon cease to be useful.

You have already seen how you can keep your documentation right with your tests and how you can generate examples directly from your requests in Postman. Take advantage of that and make sure your documentation stays up to date. Postman will take care of a lot of the work of it for you by updating all the documentation automatically every time you publish.

There are some specification tools that can help automatically generate documentation. These kinds of tools can help keep documentation and tests up to date with the latest code changes. I will take you through some of those in more detail in *Chapter 4, Considerations for Good API Test Automation*. In that chapter, I will particularly focus on the Open API specification, as it is a powerful and popular API specification tool, but there are other API specification tools that we can use.

There is an ongoing debate in the API development community that mirrors broader debates in the software development community as whole. The debate boils down to how much time you should spend upfront on design. Some will argue that since the only good software is software that helps someone solve a problem, we need a "ship first" mentality that gets our ideas out there. We then fill out the design based on the kinds of things clients actually need and care about. Others will argue for a "design first" approach where you rigorously define the API behavior before you write any code. As with most things, you are probably best off avoiding either ditch and finding the middle ground between them. Modern tooling can help us do this. For example, there are tools that will allow you to create simple designs and then use those designs to get feedback from clients. Since this is a chapter about API design, I do want to spend a bit of time talking about a specification language that is meant to help shift the focus from merely documenting your API to helping with API design.

RESTful API Modeling Language

RAML, which stands for **RESTful API Modeling Language**, is an API specification language that, as the name implies, helps with modeling APIs. You can read more about it on the RAML website, `https://raml.org/`. RAML has some tools that can help with API design but getting into those is beyond the scope of what I want to cover in this book. For now, I just want to introduce you to this specification and let you see how you can use it to design an API that meets the design criterion I've talked about in this chapter.

Getting started with RAML is as easy as opening a text editor and typing in some text. RAML is meant to be human-readable and so the specification is written in a simple text-based format. RAML is also structured hierarchically, which makes it easy to create the kind of usable API structures that I've talked about. In the next section, I will walk you through an example of using this modeling language to design an API and leverage the power of that design in Postman. You will then get to try it out on your own as well!

Designing an API

I have talked about a lot of the theory of API design, so now I want to look at how you can use Postman to help you out with designing an API. API design does not only apply to new APIs that you create. In fact, using the principles of API design when testing an existing API is a great way to find potential threats to the value of that API, but for the sake of understanding this better, let's look at how you can design an API from scratch. If you understand the principles through this kind of example, you should be able to use them on existing APIs as well.

Case study – Designing an e-commerce API

Let's imagine that we want to design an API for a very simple e-commerce application. This application has a few products that you can look at. It also allows users to create a profile that they can use when adding item to their cart and purchasing them. The purpose of this API is to expose the data in a way that can be used by both the web and mobile application user interfaces. Your team has just been given this information and you need to come up with an API that will do this.

So, let's walk through this and see how to apply the design principles we've covered. I will start with a simple RAML definition of the API. The first thing we need is to create a file and tell it what version of RAML we are using. I did this by creating a text file in Visual Studio Code (you can use whatever text editor you prefer) called `E-Commerce_API-Design.raml`. I then added a reference to the top of the file to let it know that I want to use the 1.0 version of the RAML specification:

```
#%RAML 1.0

---
```

I also need to give the API a title and to set up the base URI for this API, so next I defined those in the file:

```
title: E-Commerce API
baseUri: http://api.ecommerce.com/{version}
version: v1
```

Defining the endpoints

This is a made-up API so that baseURI reference does not point to a real website. Notice also how the version has been specified. Now that I have defined the root or base of the API, I can start to design the actual structure and commands that this API will have. I need to start with the purpose of this API, which is to enable both a website and a mobile app. For this case study, I am not going to dive too deep into things like creating personas. However, we do know that this API will be used by the frontend developers to enable what they can show to the users. With a bit of thought, we can assume that they will need to be able to get some kind of product information that they can show the users. They will also need to be able to access a user's account data and allow users to create or modify that data. Finally, they will need to be able to add and remove items from the cart.

With that information in hand about the purpose of the API, I can start to think about the usability and structure of this API. The frontend developers will probably need a /products endpoint to enable the display of product information. They will also need a /users endpoint for reading and maintaining the user data and a /carts endpoint that will allow the developers to add and remove items from a cart.

These endpoints are not the only way that you could lay out this API. For example, you could fold the carts endpoint into the users one. Each cart needs to belong to a user, so you could choose to have the cart be a property of the user if you wanted. It is exactly because there are different ways to lay out an API, that we need to consider things like the purpose of the API. In this case, we know that the workflow will require adding and removing items from a cart regularly. Developers will be thinking about what they need to do in those terms and so to make them call a "users" endpoint to modify a cart would cause extra data to be returned that they do not need in that context, and could also cause some confusion.

Now that I have picked the endpoints I want to use in this API, I will put them into the RAML specification file. That is simply a matter of typing them into the file with a colon at the end of each one:

```
/products:
/users:
/carts:
```

Defining the actions

Of course, we need to be able to do something with these endpoints. What actions do you think each of these endpoints should each have? Take a second to think about what actions you would use for each of these endpoints.

My initial thought was that we should have the following actions for each endpoint:

```
/products:
    get:
/users:
    get:
    post:
    put:
/carts:
    get:
    post:
    put:
```

Think about this for a minute, though. If I only have one endpoint, /carts, for getting information about the carts, I need to get and update information about every cart in the system every time I want to do something with any cart in the system. I need to take a step back here and define this a little better. The endpoints are plural here and should be representing collections or lists of objects. I need some way to interact with individual objects in each of these categories:

```
/products:
    get:
    /{productId}:
        get:
/users:
    post:
    get:
    /{username}:
        get:
        put:
/carts:
    post:
    get:
    /{cartId}:
        get:
        put:
```

Here, I have defined **URI parameters** that enable users to get information about a particular product, user, or cart. You will notice that the POST commands stay with the collection endpoint as sending a POST action to a collection will add a new object to that collection. I am also allowing API users to get a full list of each the collections as well if they want.

Adding query parameters

In *Chapter 1, API Terminology and Types*, you learned about query parameters. Looking at this from the perspective of the users of the API, I think it would be helpful to use a query parameter in the carts endpoint. When a user clicks on a product and wants to add that product to their cart, the developer will already know the product ID based on the item the user clicked on. However, the developer might not have information about the cart ID. In this case, they would have to do some sort of search through the carts collection to find the cart that belonged to the current user. I can make that easier for them by creating a query parameter. Once again, I am using the design principles of usability and purpose to help create a good model of how this API should work.

In RAML, I just need to create a query parameter entry under the action that I want to have a query parameter:

```
/carts:
    post:
    get:
        queryParameter:
            username:
    /{cartId}:
        get:
        put:
```

I have designed the structure of the API using the principles I laid out, and hopefully you can see how powerful these principles are in helping you narrow down a broad space into something manageable and useful. When it comes to creating a RAML specification for an API, you would still need to specify the individual attributes or properties of each of the endpoints and query parameters that you want to create. I won't go into all those details here. You can look at the RAML tutorials (https://raml.org/developers/raml-100-tutorial) to learn more about how to do this. I didn't give enough information about this imaginary API that we are designing to fill out all the properties. We don't know what information each product or user has for example. In real life, you would probably get this information based on what is in the database and then build out the examples and attributes based on that.

Using the RAML specification in Postman

This might not be a fully fledged API specification, but it is enough for us to use in Postman! Click on the **Import** button in Postman and then click on **Upload Files** and select the `.raml` file from this case study. Ensure that both the request and response parameter generation options are set to use schema and click on **Import**. Postman will parse the specification for you and automatically create a collection with calls defined for each of the endpoint and action combination that you created in the specification file. Pretty cool, isn't it?

Once you have learned some more Postman features, I will show you how to use these concepts to dive a lot deeper into the design process for APIs. For now, though, I want you to be able to think about how API design intersects with the quality of the API. In fact, I want to give you a little challenge to try out.

Modeling an existing API design

You have been learning how to think through API design. I gave you some principles for this and then walked you through putting the principles into practice in a case study. Now I want you to see if you can use these principles on an API that you are currently working on. If the company you are working at does not have an API that you can use, you can of course just find a public API to try out this exercise with.

Using the API you have selected, work through the following steps to apply the principles of API design:

1. Add each of the endpoints to a RAML file. Make sure to follow the hierarchy of the API in that file.

2. Spend a bit of time thinking about what the purpose of the API is and reflecting on if the structure that you see here fits with that purpose. What other ways might you design the API? Could you improve the layout to better fit the purpose?

3. If you were designing this API, what actions and query parameters would you give to each endpoint? Create a copy of the file and fill it in with what you think you would do with this API.

4. In the original file, add in the actual actions and query parameters that the API has. How do they compare to the ones that you made in the copy of the file?

If you want, you can import the file into Postman and as you learn more about testing and other features that you can use in Postman, you will already have a collection of requests ready to use.

Summary

Designing an API takes careful thought. An API is software and the whole reason we write software is to help people solve problems. APIs need to solve a problem, and the better they solve that problem, the better quality they are. One thing that can help with API quality is to have a well-designed API. A well-designed API is one that is designed to fulfill the purpose for which it is used. In this chapter, you learned how to think through the purpose of an API by coming up with personas. You also learned some questions that you can ask to get to heart of why an API needs to exist in the first place.

This chapter also showed you some way to structure and document APIs. You learned about API specification and how you can use RAML to create design driven specification for an API. And, of course, you also got to try these things out and put them into practice! With a firm grasp of principles of API design, you are ready to move on to the next chapter and learn about what it takes to create good API test automation.

3
OpenAPI and API Specifications

The history of computing has been a long path toward higher and higher levels of abstraction. In the early days of the computer era, computers were programmed with punch cards and assembly languages. The invention of FORTRAN in the 1950s created a programming language that allowed programmers to write code in ways a little more similar to the ways humans work. Over the years, object-oriented languages such as C++ came along and added additional levels of abstraction. In a sense, APIs are another level of abstraction. They allow people to write "code" at a very high level that will tell computers what to do. However, we didn't stop there. As APIs became more popular, we started to develop interfaces that would allow us to specify how an API works, so that users who know nothing about the source code can easily interact with the remote service.

We call these interfaces **API specification languages**. These languages help with API development in several ways. They make it easier to share information between clients and those creating the API, and they also enable a lot of automation. They let you do things such as automatically create some kinds of tests and code. There is a lot of complexity that goes into using these specifications, but when you understand them, you will find that they help you create and maintain better-quality APIs.

There are several different RESTful API specification languages that have been created. In *Chapter 2, Principles of API Design*, I talked about RAML and how it can be used to create design-driven APIs. RAML is an example of an API specification language. Another API specification language is the **OpenAPI Specification** (**OAS**). This is the most used API specification language and much of this chapter is devoted to understanding how to use it. However, before diving into how to use it, I want to spend a bit of time talking about the value of API specifications in general.

The following topics will be covered in this chapter:

- What are API specifications?
- Creating OASes
- Using API specifications in Postman

Technical requirements

The code used in this chapter can be found at `https://github.com/PacktPublishing/API-Testing-and-Development-with-Postman/tree/master/Chapter03`.

This chapter will also use the online Swagger Editor tool. This is a simple tool that you don't need to download or install.

What are API specifications?

Some APIs follow strictly defined protocols. However, RESTful APIs follow an architectural style that was laid out by Roy Fielding in his doctoral dissertation. This means that there are general principles laid out that they follow, but there is not a strict protocol that they must adhere to. This balance between structure and flexibility has been a powerful concept and has contributed to the widespread adoption of this kind of API architecture. There is no such thing as a perfect solution, however, and this is no different. One of the benefits of SOAP APIs is that the structure must be specified following strict programmatic rules. This means that the API definition must be written in a way that computers can easily understand. This makes it easy to create a lot of general-purpose automation for these kinds of APIs. If a computer can understand the layout of an API, you can automatically generate some kinds of documentation, tests, and even code from that specification.

Without that strict specification, each RESTful API may have some nuances to it that are different from others. As humans, this is generally fine to manage. We can quickly and easily figure out where those differences are and accommodate for them. Computers struggle with this, however. Things must be very clearly and explicitly laid out for a computer to use it. This challenge with RESTful APIs was recognized pretty early on, and so some API specification formats were proposed.

API specifications provide a structured way to define an API. If you follow the rules of the specification, you can interact with the API at a higher level of abstraction. For example, an API specification could be used to automatically create mock servers that you can use for testing and experimentation during development. You can also do things such as automatically generate documentation and contract tests. You can even use these specifications to generate some kinds of code, for both server implementations and client-side code that calls the API.

API specification terminology

There are a few different terms that are worth understanding when it comes to using API specifications. I've been talking about API specification languages. Another term for this is an **API description format**. You can follow the API description format to create an **API description** itself, which is the actual metadata that describes what the API contains and can do. There are multiple API description formats, and there are also tools that will allow you to take an API description that is written in one format and convert it to another.

I have been using the term **API specification**, which is a kind of umbrella term that covers all the different types of description formats and documents. It is used a bit fluidly in the industry (as most terms are), but I will use it in this way as a term that means both the different formats or languages and the **API description documents**. API description documents are documents that contain a description of a particular API written with a certain API description format. I will usually use the more generic term "API specification" when talking about these documents though.

As you can see, there is some complexity with using API specification languages, so let's take a minute to review a few of the main ones before diving into how to create and use an OAS in Postman.

Types of API specifications

There are three main RESTful API specification languages: **RAML** (`https://raml.org/`), **API Blueprint** (`https://apiblueprint.org/`), and **OpenAPI** (`https://github.com/OAI/OpenAPI-Specification`). Previously, OpenAPI was called **Swagger**, so if you hear anyone talking about Swagger, just realize that it is the same thing as OpenAPI. I will be talking extensively about OpenAPI/Swagger later in this chapter and I've already talked a bit about RAML, but let's take a quick look at a comparison between these different specifications.

RAML

I already showed you an example of how to use the **Restful API Modeling Language** (**RAML**) to define how an API works in *Chapter 2, Principles of API Design*. This specification language uses the YAML format. YAML is a human-readable file format that makes it easy to structure data by following a few simple rules. The rules for structuring YAML are in the YAML spec (`https://yaml.org/spec/1.2/spec.html`). Since YAML is designed to be human-readable, it is quite easy to get started with and helps to make RAML intuitive to understand. Much of the structure is built in a way that matches how you should think about and design APIs. This makes RAML a good choice if you are trying to create "design-first" APIs where you plan out the API ahead of time and then create an API that matches that design.

RAML is supported by Postman and is probably the second most popular API specification language. Although not as popular as OpenAPI, it has broad community support as well, and so if you are looking for a design-first approach, it may be a good choice

API Blueprint

The API Blueprint specification uses **Markdown** as the format. You can read more about Markdown here: `https://www.markdownguide.org/cheat-sheet/`. Using Markdown makes specifications written in this format more readable. In fact, it reads almost exactly like consumer-facing documentation. It is also very easy to understand and get started with. However, it isn't as widely supported by the community. If you want to use it in Postman, you have to first use a tool to convert it into a format that Postman can use.

The API Blueprint format is integrated into some tool stacks such as apiary (`https://apiary.io`), but if you are working with Postman, it is probably better to choose a different API specification language if you can.

OpenAPI/Swagger

The most used API specification language is OpenAPI. Since it was originally called Swagger, many of the tools that support the OAS are called Swagger tools, while the specification itself is called OpenAPI. This specification language is flexible and powerful and has a lot of tooling to support it. You can directly import descriptions written in this format into Postman, and you can use a lot of other tools to automate things related to it as well. This large toolset and broad adoption has in some ways made it the de facto standard for API specifications. If you aren't sure which specification you want to use, it's probably best to just default to using OpenAPI.

There are some other niche API specification languages out there, but for the remainder of this chapter, I want to focus on how to use OpenAPI. The OAS is the most popular specification, and if you do a lot of API testing, you will probably come across an OAS file at some point. In the next section, I'll show you how to create an OAS.

Creating OASes

I won't spend a lot of time on the Swagger tools that are used for OASes, but I do want to give you at least an introduction to the subject so that you can use these tools in your API testing if you want. In this section, you will learn how to create and edit OASes in the Swagger Editor. You will also learn what an API schema is and how to codify one in an API specification. In order to demonstrate these things, I will use the Swagger Petstore API. This is an example API that already has the OAS built for it. It is a good way to get started with using OpenAPI and is used in their documentation a lot as well.

The OAS enables a lot of value, but there is quite a bit to it as well. In this section, I will quickly skim through using it. I will also develop these themes more deeply by working through some more examples in *Chapter 11, Designing an API Specification.*

The Swagger Editor is an online tool for editing the OAS. You can access it at `https://editor.swagger.io/`. When you first open that in your browser, it will load the OAS for the example Petstore API. If you have used the editor before, it might not be there, but you can easily load it by going to the **File** menu and choosing the **Import URL** option, and then putting in the URL `https://petstore.swagger.io/v2/swagger.json` and clicking **Ok**. By default, the editor loads the 2.0 version of the spec. However, I want to use version 3 since that is the latest version of the spec. To convert it, use the following steps:

1. Click on the **Edit** menu.
2. Choose the **Convert to OpenAPI 3** option.

    You will get a warning letting you know that the current values will be overwritten.

3. Choose the **Convert** option, and the spec will be converted for you.

On the right-hand side, the editor shows a preview of the documentation that can be produced from the specification. You can play around with the actual specification in the left-hand panel and immediately see the result on the right. Try it out yourself and see. Look through the specification and under the `put` action for the `/pet` endpoint in the `paths` section, change the summary to say `Modify an existing pet` instead of `Update an existing pet`. Note that when you do that, it immediately updates the text in the `PUT` action of the `pet` endpoint, as shown in the following screenshot:

Figure 3.1 – Modifying the spec modifies the documentation

Now that you know how to use the Swagger Editor, let's take a closer look at the specification itself to make sure you understand how to create one for your own APIs.

Parts of an OAS

The first section I want to dig into is the `info` section. This is where the base data for the API object is defined. At a minimum you will need to include the `title`, `description`, and `version` options. There are a few other optional high-level tags that help specify metadata about the API. These tags are helpful but not necessary for describing your API. The following screenshot shows different options in the `info` section:

```
info:
  title: Swagger Petstore
  description: 'This is a sample server Petstore server.  You can find out more about    Swagger
    at [http://swagger.io](http://swagger.io) or on [irc.freenode.net, #swagger](http://swagger.io/irc/).
      For
    this sample, you can use the api key `special-key` to test the authorization      filters.'
  termsOfService: http://swagger.io/terms/
  contact:
    email: apiteam@swagger.io
  license:
    name: Apache 2.0
    url: http://www.apache.org/licenses/LICENSE-2.0.html
  version: 1.0.0
```

Figure 3.2 – Options in the info section of an OAS

The next section in this file is the `paths` section. This section is critically important and there are a lot of options in here. Obviously, it is the place where you define your endpoints, and under each endpoint, you can define the various actions available on that endpoint. You can also define a lot of detail about each endpoint/action combination, things such as what kind of responses this endpoint can give and what kind of data it requires, as well as descriptions of what the API does. As you can see, this section contains the bulk of the API description. This is a pretty simple API and it takes up nearly 600 lines in this specification. A lot of the pieces in this section are optional depending on how you have laid out your API, but let's walk through the `/pet` endpoint to get a bit more of a feel for this.

The first thing that is defined is the actual endpoint itself (`/pet`). The next thing you specify is what actions you can do on that endpoint. This can be called with either `put` or `post`. The next things under those verbs are some parts of the spec that define some information about the endpoint. These include things such as `summary`, `operationID`, and the request body description. Most of these kinds of keys are optional but can be helpful for documenting and organizing your API.

The `requestBody` section defines what needs to go into the body of the API call. In this section, we need to define the content type (it can be either `application/json` or `application/xml` in this example) and then under it, you need to define the schema or structure that this content needs to adhere to. You will notice that the schemas are referenced using a `$ref` key. This is merely a key that points to values that are stored in another part of the document. You could spell out the entire schema directly in this part of the document. However, in this case, the same schema is being used in multiple requests and so it has been moved to another section of the document called `components`. This makes it possible to reference the same thing from multiple places.

Another important part of any API call is the response. The spec defines what should happen for each response that the API can give in the `responses` section. These responses are described in the spec under the different HTTP error codes that you want your API to support. The specification also lays out the `security` options for each action on the endpoint. The actual definition of the security options for the API can be found in the `securitySchemes` section near the bottom of the file.

One final option you will see in the Petstore spec is the `x-codegen-request-body-name` option. This option is used when you use the Swagger code generation tools to create server code. It tells the code generator what name to use in the underlying code. When first getting started with using OASes, you don't need to worry too much about options like these, but it does demonstrate that there are other powerful options available. You can find a full list of all the parameters that you can use in your specifications on the documentation page here: `https://swagger.io/specification/`. In the following screenshot, you will see some examples of path specifications:

```
33  paths:
34    /pet:
35      put:
36        tags:
37        - pet
38        summary: Update an existing pet
39        operationId: updatePet
40        requestBody:
41          description: Pet object that needs to be added to the store
42          content:
43            application/json:
44              schema:
45                $ref: '#/components/schemas/Pet'
46            application/xml:
47              schema:
48                $ref: '#/components/schemas/Pet'
49          required: true
50        responses:
51          400:
52            description: Invalid ID supplied
53            content: {}
54          404:
55            description: Pet not found
56            content: {}
57          405:
58            description: Validation exception
59            content: {}
60        security:
61        - petstore_auth:
62          - write:pets
63          - read:pets
64        x-codegen-request-body-name: body
65      post:
```

Figure 3.3 – Examples of a path's specification

The `paths` sections lay out most of the details of what each endpoint can do, but as I noted earlier, the schema for the bodies of these requests is defined in another part of the document called `schemas`. Let's look at that section of the specification. However, before doing that, I want to take a moment to make sure you understand what is meant by the term schema.

Defining API schema

At its most basic, a **schema** is just a plan, usually in the form of a model or theory. Schemas are common in software development. For example, databases have schemas that show how the various tables are connected to each other. In a similar way, an API can have a schema. An API schema shows how the data should be structured. It will specify what a response should contain, and what data you need to include in the body of POST or PUT requests.

In the example spec that we are looking at, if you scroll down to near the bottom of the file in the editor (around line 596), you can see where the schema definitions start. In many ways these are the core of the spec. They define what the incoming and outgoing data in the API calls need to look like. Continue scrolling down to where the Pet schema is defined (around line 669), and you can see how this works in practice. Any request that uses this schema is required to have a `name` field and a `photoUrls` field. The `name` field needs to be of the `string` type and the `photoUrls` field needs to be an **array of strings**. There are also some other optional fields that you can include, such as `status` and `tags`. Another interesting thing to note is that the optional `category` field references another schema. In other words, to fully see the schema, we have to scroll up to the section that has the `category` schema in order to see that it is an object with an ID and name.

It can feel a bit overwhelming to put this all together like this but having a well-defined schema like this helps you do all kinds of cool things. I have obviously skimmed quickly through this, but as I mentioned earlier, I will flesh this out in more practical detail in *Chapter 11, Designing an API Specification*. We have seen how you can use OASes with the Swagger tools, but now let's take a look at how you can use them in Postman.

Using API specifications in Postman

You can use API specifications to simplify work in many areas. In this section, I will show you some things that you can do with them. You will learn how to create mocks and tests from a spec with only a few clicks. I will also show you how to use them to do some validation so that everything in your request and elements are consistent.

Since this book is about learning how to use Postman, this section will be devoted to showing you how to use OASes in Postman. However, it is worth noting that you can also use them in other cool and interesting ways as well. For example, in the Swagger Editor, if you go to the **Generate Server** menu, you can see several different languages , and you can generate the code in the language of your choice. You can also generate client-side code using one of the options from the **Generate Client** menu.

Another powerful Swagger tool that makes OASes is SwaggerHub (`https://swagger.io/tools/swaggerhub/`). This is a place where you can share your specification with your team to have one single source of truth for what your API does and how it works. In addition to helping you with coding, an OAS can help you with a few testing tasks. Let's look at those now.

Creating mocks from an OAS

Using an OAS in Postman is as easy as importing it and doing a few setup steps. First, you will need a specification file to import. In order to get one, use the following steps:

1. Use the **Save as YAML** option from the **File** menu in the Swagger Editor to save the Swagger Petstore spec file.

   If you prefer, you can instead use the `petstore_openapi.yaml` file that I have provided in the GitHub repository for this course (`https://github.com/PacktPublishing/API-Testing-and-Development-with-Postman/tree/master/Chapter03`).

2. In Postman, choose the **Import** button at the top left of the application.

3. Click on the **Upload Files** button and navigate to the `.yaml` file that you just downloaded.

4. You can leave all the settings at their default values and click on **Import**.

5. This will automatically import the API and create a collection. Click on **Confirm and Close**

6. Once the import has completed, click on the API in the navigation tree and go to the **Define** tab.

You should see the API definition data. At this point, there are several different things Postman can automate for you. You could generate a collection for documentation and testing purposes, or you could generate a few different kinds of tests, including integration tests and contract tests. For now, I want to set up something called a mock server. I will go into a lot more depth on what mock servers are and how to use them in *Chapter 12, Creating and Using a Mock Server in Postman*, but at this time, I want to walk you through setting one up so that you can use it for some other examples later in this chapter. Don't worry too much about understanding the details of what is going on at this point. If you use the following steps, you should be able to set up a mock server that will do what you need in order to follow along with the examples in this chapter.

Follow these steps to set up a mock server:

1. Go to the **Develop** tab of the API and choose the **Create new mock server** option from the **Add Mock Server** link:

Figure 3.4 – Creating a new mock server from an API spec

2. Since Postman has already automatically created a collection, leave the **Use an existing collection** option selected, and click on **Select Collection and Continue**.

3. Name the mock server `Swagger Petstore Mock Server`.

4. Click on **Create Mock Server** and close the dialog.

   Postman will automatically create a mock server for you based on the imported specification file!

Creating a mock server is simple, but in order to use it, you will need to create some examples as follows:

1. Switch to the **Collections** tab in the left-hand navigation panel.

2. Expand the **Swagger Petstore Collection** collection that you created, and then expand the `pet` and `{pet Id}` folders.

3. Click on the **Find pet by ID** GET request.

4. Set the value of the `petId` variable to 1:

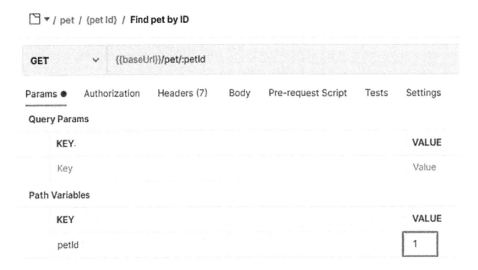

Figure 3.5 – Set petId to the first pet

If you mouseover the `baseUrl` variable, you can see that the request is going to be sent to the swagger server. We will use the data this server gives as the basis for our mock data, so go ahead and send that request.

5. Once the request has returned, click on the **Save Response** option, and choose the **Save as example** option:

Figure 3.6 – Adding an example

You can leave the name as the suggested value. You can find the saved example in the navigation tree under the **Find pet by ID** request, and you should now be ready to make a call using the mock server.

6. In the left navigation panel, click on the **APIs** tab and choose **Swagger Pet Store API**.

    If you mouse over the Swagger Petstore mock server, you should see a **Copy URL** option.

7. Click on the **Copy URL** option to copy the URL of the mock server.

8. Now, add a new request. You can click on the plus button to add a new request tab:

Figure 3.7 – Adding a new request tab

9. Paste the mock server URL that you copied into the request URL field, and then add `/pet/1` to the end of it.

10. Send the request and you will get back the example response that you saved.

As I said earlier, this just scratches the surface of how to work with mock servers. I will show you more on how to set up and use mocks in *Chapter 12, Creating and Using a Mock Server in Postman*. For now, note that using an OAS makes it very easy to set up a mock server in Postman. Creating mocks directly from a specification file can be very useful, but it is far from the only thing that you can do with these specifications. Another useful thing you can do with an OAS in Postman is to use it to create tests. Let's take a look at how to do that in the next section.

Creating tests from an OAS

When it comes to creating tests, you have a few different options in Postman. If you look on the **Test** tab of the Swagger Petstore API that you created, you can see that there are options to add a **Test Suite**, **Integration Tests**, or **Contract Tests**. Each of these options will create a collection for you so that you can use them to set up those types of tests. I will cover the actual details of creating these kinds of tests in future chapters.

There are, however, some things that we can look at now without getting into all the details of how to create test scripts:

1. Make sure you have **Swagger Pet Store API** selected on the **API** tab in the left-hand navigation panel.

2. Select the **Test** tab, and then click on **Add Contract Test** and choose the **Create new contract test** option.

3. Name it something such as `Pet Store Contract Tests` and click on the **Create Contract Tests** button.

In the background, Postman will add a collection for you with all the requests defined for each of the endpoints defined in the specification. At this point, there are a couple of ways that Postman can help you with validation. Postman validates that data in requests that you send matches with the data defined in the specification. It can also validate that the structure and layout that the requests have in a collection or mock match with the spec. In the Postman documentation, this is called **validating requests** and **validating elements**, so I will use the same terminology here. Let's take a look at these in more detail in the next sections.

Validating requests

With request validation, Postman checks that all the data sent and received when requests are sent matches the API specification. It might be hard to visualize what I mean by that sentence, so let's look at it in action:

1. With the Swagger Petstore API active, go to the **Define** tab and you will be able to see the specification that you imported.

   Earlier I showed you how to use the Swagger Editor to modify the specification. You can do the same thing right here in Postman itself.

   Now, let's modify the schema so that it is incorrect. This will allow you to see a validation error. It is usually a good idea to check your tests like that and make sure they will actually fail. To do this, do the following.

2. Scroll down to the `components` section where the schema for the various endpoints are defined and go to the schema for the `pet` endpoint (this should be around line 607).

3. In the properties for this, change the `type` of the `name` field from `string` to `integer`:

```
669    Pet:
670      required:
671      - name
672      - photoUrls
673      type: object
674      properties:
675        id:
676          type: integer
677          format: int64
678        category:
679          $ref: '#/component
680        name:
681          type: integer
682          example: doggie
```

Figure 3.8 – Changing the pet name type to integer

This should create a scenario where if we get a response back that contains a string in this field, the validation will fail since the API description now says that this field should be an integer.

4. Click on the **Save** button at the top of the file.

You have changed the schema for this endpoint to be incorrect, so now let's see whether Postman will catch this.

5. In the left-hand navigation panel, go to the **Collections** tab and expand the **Pet Store Contract Tests collection**.

6. Expand the `pet` folder and then the `{pet Id}` folder.

7. Click on the **Find pet by ID** request.

8. Send the request, and once it returns, Postman will notify you that there is one issue.

There should be a little yellow warning exclamation by the title of request:

Figure 3.9 – Warning about request issue

You can click on this warning to see the error and you will see that it says that the response body property "name" should be an integer. In the spec, you said that the `name` property should be an integer, but when the request came back from the server, it came back as a string. Postman used the spec to compare what results it was getting back from the server and since there was a difference between what the server gave and what the specification said it should give, it flagged up a warning.

Obviously, in this case, the specification was wrong, but if you had a specification that correctly defined the data type and then you got back something you weren't expecting, this could be valuable information. Perhaps a developer changed something in the API, and you need to update the documentation or even the UI that is using that API. Knowing that something has changed is an important part of setting up an API test.

> **Note:**
> Don't forget to go back to the specification on the **Define** tab of the API and change the `name` type back to `string`.

Request validation is a powerful way to use an API spec to give you valuable information, but it is not the only kind of validation that Postman can do with this information. It will also do element validation, so let's look at that next.

Validating elements

Element validation is a check that Postman does to ensure that the way you have set up various elements (collections, mock servers, and so on) within Postman matches up with the structure expected by the specification. Let's look at how this type of validation works:

1. On the **Test** tab of the **API** panel, go to the **Pet Store Contract Tests** collection that you created earlier and tap the **Click to validate** button.

   The validation will run for a second or two and then it will show a warning saying issues found.

2. If you click on this warning, you can choose the **Review Issues** button to look at those issues.

   This will open your Postman dashboard in the browser window and show you where the issues are. In this case, the issues are mostly because we have placeholders such as `<long>` in some fields instead of actual example values.

3. In order to keep things clear, just choose the **Select all changes** option at the bottom of the page, and then click the **Confirm Change to Collection** button to update all the changes.

This will update the way the requests in the collection are set up, so that they match the data in the specification file. Now that those changes have been updated, let's look at creating an actual failure so that we can verify that this validation is working:

1. Return to Postman and go to the **Collection** tab in the navigation panel.

2. Click on one of the requests (say **Finds Pets by tags**) and change the URL (for example, you could change the text pet in the URL path to be store instead):

Figure 3.10 – Changing the request URL

By doing this, you are in essence taking away the /pet endpoint and creating a new endpoint called /store. However, the specification does not have information about a /store endpoint and it does have information about the /pet one. This means what we have defined in the collection does not match with what has been defined in the specification.

3. Save the request changes and then go back to the **Test** tab of the **API** panel.

4. **Pet Store Contract Tests** will still have an **Issues Found** button beside it from the previous issues. Click on that button and choose the **Validate Again** option.

5. Once the validation has completed, click on the **Review Issues** option.

    This will open a tab in your browser where you will see that it gives you a warning about an extra request that has been found and about one that is missing:

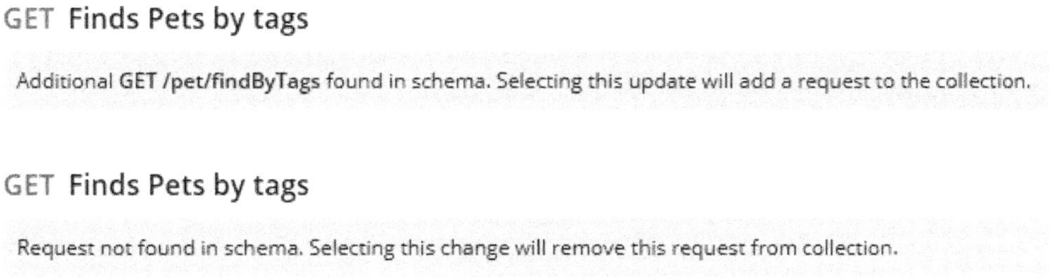

GET **Finds Pets by tags**

Additional **GET /pet/findByTags** found in schema. Selecting this update will add a request to the collection.

GET **Finds Pets by tags**

Request not found in schema. Selecting this change will remove this request from collection.

Figure 3.11 – Element validation errors

Since we changed the URL of the request, it is now set to an endpoint that does not exist in the specification and so you can see the error about the additional request. Also, by changing the path you made it so that the request is calling a path that does not exist in the specification and so you get a warning about the request not being found.

This element validation helps you to see whether the way that you are setting up your tests gets out of sync with the specification. It helps to make sure that everything is consistent.

Summary

API specifications give you a lot of power in your testing. You can use them to keep documentation, tests, and even underlying code all in sync with each other. In this chapter, you learned how to use them to reduce the work in generating mocks and collections in Postman. You have learned how to create an OAS to document an API. You can also read API specs that others may have made, and you have the ability to use those in Postman. You have learned how to leverage an API specification to help you automatically create tests and mocks in Postman. You have also learned how to validate that tests in Postman are set up to be consistent with the documentation and code produced from a specification. In addition to that, you have learned how to use specifications in Postman to verify that the data being sent and received from a request is in the proper format. Taken as a whole, you have gained a lot of useful skills for using an API specification to help with testing and designing high-quality APIs. Creating and maintaining API specifications can be a bit of work, but they help with many aspects of API building. You are now able to create and use OASes in Postman!

The ability to use API specifications will let you create APIs that are characterized by consistency. This is an important factor in API design and quality, but we also want to be able to automate things. In the next chapter, I will take you through some of the theory of how to create good test automation. API specifications help give some structure and organization to API testing but there is so much more that you can do with Postman. Let's dive into that in the next chapter!

4
Considerations for Good API Test Automation

In 1811, an angry group broke into a factory in the town of Nottingham in the UK. They started smashing machinery and equipment and destroyed much of the factory before fleeing. These men had been angry and upset for some time. They had issued manifestos and sent threatening letters, but on this day, they took the even more radical step of destroying the machines in this factory. Why were they so upset?

Well, to sum it up in a word: automation.

These men were skilled artisans. They were weavers and textile workers who had dedicated their lives to the craft of making clothes, and they did not like the new machines that were able to make cloth much more quickly and cheaply than they ever could. They claimed to be following the orders of a man named Ned Ludd and called themselves Luddites. This term has entered our modern vocabulary as a description of those who dislike new technology, but the origin of it goes back to the protest movement in which artisans were afraid of losing their jobs to automation.

The debate sounds similar to some of the debates in our society right now, although thankfully, we don't seem to have people going around and destroying property in relation to this issue. But the fact is, like it or not, our society has been on a steady path of increased automation for the past 200 years. We have added more and more automation to our factories, but we didn't stop there. We now live in a world that is saturated with cheap and accessible computing power. We have used this power to automate many things in life – I am typing this up on a computer, for example – and we continue to find more and more things to automate.

I rather enjoy the philosophy of automation – when is it helpful and when is it not? But that discussion is outside the scope of this book. What I want to focus on in this chapter is how we can best use test automation. The Luddites framed the debate in terms of a conflict between artisans and automation. I want to reframe that debate a bit. I want to help you become an artisan *of* automation. Automation is here to stay, and I think that, overall, is a good thing. It allows us to extend our capabilities as humans and to do more good than we could have otherwise, but that doesn't mean that all automation is good.

Automating something isn't just a matter of taking a manual task and turning it into a set of algorithmic steps that a computer can do. It requires careful consideration to ensure that it is actually helpful. Doing the wrong thing faster isn't helpful; it's destructive. Creating automation that takes more work to maintain than the work it saves isn't doing any good either. There are plenty of ways to create bad automation. In this chapter, I want to help you understand how to create good automation.

This chapter will lay some foundations that will be built on a lot in future chapters, but you will still find that you have a lot of practical skills to use by the time you get through the material in here. We will be covering the following topics in this chapter:

- Exploring and automating
- Organizing and structuring tests
- Creating maintainable tests

By the end of this chapter, you will be able to create useful test automation, choose what to include (or not) in automated API tests, create well-structured tests suites, use variables, understand variable scopes in Postman, use best practices when deciding where to create Postman variables, and explain the importance of logging and reporting for creating maintainable tests.

Let's get started!

Technical requirements

The code that will be used in this chapter can be found at: `https //github.com/ PacktPublishing/API-Testing-and-Development-with-Postman/tree/ master/Chapter04`.

Exploring and automating

It is easy to think of test automation as a way to quickly do the things that we could do in a manual way. There can be times where this is true. If you are doing some tedious, repetitive work that requires doing the same thing over and over again, by all means automate it if you can! However, there is danger that comes with this kind of thinking as well. If you start to think of automation as replacing what humans do, you will end up making poor automation. Manual and automated testing may have the same goal of reducing the risk of shipping bugs to clients, but the way that they achieve this goal is radically different.

For example, a manual test that is meant to help you figure out if a change to the API has caused issues will be guided by what you, as the tester, know about the change you've made. It will also be influenced by the tester themselves. If you are familiar with the API, you will try and observe different things than someone who is not. You will notice things and possibly even slightly alter what you are doing. Even if you are trying to follow a strict script (which is not a form of manual testing I would generally encourage), there will be variations and changes in what you, as the tester, do from one time to the next. There might be minor changes in the system that you know are fine and you just skip over them. There might be other things that you see that aren't related to the change at all that you make note of. Even when scripted, testing being performed by humans in this way always has an element of exploration built into it.

On the other hand, an automated test that is meant to help you figure out if a change to the API has caused issues, will do exactly the same things it did last time and check all the same things in the same way. It will not notice any incidental changes that might be problematic. If there are minor changes that don't really matter, it won't know that and might fail for the wrong reason. Compared to exploratory testing, automated tests are less comprehensive and more brittle. But it's not all bad news. There is a reason we value automated tests as an industry. They can be much faster to run and can look at variations and details that it can be hard to see when you're doing exploratory testing.

I have summarized the differences between exploratory (or human) testing and automated (or machine) testing in the following table:

	Exploratory (Human) Testing	Automated (Machine) Testing
Benefits	• Better judgment • More coverage per test • Easier to maintain	• Faster • Improved data manipulation
Cons	• Slower • Can be tedious	• More brittle • Less coverage • Harder to maintain

Table 4.1 – Exploratory/automated testing comparison

A good test strategy will include a good mix of automated and exploratory tests, but even when you're using a good balance of the two, it is important to understand how to create good test automation. By knowing the benefits and downfalls of automated testing, how do you go about making good test automation that will help reveal issues?

Exercise – considerations for good API test automation

In the next section, I will go over what I think are some approaches that you can use to create good test automation, but don't just take my word for it. Before you read through the next section, pause for a moment and think about what things you think are important for good test automation.

Write down a list of some factors (maybe two or three of them) that you think would be important when creating test automation. After reading through the next section, compare your list to the things I will be talking about. What is the same? What is different? What do you think of the differences? I will be sharing a few considerations here, but by no means are they the only possible things to think about. Entire books have been written on test automation. The quick review I will provide here certainly does not cover everything.

Writing good automation

When it comes to writing good test automation, you need to focus on a couple of things. The most important thing is to understand what you are trying to do. What kind of application are you testing and where might things go wrong? How bad is it if certain things go wrong? How often do you need to check certain things? All these things can help you make the decision of testing with an automated script or doing so by hand.

Once you have decided on the approach, though, there are a couple of other things to keep in mind. This book is about API testing, and APIs lend themselves very well to test automation. They are usually designed to be interacted with programmatically, but that doesn't mean there is nothing to think about when you're automating them. If you look at the benefits and drawbacks of using test automation in the preceding table, you can see some of the considerations we should be thinking about when it comes to test automation.

Automated testing is more brittle than manual testing. If you have ever worked with UI testing frameworks (for example, Selenium tests), you will be aware of this fact. Tests break – often for reasons that have nothing to do with finding bugs. Lower-level testing, such as calling API endpoints, has less dependencies and so are a bit less brittle, but they still break. Good test automation will create tests that are easy to fix when something changes. Software changes and good test automation will take that into account. I'll dive a bit deeper into how you can create maintainable tests later in this chapter.

Another important factor in creating good test automation is being organized. One of the benefits of test automation is that it can run the same tests over and over again. Automation can run much more quickly than a manual test, and computers don't get bored of doing repetitive tasks. You want to be able to leverage this power in your tests. In order to do this, you will need to have some kind of reporting in place that lets you know if there are test failures. You want these reports to be actionable so that they can help you pinpoint where there might be bugs, or where you might need to fix tests. This is much easier to do if your tests are well-structured.

Types of API tests

There are several types of API tests that lend themselves well to automation. **Contract testing**, which we will dive more deeply into in *Chapter 13, Using Contract Testing to Verify an API*, is a powerful form of API testing that you can use to verify that your API is meeting a given contract, which is usually specified in some sort of specification language such as OpenAPI.

You can also create **integration** or **workflow** style API tests where you are testing that you can accomplish a certain workflow. This kind of testing would typically involve calling multiple endpoints. For example, you might POST something to create a new item and then call another endpoint to verify that that item has been correctly created, and is also accessible in other parts of the system. Another example would be to GET an object such as a shopping cart and then use information in that response to GET some related information, such as details about the products in the cart.

Of course, you can also just create simple **endpoint tests** that call an endpoint with various kinds of inputs and verify the results. One important thing to consider here isn't so much a type of API testing as it is a style of test that should be run. You should check some negative test scenarios. What happens if you put in bad values or incorrect data? Like any good testing, API tests should not just consider what happens when things go right. They should also look at what happens when things go wrong.

One main category of tests where things can "go wrong" is **security testing**. I will talk a bit more about security testing in *Chapter 5, Understanding Authorization Options,* when I get into authorization and authentication, but it is an important style of testing to consider in APIs. APIs expose a lot of power and flexibility to end users (and that is partly why many companies make them), but in doing so, it is easy to miss things that could allow user access to things they should not have. Many security breaches in recent history have come from problems in APIs. I can't dive too deep into that topic in this book, but I will show you some basic things that you can do in Postman to check for API security.

Another type of testing that is worth mentioning here is **performance testing**. Postman isn't really designed as a performance testing tool, but you can get some basic performance data out of it. I will not be talking much about performance in this book, but it is an idea worth keeping in mind as you consider API quality. Performance can have a big impact on the customer's perception of quality, and APIs can often be performance bottlenecks as they involve network latency and other difficult to control factors.

As you can see, there are a lot of different ways to approach testing an API. One of the most important things you can do when trying to create good test automation is to be carefully structured in how you go about creating these tests.

Organizing and structuring tests

As the saying goes, an ounce of prevention is worth a pound of cure. This is good general life advice and is also true in test automation. Taking a bit of time to structure and organize your tests when you are starting will save you a lot of time later, when you are trying to understand test failures or reports on test effectiveness. Postman understands this philosophy and makes it easy to keep tests well-organized.

It is too easy to spout off a bunch of theory that you will skim over and not fully understand. In order to keep this practical, I will try to walk through a concrete example. I will once again use the Star Wars API for this (`https://swapi.dev/`). So, how would you go about structuring the tests for this API?

Creating the test structure

Let's start with the obvious thing – collections. One way you can think of a collection is as a folder that you can collect items, such as other folders and tests. You may already have a Star Wars API collection if you did the case study in *Chapter 1, API Terminology and Types,* but if not, I have provided a collection in the GitHub repository for this course. You can import that collection into Postman by following these steps:

1. Go to this book's GitHub repository (`https://github.com/PacktPublishing/API-Testing-and-Development-with-Postman`) and click on the **Code** drop - down arrow and download or clone the code.

2. Go to the **File** menu in the Postman application and choose the **Import** option.

3. Click on **Upload Files** and navigate to where you downloaded the files from GitHub. Then, go to the `Chapter04` folder.

4. Choose the `Stars Wars API_Chapter4_initial.postman_collection.json` file and click **Open** and then **Import**.

This will create a collection for you that you can use for the rest of this section. You can find the collection in the **collections** navigation tree in Postman.

This API has six different resources. We could just create requests directly in the newly created collection for each of them, but that would get a bit messy. For example, the `/people` resource gets a list of all the people in the service, but you can also get information about specific people. If we want to be able to test different things, we will need to include several different calls to the `/people` resource.

Instead of creating a request for this resource, I will create a folder in the Star Wars API collection for the people resource. I can do this by clicking on the **View more actions** menu beside the collection and choosing the **Add Folder** option from that menu. I will then name that folder **People**. I can repeat this for the rest of the resources in this API (Films, Starships, Vehicles, Species, and Planets):

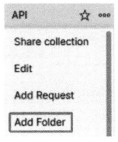

Figure 4.1 – Adding a folder to a collection

Now, with folders in place for each endpoint, I want to stop and think about what type of tests we are creating here. Although this service does provide a schema for the different resources that I could use to verify some of the results, it doesn't provide the kind of specification that I would need to create contract tests, so I won't worry about that kind of testing for now. I also won't worry about performance and security testing on this API. That leaves integration testing and endpoint testing. We will want to verify the various endpoints, so I will want endpoint tests. There are no direct workflows that we need to check here from a business sense, since this is just a "for fun" application, but there are still some interesting workflows that we might want to consider. For example, each of the resources cross-links to other resources. A call to a /planets endpoint gives links to people that live on that planet, along with other links. Each resource does this and provides links that point to other resources. This kind of linking creates some interesting possibilities for testing. You could check a planet's resources and see that it points to certain people, and you can check those people links to ensure that they have references to that planet. Tests like this could be a simple way to validate data integrity.

It seems like we want to create both kinds of tests, so the next thing I will do is create a folder in the collection called Integration Tests. Taken as a whole, these folders provide the basic structure for how we want to approach testing this API, but how do we organize these tests?

Organizing the tests

The first thing you need to do is to put the endpoint tests for each resource in the appropriate folder. I will start with the People folder. Click on the menu beside the folder and choose the **Add Request** option:

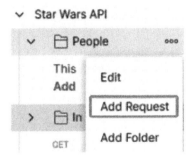

Figure 4.2 – Adding a request to a folder

Name the request `Get All People`, click on the request in the tree, and set the request URL to `https://swapi.dev/api/people/`. This endpoint gives back the list of all people. In *Chapter 6, Creating Test Validation Scripts*, I will show you how to create checks to validate this data, but for now, I'll just focus on how to organize these tests. Each person in this list has their own endpoint, and we could create a request for each one. However, doing that could get very unwieldy. Instead, I will just sample one of the individual people endpoints. Once again, add a request to the folder and name this one `Get Person Details`. Set the request URL to `https://swapi.dev/api/people/{{peopleId}}`. Note that in this case, I have set the ID to be a variable enclosed in double curly braces. This is because I don't want to hardcode a particular value, but rather want to be able to try different characters at different times.

When it comes to organizing tests, sharing variables between them is very important. You have typed in a variable, but when you hover your mouse over it, you will see that it is an unresolved variable:

Get Person Details

Figure 4.3 – Unresolved variable

This warning is here because, by surrounding it with double curly braces, you told Postman that you want to use this `peopleId` variable, but you have not assigned that variable any value. There are a few different places in Postman where you can store variables. The first place is in the collection itself. These are aptly named **collection variables**, and we will discuss them in more detail later. In this case, I want you to save this variable as an environment variable, so let's look at how we can do that now.

Environments

In order to create an environment variable, you will need an environment that you can save the variable in. You can create a new environment in Postman by following these steps:

1. Click on the **New** button and then choose the **Environment** option on the resulting popup.

2. Name it SWAPI Environment.

3. Add a new variable called peopleId with an initial value of 1:

Figure 4.4 – Adding a new environment

4. Click on **Save** to add this new environment and then close the **Manage Environments** tab.

Now that you have the variable defined in an environment, return to the **Get Person Details** request. The variable will still be unresolved, and that is because you need to tell Postman which environment you want to use. To do that, click on the dropdown near the top-right of the screen and choose **SWAPI Environment** from the list:

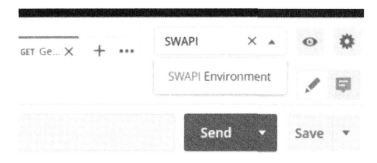

Figure 4.5 – Choosing an environment

Now that you have set the environment, if you mouse over the `peopleId` variable, you should see that it is now set to `1`:

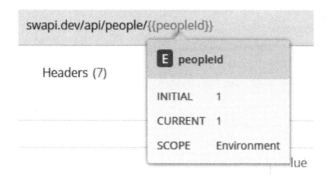

Figure 4.6 – Variable defined

Environments are a great way to organize data for your tests. In *Chapter 6, Creating Test Validation Scripts,* we will cover the different ways that we can share data and manipulate variables in the environment, which will make the concept even more powerful. Environments allow you to manage your variables in one place. This is very helpful if you need to make changes, or just need to understand what variables you have set up. Instead of looking through every endpoint to see what might be defined and trying to decide if you can change things in them, you can collect all the variables in one place and see what you can change at a glance.

Collection variables

I mentioned earlier that you can also store variables in the collection, so let's look at how that works. You have created a couple of requests already and each of them starts with the base URL `https://swapi.dev/api`. Instead of repeating that on every request that you put in the collection, let's turn it into a variable:

1. Go to each of the requests that you created earlier and replace the `https://swapi.dev/api` URL with a variable called `{{baseUrl}}`.

2. In the collection navigation pane, go to the **View more actions** menu for the collection and choose the **Edit** option.

3. Go to the **Variables** tab and create the `baseUrl` variable, setting the initial value of it to the base URL (`https://swapi.dev/api`).

4. **Update** the collection.

The variable will now be defined in all the requests that you are using it in. You can also use that variable when defining any new requests for this API.

Choosing a variable scope

You now know of two different places you can store variables in Postman (environments and collections). There are a couple of other places where you can store variables (for example, you can make global variables), but how do you decide where to store variables? How would you decide if you should put a variable into an environment, or in a collection, or somewhere else? Well, in order to answer that question, let's look at the different places where you can have variables in Postman and understand how they relate to each other.

How scopes work

When you store a variable in a collection or an environment, Postman will give that variable a **scope** that corresponds to where you have stored it. When you're trying to resolve a variable, Postman will look for it in a defined order in each of the scopes. Scopes allow a variable to be used in broader or narrower parts of the application. If you define a variable in the global scope, you can use it in any request anywhere in the application, but if you define it at the narrowest scope, it will only be available during one particular iteration of a test. So, what are the available variable scopes in Postman? In order from the broadest to the narrowest scopes, they are as follows:

- Global
- Collection
- Environment
- Data
- Local

When resolving a variable, Postman will use the narrow scope in which that variable exists. Let's take a look at a concrete example illustrating this.

You have already created the `baseUrl` variable in the Collection scope. Now, we need to create a variable with the same name in the SWAPI Environment. You can do that by following these steps:

1. Click on the **eye** icon (**Environment Quick Look**) beside the environment dropdown.

2. Choose the **Edit** option to make changes to the environment:

Figure 4.7 – Editing an environment

3. Add a new variable called **baseUrl** and give it silly value such as **bob**.

4. **Update** the environment.

5. Go to one of the requests and mouse over the `baseUrl` variable.

You can see that it now has a value of `bob`, and you can also see that the scope of this variable is `Environment`. Even though, in the collection, the variable with the same name contains the site URL, the value being used comes from the variable defined in the environment since an environment is a narrower scope than a collection:

Figure 4.8 – Variable values coming from the narrowest scope

Don't forget to go back into the environment and clean things up by deleting the silly variable that you made! To do that, edit the environment again and then click on the **X** that shows up beside the variable when you mouse over the field:

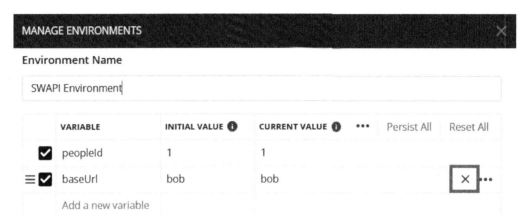

Figure 4.9 – Deleting a variable

You now understand how Postman determines which value to use when variables are defined in different scopes, but how do you know which scope to create a variable in? Let's do a quick overview of the different scopes and discuss when you would want to use each of them.

Global scope

The first scope we will discuss is the **Global** scope, which defines variables that are accessible globally or anywhere in the application.

You may want to use global variables when experimenting with sharing data between different tests or collections, but in general, you want to try and avoid using global variables. They are, by definition, available everywhere and if you use them, it is likely that you will end up eventually giving a variable in another scope the same name as the global variable. Postman will, of course, use the narrower scope, but this can still lead to confusion, especially when you're trying to debug failures.

You can add and edit variables in the global scope by using **Environment Quick Look**, and then choosing the **Edit** option in the **Globals** section:

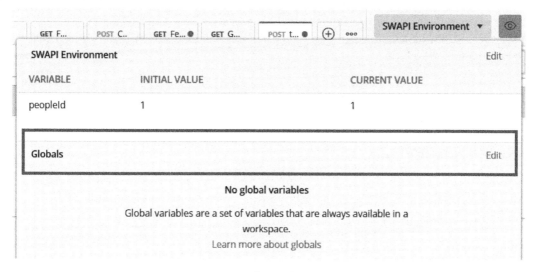

Figure 4.10 – Editing global variables

Variables in the global scope are the most widely available and the last ones that Postman uses when trying to resolve a variable value. Let's continue with the slightly narrower collection scope.

Collection scope

Variables defined in the collection are available for all the requests in that collection. They are not available in other collections, but any request in that collection can use them. You want to create collection variables when you need to share the data between multiple requests in the collection, and that data will stay the same. An example of this is an application URL. Every request will need it, and it should stay consistent. Another example would be doing some setup work with a pre-request script (I will show you how to do this in *Chapter 6, Creating Test Validation Scripts*) and then storing that data in a collection variable.

Environment scope

Environments allow you to define a set of variables that belong to a certain context. For example, many companies will have testing sites and production sites. You might also have a staging environment or want to run tests on a local build. Each of these environments might require some minor changes needing to be made to the variables being used, so in these cases, you would want to create variables that live in the different environments.

For example, if you had staging, testing, and local sites that you wanted to test against, you might define an environment in Postman for each of those sites, and then in each of those environments create a URL variable that points to the correct endpoint for each of those environments. It is important to note that in these cases, you should try not to also have the same variable defined in the collection. This will lead to confusion and is not a good practice.

Another time you might store variables in an environment is if you want to try some API endpoints as different users. You might want to try as an administrator and a regular user, for example, and so you could create environments for each of those users. These will store the login information for them and maybe some specific variables that store expected results for those different users.

If you find yourself with only one environment for a collection, you are probably better off just creating variables directly in the collection instead of adding the additional complexity of an environment.

Data scope

Most variables will be defined in collections and environments. However, in *Chapter 7, Data-Driven Testing*, I will show you how to do data-driven testing in Postman. This kind of testing imports data into Postman from a CSV or JSON file. Postman will create variables in the data scope from this imported data. You cannot create these kinds of variables yourself within Postman, but you should be aware of the kinds of variables that you have defined in your collections or environments when you are creating your input data files. The scope of data variables is narrower than that of collections or environments, so any variables defined in this scope will overwrite values defined in those broader scopes.

Local scope

The narrowest scope you can define variables in in Postman is the local scope. You can only create variables in this scope using request scripts (which I will talk about in *Chapter 6, Creating Test Validation Scripts*). They are temporary variables that do not persist between sessions, but since they are the narrowest scope, they do allow you to override values that have been set in collections or environments. Sometimes, this is desirable as it lets you override a variable in one request while still using it in all the other requests in a collection, but you should be careful that you are not accidentally overriding them either.

Variables and the different scope that they can be stored in give you a lot of power, control, and flexibility when it comes to creating and organizing tests. They also help with creating tests that continue to be valuable over time.

Exercise – using variables

Hopefully, at this point, you have a pretty good grasp of the various variable scopes, but I want you to try this out, both to cement these concepts in your mind and to prove to yourself the order in which Postman resolves the scopes:

1. Create a global variable called `base_url` and set its value to `https://swapi.dev/api`.

    What are some potential problems with this?

2. Create a new collection called `jsonplaceholder`.

3. Add a request to that collection and set the URL of the request to `{{base_url}}/todos/1`.

4. Mouse over the variable in the URL field.

    What value does it resolve to?

5. Create an environment called `jsonplaceholder Env`.

6. Add a variable to the environment called `base_url` and give it a value of `https://jsonplaceholder.typicode.com/`.

7. Go to the request you made in the **jsonplaceholder** collection and ensure that the **jsonplaceholder env** environment is selected.

8. Mouse over the `base_url` variable in the URL.

    What value does the variable resolve to? Why?

Effective use of variables is an important factor in test automation. Take some time and make sure that you understand this. Good management of this will help you create maintainable tests, but there are other factors that are important as well. Let's look at some of them.

Creating maintainable tests

One of the things that frequently gets forgotten in conversations about test automation is that they take time and work to maintain. The "sales pitch" for test automation is that we can run the same test over and over again "for free" but of course, that is not true. Leaving aside the hardware and software costs of running these tests, there are maintenance costs. Tests don't always pass. Sometimes, failures are due to finding a bug, but other times, it is just because the code has changed and the test needs to be updated, or because of some kind of flakiness in the system that we don't need to worry about too much. Well-written tests take these considerations into account. They assume that there will be failures in the future that need to be debugged. So, how do you set yourself up to make sure that your tests are maintainable?

Using logging

One of the ways in which you can make it easier to figure out failures is by having good logging options set up in your tests. You can view the logs in Postman using the console. You can either open a standalone console, by going to the **View** menu and choosing the **Show Postman Console** option, or you can open an in-app console by using the **Console** icon at the bottom of the application:

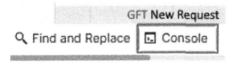

Figure 4.11 – Opening the Postman Console

The console will show you further details about the requests, along with any errors or warnings. It is also the place where any `console.log()` commands that you set up in your scripts will print to.

Maintainable tests also include some things that I have already talked about, such as writing good documentation and organizing your tests in a logical way, but another consideration for writing maintainable tests is having good test reports.

Test reports

Any automated test system needs to report on the results in some way so that you can find out if there are any issues to investigate. Postman will report on results directly in the application or command line. Many of the reporters built into Postman require that you have an Enterprise or Business plan.

However, there are some free reporting tools available, including a number of third-party reporters. `newman-reporter-htmlextra` (`https://github.com/DannyDainton/newman-reporter-htmlextra`), written by Danny Dainton, is probably the best one available. This reporter works with the Postman command-line runner known as **Newman**, which I will show you how to use in *Chapter 8, Running API Tests in CI with Newman*. In that chapter, I will also show you how to use the test reporter, but for now, keep in mind that good test reporting will help with creating maintainable tests.

Summary

This chapter has been filled with ideas on how to create long-lasting and valuable test automation. Over the next few chapters, I will take a lot of the foundations we've laid here and show you how to use various features in Postman. This will help you put the topics from this chapter into practice in your testing.

You have learned the strengths that test automation brings to the table and how to use those strengths to your advantage when creating a test strategy. You have also learned about different types of API tests that you can create, including contract tests, integration tests, endpoint tests, and performance and security tests.

I also showed you how to use Postman to organize and structure variables in ways that will help you understand what an API is doing and what you might need to do if tests fail. I also showed you how to use variables in Postman and where to store them. You now know which scope to use for different kinds of variables and understand how Postman will resolve variables values if there are conflicts between those scopes.

In addition, you have learned the importance of logging and test reporting when it comes to creating API tests. I gave you a few exercises to work on, but the truth is that this information might still feel a little abstract at this point, and that is ok. These are important principles to understand. I will build on them and make them much more concrete as we progress through this book. You will see how important these foundations are and how to use them in practice as you learn more about Postman.

In the next chapter, we will look at some concrete ways that you can use Postman to do authorization in APIs. We will see how authorization works in APIs, as well as how to set up and use various authorization options within Postman itself.

Section 2: Using Postman When Working with an Existing API

This section will help you to use Postman to test and improve the quality of existing APIs.

This section includes the following chapters:

5
Understanding Authorization Options

In 2017, Equifax, a large credit reporting agency, announced that they had been hacked. Data from 147 million of their users had been stolen. Years of lawsuits and fines followed and by the time everything had been paid out, the hack cost Equifax more than 1.7 billion dollars.

Although this is one of the most expensive hacks in history, it is far from the only one. Many thousands of companies have been hacked and lost data. The cost of these hacks might range from dollar amounts that end in billions, to those that are "only" in the millions, but the fact remains that security is an extremely important part of any application.

One of the most common ways that attackers get into systems is through APIs. In the Equifax case, the attackers got in initially due to an unpatched server, but then, they were able to extract data for several months by using the APIs that Equifax provides. APIs are meant to be interacted with programmatically. That's the whole reason we make them, and it allows for all kinds of powerful interactions. However, it also means that nefarious actors can use their power too. Security is important at every level in an application, but APIs are one of the most important places to think very carefully about it.

In this chapter, I will show you some of the strategies that can be used to make APIs more secure. I will also show you some of the things you can do to test for security issues. An important factor of any security system is being able to control who has access to the system and what things they can do. Many APIs have authorization options that give control over these things. These options are obviously important, but they can create some challenges when testing an API. They add additional testing considerations since you need to make sure that they correctly restrict things.

It is important to test for those kinds of things, but authorization can also make it harder to do other API tests. Even if you are not trying to test the authorization options in an API, you will still need to interact with those options when doing other tests on that API.

There are a lot of different ways to set up authorization in an API, and Postman has tools that help you work with APIs that have various types of authorization options. I will spend a good portion of this chapter showing you how to use those tools so that you can effectively test your APIs. In this chapter, I will cover the following topics:

- Understanding API security

- API security in Postman

- Security testing with Postman

By the end of this chapter, you will have a good grasp of a lot of concepts related to API authorization. This will include things such as the following:

- The ability to use the various authorization options in Postman to let you access API calls that require authentication to use

- Authorization and authentication and their use in API security

- Skills that will allow you to deal with various kinds of API authorization

- Using secured API calls regardless of the type of authorization they use

- Being able to set up calls using OAuth 2.0 and other workflows that grant authority implicitly

- The ability to do several kinds of security testing including fuzzing, command injection, and authorization testing

- Learning how to integrate Postman with other security testing tools and specifically learn how to use it with Burp Suite

Understanding API security

API security is an important topic. This section will introduce some of the basic concepts and terminology used in API security. Later sections in this chapter will walk you through the various ways to authorize an API. However, before I show you how to use those, I want to talk a bit about what authorization even is. I have been using the term authorization, but the reality is, securing an API (or a website) involves two things. It involves **authorization** and **authentication**. These are important topics that underpin all security testing. Although they are often used interchangeably, understanding the distinction between them will help you to effectively test APIs with these options. In this section, we will explore what these two concepts are and how they relate to each other.

Authorization in APIs

Authorization is how we determine what things a given user is allowed to do. So, for example, if you imagine an online learning platform, you might have different sets of permissions for different users. You might have some users that are students and can only see data in certain ways. A student user might only be able to see a grade mark, while another user who is a teacher might be able to actually modify the grade. There are many additional ways that you might want to authorize a user. If we continue thinking about an online learning platform, the teacher may only be able to modify grades for courses that they teach, and students should only be able to view their own grades and not the grades of their classmates.

Authorization is how we determine which things you have been given permission (are authorized) to do. In an API, this can take the form of determining whether you are authorized to use different endpoints or certain methods on an endpoint. For instance, some users might not be allowed to use a certain endpoint at all, while in other cases a user may be allowed to use an endpoint to GET data, but not to DELETE or modify the data. There may also be cases where an API might return different information depending on the kind of user that you are. An API call that returns data about a user's grades might return information about the actual grade along with some public feedback if you call it as a student, but it might return some additional private comments if you call it as a teacher.

Authorization is a very important aspect of API security. Just because an API requires a username and password to use it, does not necessarily mean that it is well secured. You still need to test that different types of users only have access to the things that they should. In APIs, you especially need to be careful of the way that different relationships and pieces of the API work in revealing information. I have seen a case where an API blocked direct access to certain data for a type of user. However, as that same user, I could see the data if I viewed an object that was a hierarchical parent of the object I wasn't supposed to see. There are often many different paths to the same data, and you want to think carefully about what those paths are when you are testing that the authorization is working correctly.

Authentication in APIs

The concepts of authentication and authorization often swirl together in our minds as one thing, but there is actually a meaningful distinction to be made between them. You have already seen how authorization is about what things you are allowed to do given that you are a certain kind of user. Authentication is about determining whether you really are that kind of user. In other words, are you who you say you are?

This might be clearer if you think of a physical authentication/authorization system. Think of a spy movie or a heist movie. In these kinds of movies, the characters need to somehow get into a place they aren't allowed to go. They don't have authorization to go there. Maybe they want to break into a bank vault and steal some valuable jewels. There are certain users that are authorized to go into that bank vault. Maybe the bank manager and the owner of those jewels can go into the vault, but most types of users do not have the proper authorization to go in there.

However, how do we know which type of user you are? How do we know if you are the owner of the vault or a thief trying to steal the precious jewels? This is where authentication comes into play. You might have to enter in a combination on the lock, or maybe scan your fingerprint or retina to prove to the system that you are the owner and not a criminal. Authentication is about proving that you are who you say you are. Authorization is about making sure that you can only access the things you are allowed to access. Once you have scanned your fingerprint, the system knows who you are – it has authenticated you. The security system then needs to only allow you access to the security deposit box that the user with that finger is authorized to use.

If we take this back to the idea of API authorization and authentication, authentication involves putting in a password or providing a key that proves that you are who you say you are. Once you have done that, authorization determines which data you can see and interact with.

Both of these pieces are crucial to a properly working security system. The two concepts often get conflated and you will hear one term or the other used to describe them both. This is fine as long as you are aware that there are these two different aspects at play. We need to have some way to verify that someone is who they say that are (a password, for example), but then we also need a set of rules or permissions that allow that authenticated user access to the correct set of resources.

Now that you have the big picture view of security, let's take a look at how to deal with security in Postman.

API security in Postman

Now that you understand what authorization and authentication are, it's time to look at how to use this knowledge in Postman. Postman has a lot of built-in options for dealing with API security, and in this section, I will show you how to use each of them. When I was getting started with API testing, I found that figuring out how to authorize and authenticate myself was one of the hardest parts of API testing. I hope that this section will help you figure out how to handle API security on any APIs you are testing. In the previous section, I talked about the distinction between authorization and authentication. However, as I mentioned, sometimes those two terms are conflated. Postman uses the terminology of "authorization" to combine both of these concepts, so as I show you how to do this, I will generally stick to using that term as an umbrella term for both authentication and authorization.

In this section, you will learn how to use the various authorization options in Postman. I will go over some common ones such as bearer tokens, and also walk you through the details of how to use OAuth 2.0. In addition, you will learn how to use many of the less common authorization options as well so that you will be ready to test regardless of the type of authorization your API uses.

Getting started with authorization in Postman

Authorization details can be set directly on the **Authorization** tab of a request. In order to do that, do the following:

1. Navigate to a request through the **Collections** tab in the navigation panel.

2. Open the request by clicking on it and you will see an **Authorization** tab.

3. Click on that and you will see a dropdown where you can specify the type of authorization that your API uses.

    If you click on that dropdown, you will see that there are a number of options available.

In this section, I will show you how to set up some of the more common ones from this list. If you need more details on some of the other authorization options, you can find more information in the Postman documentation (`https://learning.postman.com/docs/sending-requests/authorization/`). As you can see in the following screenshot, Postman has many authorization options:

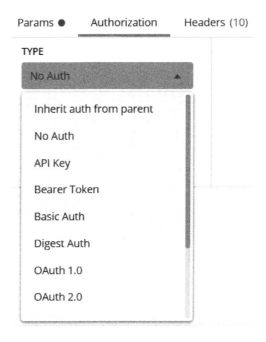

Figure 5.1 – Authorization options in Postman

The first option on this list is the **Inherit auth from parent** option. This is a powerful option that makes it much easier to manage an API. Usually when an API has authorization enabled, it will be required for every endpoint in the API. This means that any time you want to access a request in the API you will need to specify auth options. However, you aren't trying to test the authorization itself; you merely need to enter it so that you can do some other testing. In this case, it makes a lot of sense to only specify the login information in one place rather than repeating it for each request. Postman enables this by allowing you to specify authorization at the folder or collection level. If you click on the **View more actions** menu beside the collection in which your request is located and choose the **Edit** option, you will see that there is an **Authorization** tab. You can set up authorization options here, and then for any request in that collection, you can choose the **Inherit auth from parent** option to use the values you entered in the collection.

If you ever need to update your password or other login information, you can just do this in one spot and all the requests that use it will be updated. Sometimes in API testing, we want to check that different users are correctly authorized and so we might want to use different credentials for some of the API calls. To do this in Postman, you could create a folder inside your collection for each user, and in the options for that folder, you can specify authorization options that can be inherited by the requests in the folder. These options are set on a folder in essentially the same way they are on a collection.

So now that you understand how to structure, organize and set up authorization options in Postman, let's look at some of the specific options and see how to use them.

Using Basic Auth

I guess a good place to start is with a basic option. The **Basic Auth** option is used for APIs that require you to specify a username and password in order to use the API. It is probably the simplest form of API authorization, but it isn't one that is generally recommended or used in production systems. The reality is that Basic Auth is just a little bit too, well, basic for most uses. It is too easy to hack Basic Auth and so it is rarely used in production. However, it is helpful for getting a grasp of how API security works. It is intuitive since it maps well to the way you usually log into a site with a username and password. I will use the Postman Echo API, which is a service that you can use to test some different kinds of API calls. The endpoint (`https://postman-echo.com/basic-auth`) is set up to demonstrate the use of basic authorization. In order to set up basic authorization on this endpoint, follow these steps:

1. Create a collection in Postman for the Postman Echo API and add a request to it with the Basic Auth endpoint mentioned previously.

2. Click on **Send** and you will get back a `401 Unauthorized` code.

3. Click on the **Authorization** tab and from the **Type** dropdown, select the **Basic Auth** option.

   Postman will display spots for you to put in a username and password.

4. For this endpoint, put in `postman` for the username and `password` for the password.

   If you click **Send** again, you should now get back a `200 Ok` response.

After following the previous steps, you should get back a response that has "authenticated" set to true, as you can see in the following screenshot:

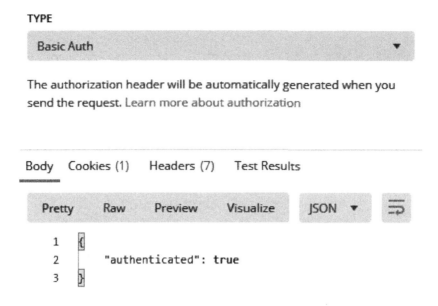

Figure 5.2 – Response authenticated with Basic Auth

Postman makes it straightforward to do this, but let's look at what is going on under the hood to make sure you understand this. If you click on the **Headers** tab, you will see that one of the headers Postman has automatically added to this request is the *Authorization* header. The value for this header starts with the keyword **Basic** and this is how the server knows that you are using the basic authorization for this request. The rest of the value for the authorization header represents a base64 encoding of the username and password that you put in.

It is important to note here that base64 encoding is not secure. If you copy the characters from this and go to https://www.base64decode.org/ and decode it, you will see that it is trivial to get back the username and password from this request. Since base64 encoding is not encryption, it is important to be careful about how you use it. If you are not using a secure (https) connection, this kind of encoding is open to man-in-the-middle attacks and so you want to be careful about using it. Most APIs don't use Basic Auth and instead rely on more complex authorization schemes.

> **Important note**
>
> The point of testing is to help improve the quality of our product, but
> unfortunately it can sometimes cause problems of its own if you are not
> careful. One area where testing has caused issues in the past is in leaking
> login information. Many build systems run tests and these build systems are
> increasingly done on web-based platforms that may be accessible to others. If
> you are running tests using platforms such as Travis, Jenkins, CircleCI, and
> others, you will want to be careful about how you store login information.
>
> Even if you are not using build systems like these, Postman has features that
> allow for the sharing of collections and tests with others. You need to think
> about what credentials you have and make sure that they are stored and shared
> in safe ways.

Basic Auth is pretty easy to understand but it certainly isn't the only, or even the most
common way to do API authorization. Let's move on to looking at how to use **Bearer
Tokens** in API authorization.

Using Bearer Tokens

Bearer tokens are a common way to set up API authorization. They have some
advantages over Basic Auth, since they can contain within them not only the concept of
authentication, but also authorization. Let's look at the example of using GitHub:

1. If you have a GitHub account, log into it.

2. Under **Settings**, go to **Developer settings**.

3. In there, you can choose the **Personal access tokens** option and generate a token.

Here, you can select scopes for this token. The scopes allow you to control what things the user of this token can do. The following screenshot shows you some of the GitHub API scopes:

What's this token for?

Select scopes

Scopes define the access for personal tokens. Read more about OAuth scopes.

☐ **repo**	Full control of private repositories
☐ repo:status	Access commit status
☐ repo_deployment	Access deployment status
☐ public_repo	Access public repositories
☐ repo:invite	Access repository invitations
☐ security_events	Read and write security events
☐ **write:packages**	Upload packages to github package registry
☐ **read:packages**	Download packages from github package registry
☐ **delete:packages**	Delete packages from github package registry
☐ **admin:org**	Full control of orgs and teams, read and write org projects
☐ write:org	Read and write org and team membership, read and write org projects
☐ read:org	Read org and team membership, read org projects

Figure 5.3 – Some of the GitHub API scopes

This provides several advantages over basic authentication since in addition to authenticating that someone is who they say they are, with this token you can also determine what actions they are authorized to use. You can also change or revoke what things the bearer of the token can do and so if the token ever is compromised, it is easier to mitigate the damage. Due to this, these kinds of authorization tokens are very common.

In order to use a token like this in Postman, you just need to select the **Bearer Token** option from the **Type** dropdown, and then type or paste in your token. If you look at the **Headers** tab for that request, you will see that Postman has added an **Authorization** header for you. You can also see that the value for this token starts with *Bearer*, which lets the server know that you are using an API token to authorize your request.

Bearer tokens are an example of a larger class of authorization methods known as **API keys**. Bearer API keys have become so common that Postman includes a separate way to set them up, but there are other ways to use API keys as well.

Using API keys

API keys can be used in a variety of different ways. In order to see this, do the following:

1. Go to the **Authorization** tab of a request in Postman.

2. Choose the **API Key** option from the **Type** dropdown.

   You will be presented with a few options.

3. Click on the **Add to** option, which will give you a drop-down choice between adding your API key to the **Header** or adding it to the **Query Params**.

API keys can also sometimes be added directly to the body of a request. However, if your API does this, you will need to manually set it up since Postman does not support this option. API keys can also be added to the **Authorization** header, and this is usually done with bearer tokens, which Postman has separated into its own category of authorization since it is so common.

Aside from using API keys as bearer tokens, one of the more common ways to pass them through the API, is still in the headers. Rather than passing it in with the authorization header though, it will often be passed as its own header. The exact way to do this will vary from API to API and you will need to look at the documentation to figure out exactly how it works. A common header used for this is the x-api-key header, although others can also be used. If you had an API that required the key to be passed in this way, you could fill it out in Postman by setting the **Key** field to x-api-key and the **Value** field to have the API key in it. You would also need to make sure that the **Add to** option was set to **Header**. If you do this in Postman, you can then look at the **Headers** tab and see that Postman has automatically added an x-api-key header with the API key value to your request.

In a similar way, you could specify the key name and value for a query parameter type of API key authorization if that was what the API required. If you do this, Postman will automatically add the key and value to the params for that request.

Basic auth and API keys are easy to understand and use, but some APIs use more advanced forms of authorization. Let's look at some of those.

Using AWS Signature

Cloud computing is fully mainstream, and many companies now use cloud computing platforms or are trying to move towards them. In many ways, Amazon has led the charge when it comes to cloud computing and the **Amazon Web Services (AWS)** ecosystem is well known and widely used. A lot of cloud computing systems and resources can be interacted with via APIs, which need to be authorized. Postman provides an AWS Signature authorization option to help with authorizing AWS APIs. Going into the details of how to set up and use AWS is far beyond the scope of this book, but if you have AWS APIs that you are testing, you may find this helpful. In many ways, the AWS Signature option is just another way to specify an API key. You specify the **AccessKey** and the **SecretKey**, which are a lot like the key and the value for the API keys option. You can also specify whether the data gets passed in as a header or a query. Which setting to use will depend on what the documentation for the particular API you are looking at ways to do.

There are a few advanced options that let you set things such as the **AWS Region**, the **Service Name**, and the **Session Token**. Postman uses these options to automatically add the headers and parameters that you need to your AWS calls. As I said, I can't get into details on how to call AWS APIs from Postman, but if you are using them, be sure to check out the AWS Signature option to help you with authorizing them.

Using OAuth

You've probably heard of OAuth before, but if you are anything like me, you've found it hard to wrap your head around this concept. There are a couple of points of confusion that, once cleared up, helped me to get a better grasp of what exactly is going on with OAuth.

The first thing to know is that the Oauth specification, while of course being about authorization, is primarily about the delegation of that authorization. What does that mean? Well, imagine that you are checking into a hotel. The whole point of being there is that you want to get into one of the rooms. Now the hotel has a key with the ability to open any of those rooms, but they understandably do not want to give you that key. Instead you go to the front desk and request access to a room. The clerk verifies that you can have access to that room, perhaps by swiping your credit card, and then hands you a key card that you can use to get into that room.

Let's diagram it out and then compare that diagram to how an OAuth flow works. The first step is that you come into the hotel and give your credit card to the clerk while requesting access to a room:

Figure 5.4 – Requesting a room

The clerk then swipes your credit card to determine that you have enough funds available. In this way, the clerk gets approval to issue you a room key and so they hand you a key card:

Figure 5.5 – Giving you an access card

You can now use that key card to access your room. In this way, the hotel owner can give you access to something without needing to issue you the key to whole hotel. They can also easily limit what you have access to and only let you in that one room and maybe the pool and weight room, while not letting you in the other rooms in the hotel. This is similar to what is going on in an OAuth flow.

Let's change the terminology in those diagrams to see how it correlates. Now instead of imagining yourself trying to get access to a room, imagine you want to play a game that needs access to some of your user data from Facebook. In the hotel scenario, you requested access to a hotel room and in this scenario, the game (or, more generically, the application), asks the authorization server for access to the data that it needs:

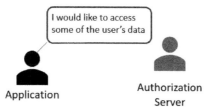

Figure 5.6 – Token request

When you were requesting access to a hotel room, the clerk used your credit card to figure out whether you should be allowed to have the access that you were requesting. In an OAuth workflow, the authorization server will prompt the user to see if the application should be allowed to have the access it wants. If you approve that access, the authorization server will then give the application a token that will give it access to the data it has requested access to:

Figure 5.7 – Token granted

A hotel gives you a key card that will open your room for you. An authorization server gives the application a token that it can then use to access the data that it needs from the resource server.

As you can see, an OAuth workflow involves a couple of steps and includes some complications, but it has a few benefits as well. It allows a third-party application to access some of your data without that application needing to be trusted with your password. It also has a lot of the same benefits as a bearer token in that you can change or revoke access if anything goes wrong in the future. This type of auth has become very popular. Many of the big tech companies, such as Twitter, Facebook, and Google, allow you to use your accounts with them to log into other applications. OAuth isn't simple to use, but it is supported by Postman and is a powerful and common authorization option. Let's look at how to use it in Postman.

Setting up OAuth 2.0 in Postman

The workflow described previously is an OAuth 2 workflow. There are several slightly different flows that can be used with OAuth depending on what kind of application it is. The exact steps that you will need to use will vary a bit from application to application and you will need to follow up with the documentation for your application to figure out exactly what to do, but in order to help you understand that, let's walk through an example showing how to set this up. For this example, I will use the Imgur website (`https://imgur.com/`). If you want to follow along with this, you will need to create an account with that site if you don't already have one.

Before setting up an authorized call, let's first try calling one of the Imgur API endpoints without using authorization by following these steps:

1. Create a collection and name it `imgur`.

2. Create a request in that collection. Name it something like `my account images` and set the endpoint to `https://api.imgur.com/3/account/me/images`. This endpoint will give you a list of all the images that belong to your account.

3. Send the request and you will notice that you get back a `401 Unauthorized` error.

In order to successfully call this endpoint, you will need to get an authorization token. To get this token with the Imgur API, you will need to use OAuth. Before you can set up an OAuth login, you will need an application for it to log into. Let's take a look at how you can do that.

Register an application

Imgur makes it quite easy to create an application. Simply go to `https://api.imgur.com/oauth2/addclient` (ensuring that you are logged in) and fill out the information in the form. Name the application something like `My Postman Test Application` and leave the authorization type option to use OAuth 2 with a callback URL.

The callback URL is the spot users of the application you are creating will be redirected to if they successfully authorize. In this case, we don't have an actual callback URL that we want to redirect users to, but we can use a dummy URL that Postman provides for this purpose: `https://www.getpostman.com/oauth2/callback`. Type or paste this URL into the **Authorization callback URL** field and then add in your email and description if you want and click on the **Submit** button to create your Imgur application. At this point, you may want to copy the client ID and secret as we will use them later. Make sure to keep them somewhere safe though.

Now that you have an application, we can look at how to set up auth in Postman using OAuth 2.

Getting an OAuth 2 access token

Go back to the request where you are trying to get all the images that belong to your account and go to the **Authorization** tab. On the **Type** dropdown, select the **OAuth 2.0** option. As I explained earlier in this chapter, the OAuth workflow requires making a couple of API calls. First, the application you made will need to go to the authorization server and let that server know that it wants a token. This server will check with the user and make sure they are OK with giving the application a token and if they are, it will return the token and redirect to the callback URL.

These steps can be performed manually, but Postman has set it up so that it can do some of this automatically in the background for you. In order to use that functionality, click on the **Get New Access Token** button. This will give you a form with several fields to fill out:

- Give the token a name. Postman will store the token for you so that you can use it in other requests if you want.

- Ensure that the **Grant Type** option is set to **Authorization Code**.

- **Callback URL** needs to be the exact same as the one the application will redirect to. So, in this case, `https://www.getpostman.com/oauth2/callback`.

- **Auth URL** is the API endpoint that you call in order to ask the authorization server if you are allowed to get a token. When you call this URL, the user will be prompted to make sure they are OK with your application having access to their data. For the Imgur API, that endpoint is `https://api.imgur.com/oauth2/authorize`.

- Once your application has received authorization to proceed, it gets a very short-lived key that it can exchange for a more permanent token. It does this with the **Access Token URL**. The Imgur API endpoint for this is `https://api.imgur.com/oauth2/token`.

- In order to authorize your application, the authorization server needs to know what application it is being asked to authorize. This is where the **Client ID** and **Client Secret** fields come in. If you didn't copy them when you created your application, you can get them by going to `imgur.com` in your browser, clicking on your username, and then selecting **Settings**. On the settings page, choose the **Applications** option. You should now be able to see the **Client ID** for your application, and you can click on the **generate a new secret** option to get the **Client Secret**, which is shown in the following figure:

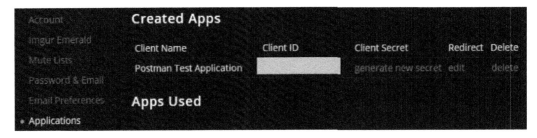

Figure 5.8 – Getting the Client ID and Client Secret from Imgur

- The **Scope** field is used if the token should have limited abilities and **State** is an additional security measure that some APIs have. You don't need to worry about either of those with the Imgur API.

- For the **Client Authentication** option, ensure that it is set to use the **Send as Basic Auth header** option.

Whew! That's a lot of information to fill out, but once you have filled out all of those fields, the form should look something like this:

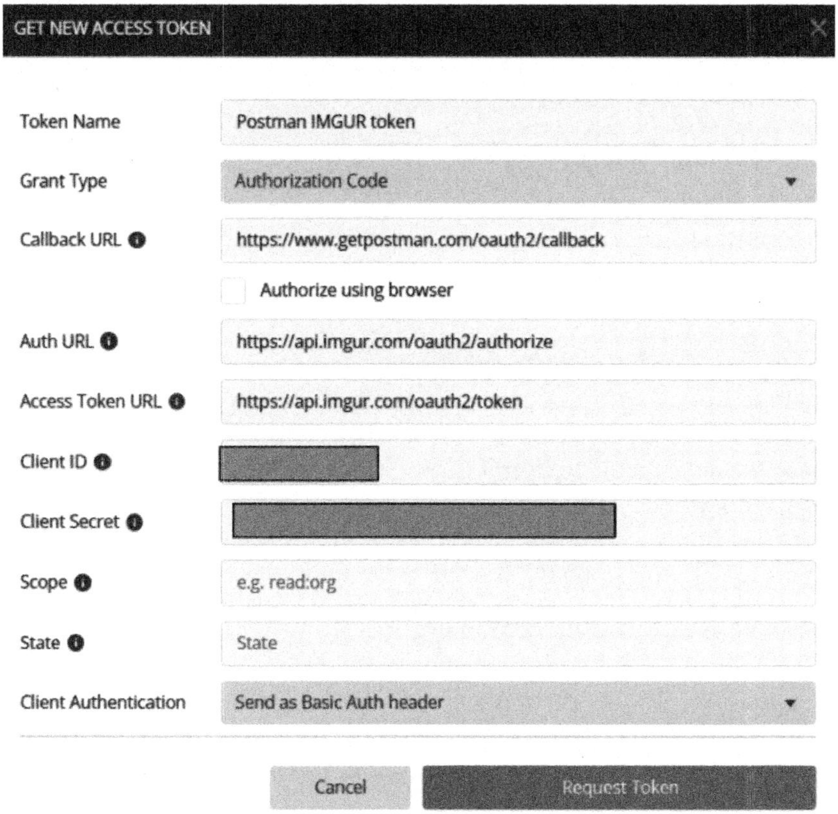

Figure 5.9 – Settings for getting an OAuth 2.0 access token in Postman

You should now be able to click on the **Request Token** button. If you have filled out all the information correctly, you will get a popup asking you if you want to allow your application access to your Imgur data. Enter your password if necessary and then click **ok**. You can then click on **Use Token** to tell Postman to add the access token to the appropriate field.

Now, if you send your request again, you should get back information about all the images that are associated with your account. If you just created your account, you might not have any images associated with your account, but you should still get back an empty list and the call should return a 200 OK status code.

As you can see, there is a lot of complexity involved in using OAuth for API authorization. Postman does give you some help with it though. I've shown you how to set it up for one API and that should give you a pretty good idea of how to do it for others. Each API, of course, is going to be different and so you are going to need to figure out things such as the token and authorization endpoints for the API you want to test. These things will usually be in API documentation. You will also need to figure out the Client ID and Secret, which might be things you need to ask others about, but once you have all that information, you should be able to set up an access token in Postman.

Try it out – set up Twitter OAuth

In order to understand something, you have to try it out on your own. OAuth can be tricky to use, and so I would challenge you to try setting it up on your own. I walked you through an example using the Imgur API. See if you can work out how to set it up so that you can use the Twitter API.

In order to get started, you will first need to apply for a developer account, which you can do by going to `https://developer.twitter.com/en/apply-for-access` and filling out the form. Once your request is approved, you will get some keys (store them in a safe place!). One of them is a bearer token, which you could use to authorize your API requests, but see if you can instead use the API key and secret to set up OAuth 2.0 access for your API calls. I don't want to give everything away for you, but I will give you a couple of hints to help you along the way.

One thing to note, is that you will need to use the Client Credentials Grant Type for the Twitter API instead of the Authorization code type that Imgur uses. You may also want to search the Twitter API documentation, or even do an online search, to help you out if you get stuck on trying to figure something out. It can be frustrating to figure out something you don't know but working through the frustration will help you learn how to do this.

OAuth 1.0

So far in this chapter, I have been using the terms OAuth and OAuth 2.0 interchangeably. Almost all APIs that use OAuth now use OAuth 2.0. Despite the similar names, OAuth 1.0 is quite different from OAuth 2.0. It does have some similar ideas and laid a lot of the groundwork for the kinds of flows that are used in OAuth 2.0 authorization. However, OAuth 1 had several limitations to it that were made much better in OAuth 2.0 and so it is not used much anymore.

Postman does still support this option, so if you are testing an API that uses it, you can do so in Postman. However, since it isn't used much in industry, I won't go through the details of setting this up. If you do need that information, you can look at the Postman documentation to help you get started with it (`https://learning.postman.com/docs/sending-requests/authorization/#oauth-10`).

Using Digest auth and Hawk authentication

Postman provides authorization options for setting up **Digest** and **Hawk** auth. These are older authentication standards that few modern APIs use. The Hawk authentication scheme is meant to solve similar problems to the OAuth 2.0 standard, but it never got widespread adoption and so although it is still used in some APIs, most new APIs will use OAuth 2.0 instead.

Digest authentication helps to make it more secure to use a username and password if you're sending your data over an unencrypted connection. Although it is more secure than just sending a plaintext password, it still has its downfalls and since most sites now use encrypted connections, it doesn't have much value in the modern API ecosystem.

Since these are not very common authentication systems and are in Postman for more historical reasons than anything else, I won't be working through specific examples of how to use them in this chapter. If you do ever find yourself working with an API that uses one of these methods, you can find some information on how to set them up in the Postman documentation.

Using NTLM authentication

NTLM stands for **New Technology LAN Manager**, and it is a set of security protocols that Windows uses to provide authentication to users. It can be used in APIs to allow users access to resources on the API based on their current Windows login information. If you are working with an API that has this kind of authentication setup, you can choose that option from the authorization type dropdown and then enter your Windows username and password.

> **A warning about passwords**
>
> Any time that you are using login credentials, you need to be careful about sharing collections or requests. This is especially important in this case, since you are using the login credentials to your computer and probably many other Microsoft accounts. Make sure to protect them carefully!

Postman will default to sending the request twice, since the first time it will get back the security values that it needs to be successful on the second try. A lot of APIs that use this kind of authentication are internal APIs, so if you need more information on setting it up for a particular API that you are working on, you may need to talk to the internal stakeholders at your company to figure out the details of it.

Using Akamai EdgeGrid

Akamai Technologies is a global cloud services company. They have a variety of services and many of those services are supported by APIs. They also have their own somewhat unique way of authenticating applications within their network and have created an authorization helper that you can use in Postman. The details of this are beyond the scope of this book, but if you need more information, you can check out the Akamai developer documentation (`https://developer.akamai.com/legacy/introduction/Prov_Creds.html`).

Some of the options for authorization in Postman are more common than others. So far, most of this chapter has focused on how to set up credentials so that you can log into an API and make the calls that you want. This is an important part of being able to test an API, but I also want you to think about why we need all these ways of authorizing and authenticating APIs in the first place. Why do we even have all the options in the API ecosystem? The reason, of course, is that there are those who want to use APIs in ways that would cause harm.

Postman has a lot of different authorization options. You may not have needed to carefully study each of them, but hopefully whichever option your API uses, you will be able to get started with it. I've shown you how to use Basic Auth, bearer tokens and API keys, and authentication for AWS APIs. You also now understand how OAuth workflows work and how you can use them in Postman. In addition, I introduced you to some lesser-known authorization options such as Digest, Hawk, NTLM, and Akamai EdgeGrid. You certainly won't encounter all of these options in one API. In fact, you might not even encounter some of them in the course of an entire career, but you now have the foundational knowledge that you need so that you can log into any API you face.

Knowing how to log into an API so that you can make the calls you want is important, but don't forget that APIs are one of the most common places that attackers target when they are trying to break into a system. In addition to being able to set up auth in an API, I want to also show you how to approach security testing APIs.

Security testing with Postman

I only have a few pages in this book to talk about security testing, so I will do my best to give you an introduction to this concept. There is an entire library of books written about security testing. This is a huge and important topic, but since it is not the main emphasis of this book, I will just touch on some of the key ideas and leave it up to you to do some more research if you want to dive deeper into this topic.

There are many people who have job titles that include the term security tester or security researcher. Many have chosen to dedicate their careers to ensuring that we have strong, useful security options in place. If you work at a company that has a dedicated security tester (or testing team), don't hesitate to use those resources. However, no matter how many resources your company has for security testing, I think that every tester should at least have a basic level of knowledge about this. Security is utterly vital to the survival of almost any company today, and the more knowledge of it we have in our companies, the better off we will be. Since I do have limited space, I am just going to focus on a couple of techniques. I have not yet covered some of the concepts that you will need for using these techniques, so for now I will give you an overview of them. Once you learn some of those concepts, feel free to come back to this chapter and review how they can be used for security testing.

Fuzzing

Fuzzing or **Fuzz Testing** is a funny-sounding term, but it is a powerful testing concept. It is powerful in its simplicity as all it involves is giving a program or service random inputs and seeing if something unexpected happens. Fuzzing is a brute-force testing method, where you keep trying different inputs, without worrying too much about whether they make sense or not, just to see what happens. Since APIs are designed to be interacted with programmatically, they are well suited to this kind of testing.

The ironic thing is that while fuzzing is a powerful testing technique, it is also a powerful hacking technique. Hackers will often try fuzzing to see if they can find vulnerabilities in an API. So why not beat them at their own game? In *Chapter 7, Data-Driven Testing*, I will show you how to set up a data-driven test in Postman. You can use tests like this for Fuzz Testing as well as other things.

Command injection

APIs allow you to send commands to web services. These commands are meant to be sent in certain ways, but that doesn't prevent users from trying to send the commands in ways that might cause problems. By formatting API queries in certain ways, you might be able to send commands that will get executed on the service. We forget it sometimes, but the cloud is just made up of computers. When you send an API request to a service, even if that service is in the cloud, that request will be executed on a computer somewhere. Let's look at an example of how that could work.

Imagine that you have an API that has an endpoint called /content. That endpoint allows you to read the contents of certain files by specifying the filename as a query parameter. You can send a call like this: /content?name=myfile.txt and it will return the contents of the file called myfile.txt from the server. Now, how is the server going to do that? Imagine that it took the naïve approach of calling the system command cat <file_name>. In this case, what would happen if you made an API call like this:

```
/content?name="myfile.txt; ls"
```

Depending on how the code is constructed, it could turn into the following commands in the server:

```
cat myfile.txt;
ls
```

In this case, you would not only get back the contents of the file, but also a list of the other files in the directory. In this example, since we are imagining that the server is directly executing commands, we can send pretty much any supported system command to the server and we are able to do what is known as **arbitrary code execution**. Thankfully, this is a contrived situation and I highly doubt any developer would read files from a server in this way, but it does illustrate how to think about this. Think about the fact that at the other end of the API call is a computer that is running some kind of code and consider whether there are things that might cause problems for that code if they were sent.

This was an example of operating system injection, but there are also other types of injection that can happen through API requests. For example, if the API causes database queries on the backend, it might be susceptible to SQL injection. You should also consider other ways that data can be injected. I showed an example of injecting it via a query parameter, but you might also be able to send injection data through the headers, body, or even cookies.

Authorization testing

APIs use authorization to determine whether an authenticated user is allowed to have access to a certain resource or command. As with anything in software testing, you should not just assume that this will work. You will want to execute tests that check whether users of certain types have been correctly gated from a certain resource. Use login credentials to try and access resources that you should not be allowed to have access to.

If an API doesn't have all the authorization correctly set up, it can be difficult to test since you would have to test all the endpoints and options in the system to be comprehensive. However, this is often impossible to do. For example, as new items or users are added to the system, it could generate new available endpoints. One thing that hackers have done in the past is to get access to data by checking sequential IDs. Imagine that you are using a site and you notice that it has a URL that looks something like this: `/someobject?id=1234`. You notice that the `1234` query parameter is showing up in several places and infer that it is your user ID. If the site that you are on is using sequential IDs for its users, you can quite easily try different IDs in that API and if the authorization hasn't been properly set up, you might be able to find information that belongs to another user. Often, some of the first user IDs in a database will be for the admin or other super users that got created very early on in the site's development. If a hacker is able to use those IDs, you could end up with a serious breach.

In order to make it more difficult for hackers or others to infer information from your system, you may want to consider using some kind of random value when using things like user IDs or other potentially sensitive information in an API URL. This is no replacement for proper security protocols, but it can help make things just a little more secure. This is sometimes known as **security by obscurity** since you are making things a little more obscure, which makes it harder for hackers and others to infer information about your system.

The idea of security by obscurity can help, but when it comes to proper API authorization, you need to consider two important things. The first is **role-based security**. I have already talked about this concept, where there are different roles that users within your system can take on. Anyone in the system who is a student would take on a student role, and anyone who is a teacher would take on a teacher role, and so on.

Trying out different roles in an important aspect of authorization testing, but there is another level of detail that is important for this as well. In the example of a learning system, someone might have a student role within the system, but that does not mean that they can access data from any course in the system. They should only be able to see data from certain courses that they are enrolled in. There isn't really a standard term for this, but it is sometimes called things such as **rights-based security** or **programmatic security**. This kind of security is often mixed up with business logic in an application and so it is a very important type of authorization to check for in your tests. I have seen cases where the user interface correctly restricts users from things they do not have the rights to, but that same security is not applied correctly in the API, meaning users can see things they do not have the right to.

You cannot fully mitigate all authorization mistakes, but when you set up tests, be sure to include negative authorization checks. Postman can be helpful for this. Once you have defined all your test cases in Postman, you can run them with different credentials to check whether they are correctly authorized. Doing this allows you to reuse your tests for security purposes.

Integrating with Burp Suite

I have talked about a few security testing approaches that you can use in Postman. There are also many other tools that are specifically designed around security testing. These tools are not the focus of this book, but some of them can be used along with Postman to enhance your security testing. A lot of these tools use network proxies to help you understand and test network traffic. I can't show you how each tool works, but I will walk you through integrating Postman with one of them so that you can get an idea of how to do this.

If you want to follow along with this at home (and I would recommend that you do), you will need to download and install Burp Suite. You can get a free community edition here: `https://portswigger.net/burp/communitydownload`. Once you have downloaded and installed it, start it up and click your way through the startup wizard, leaving the default options in place. With Burp Suite opened, you can now check that it is set up the way you need. Use the following steps to configure Burp Suite:

1. Go to the **Proxy** tab and select the **Options** sub-tab.

2. In the **Proxy Listeners** section, ensure that the **Running** checkbox beside the listener running on `127.0.0.1:8080` is selected:

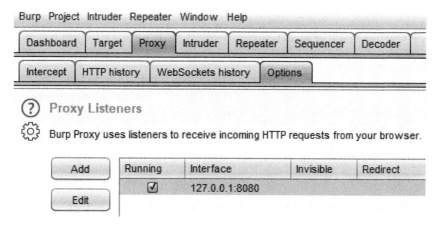

Figure 5.10 – Burp Suite proxy listener running

3. Now go to the **Intercept** sub-tab, and on click on the **Intercept is on** button to turn off intercepting:

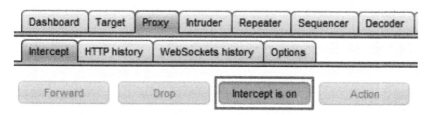

Figure 5.11 – Turn off Intercepting

Now that you have Burp Suite properly configured, it's time to set up Postman as well. Burp Suite is an internet proxy, and Postman can be set up up to route through a proxy, so that you can use it in conjunction with a proxy. In order to do this, follow these steps:

1. Click on the **Settings cog** at the top of the application and choose **Settings** from the menu.

2. On the popup, click on the **Proxy** tab.

3. You can now set up a custom proxy that will use the Burp Suite proxy. In order to do that, select the **Add a custom proxy configuration** option and then in the **Proxy Server** box, put in the IP address of the proxy server Burp Suite is using (in this case, `127.0.0.1:8080`):

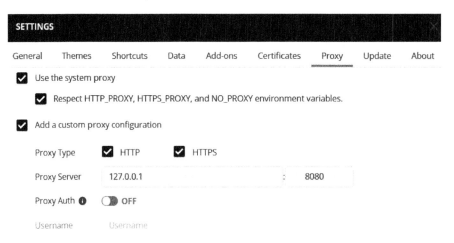

Figure 5.12 – Configure a proxy server in Postman

Since the data we send from Postman will now go through a Burp Suite, the security certificate will be from Burp Suite and will probably not be trusted.

4. In order to fix this, you can go to the **General** tab on the **SETTINGS** popup and turn off the **SSL certificate verification** option:

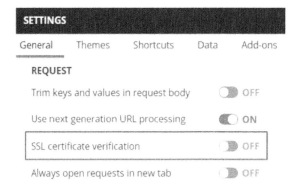

Figure 5.13 – Turn off SSL certificate verification

5. Close the dialog and then send a request from Postman.

If you go over to Burp Suite, you should see that the request has been routed through the Burp Suite proxy. You should see something similar to the following screenshot, where the API request details show up in the **Target** tab:

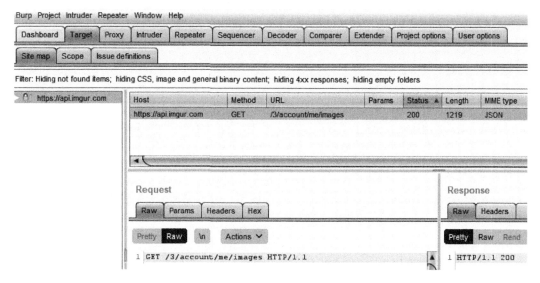

Figure 5.14 – Request captured in Burp Suite

Now that you have configured everything so that you can use Burp Suite and Postman together, you can use the security tools of Burp Suite in conjunction with the API testing tools of Postman. This book isn't about how to use the security testing tools in Burp Suite, but if you want to dive deeper into this, you can look at some of the security tests that you can do with it by looking through the documentation in the *Next steps* section of the Portswigger getting started documentation (which you can find here: `https://portswigger.net/burp/documentation/desktop/getting-started`).

I've shown you how to do this with this one particular ool, but you can also set up Postman to work with other proxies and tools like this.

> **Important note**
> Don't forget to turn off your custom proxy in Postman once you are done using Burp Suite! Otherwise, the calls that you send from Postman will seem to hang, and you will eventually get a connection or tunneling error.

Proxy tools allow you to view and manipulate data and are helpful for security testing. Although Postman itself is not a security testing tool, it can be used to help you check for security issues in your APIs. Security testing is a large, complex, and important topic. I've just scratched the surface of it in these few pages, but even if you aren't an expert on security (I'm definitely not!), don't be afraid to use what you know to check that your API is secure.

Summary

This chapter has covered a lot of territory. Security is a complex and important topic and understanding how to work with it is an important part of API testing. In this chapter, I have shown you how to think about API security and what the distinction is between authorization and authentication in security. I also showed you how to use the various Postman authorization types to give you access to secured APIs. You learned how to log in with many different authorization types ranging from Basic Auth to API keys and tokens to OAuth 2.0. I also showed you some of the other authorization options in Postman and showed you how to get started with them.

We didn't just look at how to call secured APIs in this chapter though. I also helped you get started with a few security testing techniques such as fuzzing, command injection, and authorization testing and showed you how to use them in Postman. In addition, you learned how to integrate Postman with other external security testing tools. To help with this, I showed you an example of how to integrate Postman with Burp Suite so that you could see how this might work. All in all, we covered a lot of ground in this chapter.

I hope you are excited to continue learning about Postman in the next chapter, where I will show you how to create test validation scripts. This will involve using JavaScript in Postman and will be a lot of fun as you learn how to check that requests are doing what they should be and a lot of other powerful things that Postman can help you with. Let's continue with that in the next chapter!

6
Creating Test Validation Scripts

At one company that I worked at, I was trying to figure out the value of some of the test automation scripts that we had. In order to do this, I was analyzing the test results to see which scripts were giving us the most information. One of the rules I used to determine which scripts might not be adding value was to look at scripts that had never failed. My hypothesis was that if a script had been running for some time and had never failed, it was unlikely to fail in the future and so was not giving us valuable information. I had identified several test scripts that had never failed and was looking through them. Imagine my surprise when in several of them I found assertions that where checking things such as whether `true==true` or `5 == 5`? No wonder the tests had never failed. It was impossible for them to fail.

Although these were egregious examples, the reality is that often a well-designed test suite will fail to deliver on its promise because of poor assertions. You can have a test suite that is checking all the necessary endpoints with all the correct inputs. It can have perfect coverage and be impeccably structured, but without good assertions, it isn't doing you much good.

In this chapter, I will show you how to set up good test validation scripts in Postman. Postman uses JavaScript for this. If you are not familiar with JavaScript, don't worry about it. I will walk carefully through the examples so you should be able to follow along. Postman also provides some helpful examples that you can use. You do not need to be an expert in JavaScript in order to follow along in this chapter, but I hope that by the end of this chapter you will be an expert in creating good test validation.

In addition to using JavaScript for test validation, Postman provides ways to create setup and teardown scripts. You can use these to set some things up before you run a test and to do cleanup after a test has completed. By the end of this chapter, you will be able to use all this functionality in Postman. You will be able to create test validation assertions using JavaScript in Postman, validate body and header data in API responses, use the assertions that the Postman team has created, set up variables and other data before sending a request, create workflows that include multiple requests, create loops to run the same request multiple times with different data, run requests in the collection runner, and use environments to manage and edit variables. The following are the topics that we are going to cover in this chapter:

- Checking API responses

- Setting up pre-request scripts

- Using environments in Postman

Technical requirements

The code used in this chapter can be found at `https://github.com/PacktPublishing/API-Testing-and-Development-with-Postman/tree/master/Chapter06` .

Checking API responses

Since Postman uses JavaScript for the checks in a test, it has a lot of power and flexibility built into it. I'm going to walk you through various things that you can do with this. In order to do that, it will be easiest to work with actual API calls. For that purpose, I will once again use the Star Wars API (`https://swapi.dev`). If you don't have one yet, create a collection in Postman called something like **Star Wars API – Chapter 6** and in that collection create a request called **Get First Person**. This request should call the `/people/1` endpoint from the Star Wars API. You can also download the collection from the GitHub repository for this course (`https://github.com/PacktPublishing/API-Testing-and-Development-with-Postman/tree/master/Chapter06`) and then import that package, if you would prefer.

When I made this collection, I also created a variable called `base_url` that specifies the base URL for this. I will be creating a few different requests as examples in this chapter, so it will be helpful to have that variable. If you set up the collection on your own, you will need to edit the collection and add the variable, giving it a value of `https://swapi.dev/api`. If you imported the package from GitHub, the variable should already be there for you, but in either case, you will need to go to the **Get People** request and modify the URL so that it references the variable and starts with `{{base_url}}`. Once you have that all set up, go ahead and send the request.

Being able to send a request like this is great, but if you automate this, how will you know in the future if it is working correctly? You need to add some checks to this that can verify that it is working correctly! In this section, I will show you how to add these checks. I will also show you how to check data in API response and headers and how to use some of the provided assertions so that you can check anything that you need to. The first thing I want to talk about, though, is how to check the status codes in a response.

Checking the status code in a response

The **Tests** tab in Postman is where you define the things that you want to check on each request. You can find this tab on each request. Go to the **Tests** tab for the request you made and as you can see in the following figure, the left-hand panel has several different snippets available for you to use:

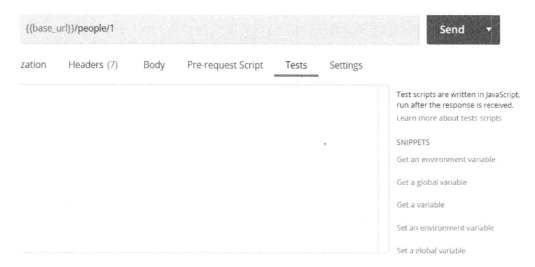

Figure 6.1 – Test snippets

These snippets are little bits of JavaScript code that Postman provides to make it easy to add some common checks to your tests. Scroll down in the list until you see one that says Status code: Code is 200 and click on that one. When you do that you will see that Postman adds some JavaScript code into the test panel. You should see a code that looks something like the following figure:

```
1  pm.test("Status code is 200", function () {
2      pm.response.to.have.status(200);
3  });
```

Figure 6.2 – Snippet checking that the status code is 200

Now, if you send the request, this code will check that the request returns a status code of 200. If the request returns any other status code, this check will fail. If you are not familiar with JavaScript, this might be a bit intimidating, so let's work through this check and see what is going on.

Using the pm.test method

In the first place, we have the pm.test function. The pm object is a JavaScript object that Postman provides that gives you access to data from your requests and their responses. It also lets you access and manipulate variables and cookies. In fact, most of the JavaScript functionality that you will use in Postman is provided through the pm object.

The test method is an asynchronous method that you can use to set up each check that you want to do. It takes in two arguments. The first one is the name of the test as a string, in this case "Status code is 200". Note that enclosing text in double (or single) quotes means that it is a string. This name will appear in the test result output, so you will want to make sure that it accurately describes what the test is doing so that you can better understand your test results.

The second argument needs to be a function that does the actual check that you are interested in. JavaScript gives a lot of shortcuts for this kind of stuff, and so you can define your function directly in the argument to the test method. In this case, the snippet is using an unnamed (or anonymous) function. This is the only spot this function is being used so it does not need a name. The function is defined by function (), which just means that you are creating an anonymous function. Since there is nothing in the brackets, we know that this function does not take in any arguments. However, the pm.test method does expect the function to return a Boolean (a value that is either true or false). It should not return a string, or an integer, or anything like that. You can do whatever checks you want inside the function, but you need to ensure that it returns a Boolean value.

The actual work that the function does is then defined inside the curly braces. So in this case the function is merely calling `pm.response.to.have.status(200);`. Tests need to take in a function like this because they run asynchronously. JavaScript is built to be asynchronous by default. This can be kind of hard to get your head around (it was for me!), but essentially it means that JavaScript (and hence Postman) will not wait for one test to finish before it goes on to the next one. In other words, if you have two tests set up for a request and the first test is doing something that takes a while to process, that test will start and then while Postman waits for it to finish, it will go ahead and start the next test. This is why we need to give the test a function. Essentially, the test will start, and then once it has the data that it needs, it will call the function that we supplied and execute the code in that function. This function that gets called is sometimes called a **callback function**, so if you hear that term, it is just referring to a function that gets passed into another function and that will be called once that function is ready. Writing with asynchronous code takes a bit of an adjustment if you are used to writing in languages that are synchronous, but by following along with examples like these you should get the hang of it quickly.

Using Chai assertions in Postman

There is one last piece to this test that we haven't looked at yet. That is the actual code that is being executed. The snippet is using the pm object to access the response data. The `pm.response` object contains various information about the response. In this example, you are getting the response and then creating an assertion on that response to check that the response has the status `200`.

Assertions in Postman are based on the capabilities of the **Chai Assertion Library**. This is a very common JavaScript assertion library and is used in many JavaScript unit testing frameworks. The Chai framework supports **Test-Driven Development (TDD)** and **Behavior-Driven Development (BDD)** approaches. Postman uses the BDD style of Chai assertion. You can read more about the various assertions on the Chai website (`https://www.chaijs.com/api/bdd/`).

Chai assertions are very nice to read. They match up well with how we would speak about the assertions in natural language English. I'm sure that you were able to figure out that when the snippet said `to.have.status(200)`, it meant that we expect the response to have a status of `200`. This readability makes it easy to figure out what a test is checking; however, I have found that it can be a bit tricky sometimes to figure out how to craft these assertions. As we go through this chapter, I will show you several different assertions. As you see (and create) more of them, it will get easier to use.

Try it out

This is very basic check, but I want you to take a couple of minutes to make sure you understand how it works. Try changing the expected status code and ensure that it fails. The test will be run after you send the request and you can view the results on the **Test Results** tab in the response section. If you click on the **Test Results** tab, you should see something that looks like this:

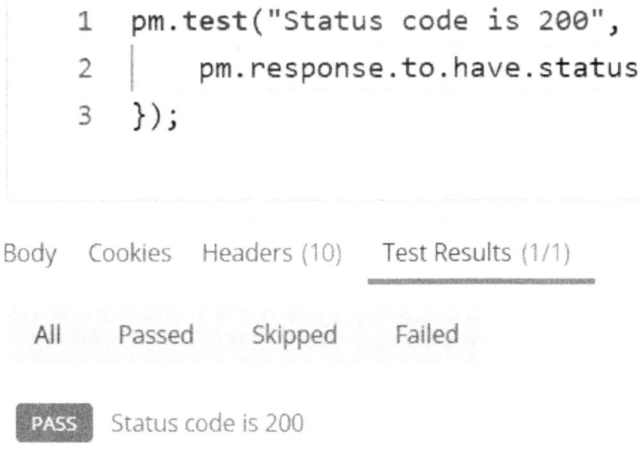

```
1   pm.test("Status code is 200",
2       pm.response.to.have.status
3   });
```

Body   Cookies   Headers (10)   Test Results (1/1)

All   Passed   Skipped   Failed

PASS   Status code is 200

Figure 6.3 – Check on the test results

The script is asserting that the response should be 200. Play around with this assertion a bit and make sure you understand what is going on. Can you make it fail? Make sure you understand how it works. I will be showing you some more assertions, but they share many of the same components as this one so make sure you fully understand what is going on here before moving on to look at how to check data in the body of a response.

Checking the body of a response

You have seen how to verify that an API response has the status code you expect it to, but there is a lot more that you can do with tests in Postman. You can check many things in the data of the response itself. I want to show you a couple of examples of how to do that, so that you can have the confidence to create these kinds of assertions on your own.

Checking whether the response contains a given string

For the first example, I will show you how to check that a response contains a string that you expect it to. The snippets are a very helpful way to learn about the available functionality, so let's use another one to look at how you can verify that the body of a request has the correct data. Scroll down in the snippets section until you see a snippet called **Response body: Contains string**. Ensure that your cursor is on the last line of the tests text field and then click on the snippet to add the code for it to the tests.

You should see a code snippet that looks like this:

```
pm.test("Body matches string", function () {
    pm.expect(pm.response.text()).to.include("string_you_want_
       to_search");
});
```

As you can see, there is a lot of similarity between this snippet and the previous snippet. It once again uses the pm.test method to define the test and we give it a function that does an assertion. In this case, the assertion is a bit different, though. You are still looking for response data with the pm.response object, but now you have the .text() method attached to it. Since the pm.response object is just that, an object; you need to turn it into a string before you can check whether it includes the string you want. This is what the .text() method does. It turns the response object into a string that Postman can search through. Replace string_you_want_to_search with a search term such as Luke. Give the test a more descriptive name as well – perhaps something like Check that the response body contains Luke – and send the request again. In the **Test Results** tab, you should now see that there are two passing tests.

Checking JSON properties in the response

Now let's look at another example snippet. This time choose the **Response body:JSON value check** snippet. You will see that the following code is added to the tests:

```
pm.test("Your test name", function () {
    var jsonData = pm.response.json();
    pm.expect(jsonData.value).to.eql(100);
});
```

There are a couple of new things in this snippet. In the first place, you can see the use of the `var` keyword. This is used in JavaScript to define a variable, so in this case, we are creating a variable called `jsonData`. The data for this variable is coming from the `pm.response` object, but this time instead of calling `.text()` to convert it into a string, the snipped is calling `.json()`, which will turn it into **JSON. JSON** stands for **JavaScript Object Notation** and it is a format that is used for storing and transporting data. It is structurally similar to a dictionary or hash map object and is a very common standard. Many APIs will return data in a JSON structure. The Star Wars API is no exception to this and so you can directly convert the response object for a call to that API into JSON.

The variable can then be used in an assertion. You can see that Postman has put in a default assertion that is expecting the value of the `jsonData` variable to equal `100`. If you send the request, you will see that this test fails with an assertion error where it tells you that it expected undefined to deeply equal `100`, as you can see in the following figure:

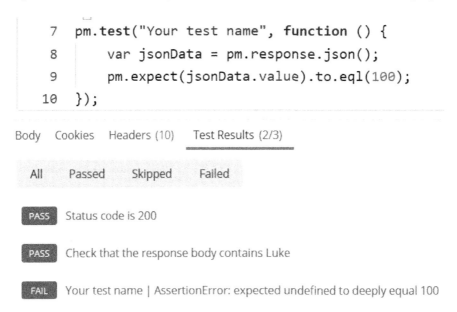

```
 7   pm.test("Your test name", function () {
 8       var jsonData = pm.response.json();
 9       pm.expect(jsonData.value).to.eql(100);
10   });
```

Body   Cookies   Headers (10)   Test Results (2/3)

All   Passed   Skipped   Failed

PASS   Status code is 200

PASS   Check that the response body contains Luke

FAIL   Your test name | AssertionError: expected undefined to deeply equal 100

Figure 6.4 – Test assertion fails

This warning sounds a bit cryptic, but all it is telling you is that it was trying to compare the two values that you gave and one of them was undefined while the other was `100`. It was expecting those two values to be equal and hence the assertion failed. This tells you that `jsonData.value` is undefined. But why? Well, in order to understand that, let's look at the console log.

In JavaScript you can log things to the console. This is similar to printing in other languages. Since Postman is using JavaScript, you can use `console.log` to print out information. This is very helpful when trying to debug something, so let's try it out here. In the line after the variable definition, add this code:

```
console.log(jsonData);
```

Now send the request again. In order to see the data that has been logged, you will need to open the console in Postman. As shown in the following figure, you can do that by clicking on the **Console** button at the bottom of the Postman app:

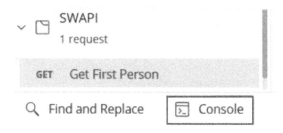

Figure 6.5 – Open the Postman console

At the bottom of the console, you should see the `jsonData` object that you logged:

Figure 6.6 – Logged object

This looks like what you'd expect to see, so why does the assertion think that things are undefined? Well, we need to look for a minute at the `.value` operator. This snippet is a bit tricky. This looks like it is a valid operator, but it is actually just a placeholder to let you know that you need to get some value out of the `jsonData` object. In JavaScript, it is easy to do that with **dot notation**. So, if you want to get the `height` field, you can just reference it by its name like this:

```
jsonData.height
```

You will need to change what you expect it to equal. In this case, it should be equal to `"172"`, so put that in to make the line look this this:

```
pm.expect(jsonData.height).to.eql("172");
```

Now if you send the request, it should pass. Don't forget to remove `console.log` and change the name to something more descriptive.

> **Important note**
> You can access the properties of objects in JavaScript using either bracket or dot notation. They both give you access to the same information, but I think that dot notation is more readable than using bracket notation, and so I will stick with that throughout this book. In dot notation, you can access the properties of an object by using the syntax `objectname.propertyName`. You can also access nested objects in this way, and so you could see something like `objectname.subobjectName.propertyName`.

This example should give an idea of the kinds of options you have for checking response data. Many APIs send responses in JSON format, and with the options you have learned about in this example, you should be able to create checks for almost anything that you might get in an API response. In order to make sure that you understand what is going on here, though, I would encourage you to explore this a bit more.

Try it out

You have a seen a couple of examples that show how to check for data in API responses. Now I want you to try your hand at this without step-by-step examples. See if you can take what you have learned and put it into practice on your own. You can play around and set yourself a few challenges on your own if you want. To help you get started, here are a few ideas of tests that you could create:

- Create a test that verifies Luke's eye color.
- Create a test that verifies the URL of Luke's home world.

If you get stuck on these, you can check out my solutions in the GitHub repository for this course (`https://github.com/PacktPublishing/API-Testing-and-Development-with-Postman/tree/master/Chapter06`). Don't look at the solutions until you have tried it out on your own, though!

Now that you know how to check data in the body of a response, it's time to look at how to check the headers of responses.

Checking headers

An API response includes a status code, a body, and a header. Sometimes, there are important things in the header that you want to be sure are getting sent back correctly. As you might guess, you can create assertions in Postman that let you check header data. Once again, the easiest thing to do is to start with a snippet – in this case, the **Response header: Content-Type header check** snippet. Choosing that snippet should add this code to the tests:

```
pm.test("Content-Type is present", function () {
    pm.response.to.have.header("Content-Type");
});
```

This is similar to the code in the body snippets. The only difference really is that the assertion has the `.header` assertion in it. This is an assertion that is specific to Postman. Postman has a Chai plugin that extends the common Chai assertions to give you access to a few custom ones that they provide. You could build this same assertion without using this custom assertion type, but it would be more complicated to do so.

Custom assertion objects in Postman

You may not have noticed, but you actually used another custom assertion object in one of the earlier examples that I went through previously. When checking the status code, the `.status` assertion is a custom assertion type. Postman has also created several other assertions like this that can make it a lot easier to assert on common response objects. I have listed the custom assertion methods that Postman provides along with examples of how to use them. These assertions are specifically designed to help you verify API response, and so you will probably use them a lot when creating tests in Postman:

- `.statusCode`: This assertion checks whether the numerical status code of the response matches the one you specify. Here's an example usage:

```
pm.response.to.have.statusCode(200);
```

- `.statusCodeClass`: This assertion checks whether the response code is in the right class. Class 2 is a status code that is in the 200s and 3 is one in the 300s, and so on. Here's an example usage:

```
pm.response.to.have.statusCodeClass(2);
```

- `.statusReason`: This assertion checks whether the reason, which is a text response corresponding to the status code, matches what you specify. Here's an example usage:

```
pm.response.to.have.statusReason('OK');
```

- `.status`: This assertion allows you to verify the status by specifying either the status code or the status reason. It is essentially a combination of `.statusCode` and `.statusReason` assertions. Here are two example usages:

```
pm.response.to.have.status('OK');
```

or:

```
pm.response.to.have.status (200);
```

- `.header`: If you only input one argument, this assertion will check for the existence of a header that matches that argument. If you specify two arguments, it will check that the given header (specified by the first argument) has the given value (specified by the second argument). Here are two example usages:

```
pm.response.to.have.header ("Content-Type");
pm.response.to.have.header ("Content-Type", "application/
json;");
```

- `.withBody`: This assertion checks that the response has a body. Here's an example usage:

```
pm.response.to.be.withBody;
```

- `.json`: This assertion checks whether the body is in JSON format. Here's an example usage:

```
pm.response.to.be.json;
```

- .body: This assertion can be used to check whether the response has a body and whether that body contains a given value. You can specify the expected value as a simple string, in which case it will check whether that string is found anywhere in the body. Alternatively, you can specify the expected value as a regular expression or as a JSON key/value pair. In those cases, the assertion will search for a match to your query. Here are some example usages:

```
pm.response.to.have.body;
pm.response.to.have.body("some text");
pm.response.to.have.body(<regex>);
pm.response.to.have.body({key:value});
```

- .jsonBody: If no argument is specified, this assertion checks whether the body of the response is in JSON format. Otherwise, it will check for the existence of the given JSON object in the body. Here are some example usages:

```
pm.response.to.have.jsonBody;
pm.response.to.havejsonBody({a:1});
```

- .responseTime: This assertion checks how long the request took. It can also be used to check whether a response time was above or below a given value or if it is within a given range. The time values are given in milliseconds. Here are some example usages:

```
pm.response.to.have.responseTime(150)
pm.response.to.have.responseTime.above(150);
pm.response.to.have.responseTime.below(150);
pm.response.to.have.responseTime.within(100,150);
```

- .responseSize: This assertion checks the size of the response. It can also be used to check whether a response size is about or below a given value of if it is within a given range. The response sizes are given in bytes. Here are some example usages:

```
pm.response.to.have.responseSize(50);
pm.response.to.have.responseSize.above(50);
pm.response.to.have.responseSize.below(100);
pm.response.to.have.responseSize.within(50,100);
```

- .jsonSchema: This assertion checks whether the response follows the specified schema. Here's an example usage:

```
pm.response.to.have.jsonSchema(mySchema);
```

These assertions can help you deal with the various responses that you will get when making API requests. This list gives some simple examples to help you get started with using these assertions, but don't stop there. You can use these assertions in combination with standard Chai library as well. For example, you could add `.not` to the assertions in order to negate any of them. Use these listed examples as starting points for building out your own assertions as you create your tests.

Creating your own tests

I have shown you several examples using the snippets that Postman has created in order to help people get started with creating tests. These snippets are a great place to start if you don't know much about JavaScript as they give very clear examples of how to do certain things. However, they are just a starting point. Since assertions in Postman are built on JavaScript, there is a lot of flexibility and power in what you can do. You may benefit from learning some basic JavaScript, but even without that you should be able to create a lot of your own assertions merely by using the snippets along with the kinds of commands you have learned about in this section.

Try it out

As I keep repeating in this book, the best way to learn is by doing, so try creating a few of your own assertions. Using the Star Wars API, see if you can create assertions to validate the following:

- Check that the server (a header) is nginx.
- Check that the response time for this call is less than 500 milliseconds.
- Check that Luke appears in 4 films.

You can check out my solutions to these in the GitHub repository for this book, but make sure you first try to figure them out on your own. Now that you have a good grasp on how to use assertions in a request, I want to look at how to share them across multiple tests using folders and collections.

Creating folder and collection tests

I have shown you how to create tests that can verify that a request is correct. Some assertions, though, might be the same across multiple tests. For example, you might have a set of positive tests that should all return a status code of 200. You can create an assertion in each of the requests that you set up, but there is an easier way to do it. In Postman, you can add tests assertions to folders and collections.

If you have several requests in a folder and you add a test assertion to the folder, that assertion will run after each request in the folder has completed. Let's look at an example with the following steps:

1. Add a folder to the SWAPI collection called Luke.

2. Drag the Get First Person request that you were working with earlier into that folder and then add another request to that folder called Luke's home world.

3. Set the URL of the request to {{base_url}}/planets/1.

4. Now, edit the folder and on the **Tests** tab, and add a test to check that Luke and his home world both appear in film 1:

```
pm.test("Check that they are in film 1", function () {
    var jsonData = pm.response.json();
    pm.expect(jsonData.films).to.contain("http://swapi.
        dev/api/films/1/");
});
```

5. Go to the Get First Person and Luke's home world requests, and for each of them send the request.

You will notice in each case that the **Test Results** area shows that Postman has run the check that was defined in the folder. You can set up similar checks at the collection level as well. Any tests that you add to the collection will run any time a request in the collection is sent. Setting up tests in the collection works the same as doing it in a folder, so I will leave it up to you to play around with that.

Being able to share tests with multiple requests is helpful, but you may also need to clean up after yourself sometimes. You might have data or variables that you don't want to persist after a request has complete and so there are times when you will need to clean up after your tests.

Cleaning up after tests

In many testing frameworks, you will have the ability to run teardown scripts. These are essentially scripts that let you clean up any variables or values that you don't want to have persist once your test is complete. Postman does not have an explicit section where you can do something like this. However, if you have stuff that needs to be cleaned up after a test, you can do so right in the **Tests** tab.

One thing to be aware of here is the order of executions. Where should you put your cleanup scripts? Should you put them in the **Tests** for a request or in a folder or collection? Scripts created at the folder or collection level will run after each request, but what order should they be run in?

After a request completes, Postman will first execute the test scripts from the collection, and then the script from the folder and finally the scripts from the request. This means that any variables created in a request test script can't be cleaned up in a collection or folder. In general, the best practice would be to clean up any variables in the same place where they are created. So, if you make a temporary variable in a collection that you want to remove when you are done, do so in the collection where you made it. I think this is the easier way to manage test data cleanup, but there may be times when you need to pass a variable around and so need to clean it up elsewhere. When doing so, knowing the execution order will help you avoid errors.

So far in this chapter I have talked a lot about running tests after a request is sent. You have seen how to use the snippets in Postman to help you get started with creating tests. You've seen how to check various parts of a response, ranging from the body to the header, and you've also seen how to use the many built in assertions that Postman provides. You can create your own tests, and now it is time to turn your attention to what you can do before a request has even been sent.

Setting up pre-request scripts

Pre-request scripts work in much the same way that tests do in Postman. In this section, I will show you how to use them to set and get variables so that you can share data between tests. I will also show you how to build a request workflow where you can chain multiple tests together so that you can check more complex workflows. All these things are great on their own, but they do beg the question of how we can effectively run these tests, and so this section will also cover how to run your tests in the collection runner.

The first thing I want to cover, though, is how to get started with pre-request scripts. These scripts use JavaScript to send commands just like the response assertions but, as the name implies, they are run before the request is sent rather than after. Now, why would you want to do that?

I have used pre-request scripts in a couple of different ways. I have had times when I wanted to test something in an API that required sending multiple API calls. In order to check the things that I wanted to check, I needed to be able to pass data that came back from one call into the next call. I could do this by assigning values to variables in the **Tests** section of the first request and then reading in those variable's values in the next test. However, there were times when I wanted to take one of the variable values and modify it slightly (for example, add one to it) before using it. In that case, I would use a pre-request script to do that.

Another example of a time I have used pre-request scripts is to test with some random data. I could generate a random number or string in a pre-request script and then use that value in the test itself. There are other ways that pre-request scripts can be useful as well, but one thing that you will often want to do with pre-request scripts is read or set environment variables.

Using variables in pre-request scripts

In *Chapter 4, Considerations for Good API Test Automation*, I explained how variables work in Postman and the different scopes that they can have. In that chapter, I showed how to create and use variables in the user interface. Postman also lets you use variables in scripts. You can use them in test scripts as well as pre-request scripts, but for now, I will focus on using them in **Pre-request Script** tab. The best way to learn this is with a couple of examples. For the first one, create a new request in the SWAPI collection called Get a Person and then use the following steps to create a pre-request script:

1. Set the URL of the request to {{base_url}}/people/{{person_id}}.

   The base_url variable should already be defined from previous examples, but the person_id variable will not yet be defined.

2. Go to the **Pre-request Script** tab for the request.

3. In the **Snippets** section, click on the **Set an environment variable** snippet. This will add the following code to the pre-request script:

   ```
   pm.environment.set("variable_key", "variable_value");
   ```

4. In the set command, change variable_key to be person_id and change variable_value to be 1.

Now if you send the command, the pre-request script will first set the person_id variable to have a value of 1 and then when the request is sent, it can use that variable in to set the URL correctly.

This example was a simple and somewhat contrived one. I did this in order to help you understand how this works, but there is a lot more that you can do with this. For the next example, we'll look at how to pass data between tests.

Passing data between tests

In order to pass data between requests, you will need multiple requests. You can use the request from the previous example for one of the requests but you will need to create a new request called Get Homeworld in the Star Wars collection. Once you've done that, use the following steps to set up that request and pass data between the two requests:

1. Set the URL of that request be {{base_url}}/planets/1.

2. On the **Tests** tab of that request, add the following code:

```
var jsonData = pm.response.json();
var planetResidents = jsonData.residents;
pm.collectionVariables.
set("residentList", planetResidents);
```

This will get the list of URLs that represent the people who live on this planet out of the response from the first request and add it to a variable called residentList. Note that in this case, we are saving the variable into the collectionVariables scope. That is so that it will be available to all requests in the collection.

3. Send the Get Homeworld request in order to create that variable.

Now that you have a variable with a list of URLs, let's see if you can use it in the Get a Person request to get the information about one of the residents of that planet.

4. On the **Pre-request Script** tab of the Get a Person request, get rid of the previous code and instead add the following code:

```
var residentList = pm.collectionVariables.
get('residentList');
var randomResident = residentList[Math.floor(Math.
random() * residentList.length)];
var splitResidentStr = randomResident.split('/');
var personId = splitResidentStr[splitResidentStr.
length - 2];
pm.environment.set("person_id", personId);
```

There is a lot of code here and some of it does things that you might not understand, so I want to walk through this one line at a time and explain what is going on:

```
var residentList = pm.collectionVariables.get('residentList');
```

This first line is just getting the data in the `residentList` collection variable and storing that data in the `residentList` local variable:

```
var randomResident = residentList[Math.floor(Math.
random() * residentList.length)];
```

You only need to use one of the URLs in the `residentList` array, and so this next line picks a random item out of that list. Don't worry too much about the details of how the code in there works. Often when I want to do something like this, I will do an internet search for something like *how to get a random item out of a list in JavaScript*. Almost always within the first couple of results you will see an example that you can use:

```
var splitResidentStr = randomResident.split('/');
```

Once you have one of the URLs, you need to get the person ID out of that URL. There are several ways to do this. The way I have done it here involves splitting the URL at the slashes. This will turn the URL into a list where each item in the list is the text that is between a set of slashes:

```
var personId = splitResidentStr[splitResidentStr.length - 2];
```

I can then use that list of the split up the URL and extract the second last item from the list to get the person ID that I need. This kind of thing can a bit tricky to figure out, but once again a bit of searching on the internet will usually help you out with stuff like this. You can also use `console.log()` to print out values along the way to help you figure out what values a variable has and how you might need to parse it in order to get the data that you need:

```
pm.environment.set("person_id", personId);
```

The final line in the script is just doing what we were doing in the previous example, but this time instead of setting the value of `person_id` to `1`, we are assigning it to have the value that we have extracted from our random person URL. You should now be able to send the request and get back data about one of the inhabitants of Tatooine.

I don't know about you, but I think that is pretty cool! At this point, you could create a test for the random person call that check that their home world is planet 1. I won't walk through the details of how to do that, but I would encourage you to try it out for yourself and run the test a few times and prove to yourself that this kind of powerful validation works! Now that you know how to pass data between tests, let's look at how you can leverage that to build workflows in Postman.

Building request workflows

In this next section of the chapter, I will show you how to use environments to help manage data that is shared between tests, but there are also a few other built-in methods that can help you manage tests that are tied together like the example we just set up. In this case, the second request depends on the first request having been run. By default, Postman will run them in the order they appear in the collection, but what if someone moves them around? In order to explicitly tie them together, we can use the `setNextRequest` method to let Postman know which request it should run next. You could do this by adding a line like this to the test (or pre-request) scripts to tell Postman that the next request to run is the `Get a Person` request:

```
postman.setNextRequest("Get a Person");
```

It is still important to note that you need to have the first request before the other one in the collection. The `setNextRequest` method will skip ahead to the next test (which means that any tests between them will not be executed). If you had your tests in reverse order (that is, first `Get a Person` and then `Get Homeworld`), the execution order would look like this:

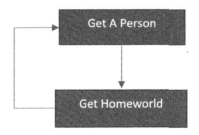

Figure 6.7 – Request execution loop

First the `Get a Person` request would run and then the `Get Homeworld` request would run. The `Get Homeworld` request would then call the `Get a Person` request (using the `setNextRequest` method). This would bring execution back to the top and so Postman would start running all the tests again. As you can see, this would lead to an infinite loop, so you want to be careful when using this method.

There are specific cases where using this makes sense, but in general I would suggest that you do not use `setNextRequest` to control flow between requests. You are better off designing your test collections well so that they run as you would want. However, there is one situation where I think looping can be helpful, and this method can help with that.

Looping over the current request

You certainly don't want to set up any infinite loops, but sometimes you might want to use the same request multiple times with different values. The `setNextRequest` method can be used to help you do this. Go to the `Get a Person` request, and let's see if you can get it to run once for each person in `residentList`.

First of all, you don't need to pull a random value out of the list, so you can comment out that line by putting two slashes (`//`) in front of it, or you can just delete the line altogether. Instead of pulling out a random value, we want to run this test once for each item in the list. In order to know which instance of the loop you are on, you will need a counter. The problem is, you can't just add a variable at the top of the script and initialize it to 0, since then the counter would be at zero every time the request is run. You will need to have a variable that is not a part of the test. I will go over environments in more detail later in this chapter, but we can do this with an environment variable. Add this line to the script:

```
var currentCount = pm.environment.get("counter");
```

This counter needs to be initialized to start at 0. You can do this by going to the `Get Homeworld` request, and on the **Tests** tab, setting the environment variable to 0:

```
pm.environment.set("counter", 0);
```

Now go back to the `Get a Person` request and set it up to use that counter to access the items in the list:

```
randomResident = residentList[currentCount];
```

This will give you the link at the index that `currentCount` is at. The counter starts at 0, so the first time this test is run, it will give you the first item in the list (don't forget that list indexes start at 0). However, we need that counter to change so that the next time we run this test, it gets the item at index 1. You can do this by set the counter to equal one more than it does right now. Add this code to the bottom of the script to do that:

```
pm.environment.set("counter",currentCount+1);
```

You can create the loop by adding this code to the next line in the script:

```
postman.setNextRequest("Get a Person");
```

This will tell Postman that the next request you want to run is the `Get a Person` test, which of course is the current test. Postman will then run this request again, but since you have added 1 to the counter, it will now use the list item at index 1 instead of index 0. The test will continue to loop over and over, but there is still one more problem. When will the test stop looping? You need an **exit condition** so that you don't end up trying to run more loops than there are items in the list. In this case, the exit condition will be when the counter has accessed the last item in the list. You can create this condition with an `if` statement that checks whether `currentCount` is less than the length of the list:

```
if (currentCount < residentList.length) {
```

This `if` statement should be placed right after you get the current value of the counter and you should put everything else in the test inside that `if` statement. At this point, you should have the script ready to go and it should look like this:

```
var residentList = pm.environment.get("residentList");
var currentCount = pm.environment.get("counter");
if (currentCount < residentList.length) {
    randomResident = residentList[currentCount];
    var splitResidentStr = randomResident.split('/');
    var personId = splitResidentStr[splitResidentStr.
      length - 2];
    pm.environment.set("person_id", personId);
    pm.environment.set("counter",currentCount+1);
    postman.setNextRequest("Get a Person");
};
```

Now that you have this script ready to go, let's look at how you would actually run it. The Postman collection runner allows you to run all the requests in a collection.

Running requests in the collection runner

You can open the collection runner from a few places in Postman, but since you know that you want to run the tests in the **Star Wars API** collection, you can start it from there by following these steps:

1. Click on the collection in the navigation panel.

2. On the resulting page, there is a **Run** button near the top right. Click on that to open the collection runner:

Figure 6.8 – Run collection button

This will show you the order that the requests will be run in along with all the requests that will be run.

3. Deselect all the requests except the Get Homeworld and Get a Person requests, and make sure those two requests are in the correct order. Your collection runner should look similar to this:

RUN ORDER

Figure 6.9 – Collection runner setup

4. Once everything is set up correctly, click on the **Star Wars API** button to run the collection.

You will see that it runs the Get Homeworld request and then it runs the Get a Person request once for each person in the list.

There are some additional things to talk about on the collection runner, and I will go through some of the options in more detail in *Chapter 7, Data-Driven Testing*, but for now, you can see that you can use the collection runner to easily run multiple tests at once.

> **Important note**
>
> Before running requests in the collection runner, make sure you have saved any changes made to those requests. The collection runner uses the last saved version for each request when running. If you have made recent changes to a request and have not saved them, they will not be reflected in the collection runner. This can be confusing and has puzzled me in the past, so try to get in the habit of always saving requests before opening the collection runner.

Passing data between tests like this can enable some cool and powerful workflows, but there are some things to be careful of with this as well. One of the biggest issues you might run into with these kinds of workflows are challenges with maintaining the tests. It can be a bit of work to track where a variable is being set or modified. In this example, I used the `collectionVariables` scope to store the variable, but you can also store variables in environments, which can make them a bit easier to manage.

Using environments in Postman

Postman environments are a place where you can create and manage variables. You can set up multiple environments for different purposes. Environments are very helpful when you need to share data between requests, and so in this section, I will show you how to use them to manage your variables. You can also manipulate variables in the environment, and so I'll show you how to do that as well so that you can also use Postman environment to help you explore or debug issues. In the first place, let's look at how to manage variables using environments.

Managing environment variables

Creating an environment is easy. Follow these steps to create one:

1. Click on the **New** button and then select the **Environment** option.

   You can give your environment a name; in this case just call it something like `SWAPI Env`. You can then start creating variables in the environment. Let's use this environment to manage the `person_id` variable that you are setting in the pre-request script.

2. Type `person_id` in the first field of the **VARIABLE** column and set the **INITIAL VALUE** to 1. The following figure shows what that would look like:

Environment Name

SWAPI Env

	VARIABLE	INITIAL VALUE ⓘ
✓	person_id	1
	Add a new variable	

Figure 6.10 – Create an environment variable

3. Save this environment and then close the dialog.

4. As shown in the following figure, in the upper right-hand corner of the app, you will see a dropdown. Click on this dropdown and select **SWAPI Env** from the list:

Figure 6.11 – Select environment

5. Now that the environment is active, send the `Get a Person` request.

   This request will set the value of the `person_id` variable to something new.

6.   Click on the **Environment quick look** icon to see what value it has been set to and you should see a panel pop up that looks like this:

Figure 6.12 – Environment quick look

Since the ID is selected randomly, you might see a different value than me for the current value, but this shows you already how this can help you manage your data. You now have one spot where you can check on what value is being used for your variable. In addition to using this to manage your environment variable, you can also use it to edit them.

Editing environment variables

One of the many benefits of environments in Postman is the ability to have all your variables in one place so that you can see and understand what is going on. However, there may also be times when you want to edit something in the environment. Perhaps you are trying to debug an issue and need to use a specific value for just one time, or perhaps you are exploring the API and want to try out some specific values. Whatever the use case, there are times you might want to do this, so let's take a look at how that works in Postman. In first place, let's add the `residentList` variable into the environment as well so that you can manage and edit it. You can add it into the environment with the following steps:

1.   Click on the **Environment quick look** icon and then select the **Edit** option to edit the **SWAPI Env** environment.

2.   Add a new variable called `residentList` and set the initial value of it to be an empty list, that is, with two square brackets like this: `[]`.

3.   Click on **Update** and then close the dialog.

4. Now go to the Get Homeworld request and on the **Tests** tab, modify the line where you are setting the variable to use pm.environment.set instead of pm.collectionVariables.set.

   This will save the variable value into the environment variable that you just created.

   Now that the variable is going to be saved into the environment, we also need to read it out of there.

5. Go to the Get a Person request and change the pm.collectionVariables. get line to instead use pm.environment.get.

6. Go back to the Get Homeworld request and send it. This will save a list of people into the residentList variable. Once again, open the environment quick look and you should be able to see this list:

Figure 6.13 – ResidentList current value

This makes it much easier to manage, but you can also edit the environment variable in here as well. Click on the **edit** icon that shows up beside the variable when you mouse over, and it will open the current value field for editing. If you wanted to, you could edit this variable. For example, you might remove all entries but one from the list if you were trying to check that the loop works if it only has one item in the list.

Environments allow you to edit variables and give you a lot of control and insight into what is going on. They are a helpful tool for you to manage your data with, and I would recommend using them to manage variables whenever possible.

Summary

Sending API requests allows you to inspect the responses and check that the API call is working the way you want it to. This is a manual process, though, and often you will need to create tests that can be run over and over again to check for product regressions. In order to do this, you need to be able to add checks to a request. This chapter has given you the ability to do that. You have learned how to add assertions that check various aspects of an API response. You have also learned about the various built in assertions that Postman provides to help you with this.

Sometimes you need to get some input data into a specific format in order to be able to check the things that you want to check. This chapter has also helped you learn how to set up scripts that can run before a request so that you can have everything in the necessary state. I also showed you how to run a request multiple times so that you can check many things in one request. This chapter also covered how to create request workflows so that you are able to check things that require multiple API requests.

In addition to being able to automatically check that API calls are working correctly, you need to be able to easily run those tests. In *Chapter 8, Running API Tests in CI with Newman*, I will show you more advanced ways to do this, but in this chapter, I introduced you to the collection runner, which allows you to run multiple tests. The chapter also taught you how to use environments to manage the variables and data that you might create in your testing scripts.

If you worked through the exercises and followed along with the material in this chapter, you should have a good foundation in place for getting started with creating automated tests. In the next chapter, I'll talk about some more advanced things that you can do with automated tests in Postman. We will be working through data-driven testing and how to set it up and use it in Postman.

7
Data-Driven Testing

One of the great things about test automation is the ability to try out many different things without getting bored. In fact, one of the heuristics I use for determining whether I should automate something is to ask myself whether what I am doing is boring. If I am working on boring and repetitive work, it's a good indicator that I might be working on something that should be automated.

Sometimes, creating test automation itself can get boring, though. You may want to create tests for several inputs to a request that are all quite similar. Creating good test cases can involve trying out many different inputs to the system. Automation is good at checking many things over and over, but it can take a lot of work to create separate requests for each of those inputs. So, rather than doing that and duplicating a lot of work, you can use something called **data-driven testing** to increase the efficiency of your automated tests.

This chapter will teach you everything you need to know to use this powerful testing technique in Postman. By the end of this chapter, you will be able to understand how to create powerful and scalable data-driven tests, use **Equivalence Class Partitioning** (ECP) to create good input for data-driven tests, define useful output for test comparisons, set up data-driven tests in Postman, create tests in Postman that can compare response results to data outputs in a file, and set up and run data-driven tests in the collection runner.

We will cover the following topics in this chapter:

- Defining data-driven testing
- Creating a data-driven test in Postman
- Challenge – data-driven testing with multiple APIs

Technical requirements

The code used in this chapter can be found at: `https://github.com/PacktPublishing/API-Testing-and-Development-with-Postman/tree/master/Chapter07`.

Defining data-driven testing

Data-driven testing is not unique to API tests. It can be used in other types of automation as well. For example, you could set up UI tests or even unit tests to use data-driven testing techniques. In this section, I will explain what data-driven testing is. I will also teach you some principles that you can use to create good inputs for data-driven tests. In addition, this section will cover how to set up good test comparisons and how to set up the outputs for data-driven tests. But what exactly is data-driven testing?

Essentially, this technique involves creating a table of inputs that map to expected outputs and then running those inputs through the system under test and checking whether the outputs of the tests match the outputs in the table. You may also hear this test technique described as **table-driven testing** or **parameterized testing**.

That is all a bit abstract, so let me try to explain it with an example to help you understand what this means. Let's imagine that you have a list of products in a catalog. You know the ID of each of the products and you also know how much they are supposed to cost, and you want to verify that each product in the system is listed at the correct price. You could create a table in a `.csv` file that looks something like this:

ProductID	ExpectedPrice
123456	$15.49
234561	$12.99
876543	$9.28
....	.....

The product IDs in this table give you a set of inputs, and the expected prices give you a set of outputs. Data-driven testing is merely the process of feeding those inputs into the test and checking that you get the expected outputs. In diagram form, it would look something like this:

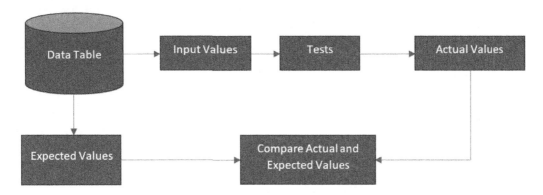

Figure 7.1 – Data-driven testing workflow

In *Chapter 6, Creating Test Validation Scripts*, we saw how to create a test that called itself multiple times so that we could loop over a set of inputs. Data-driven testing is similar. Each input in the data table will be run through the test and the result will be compared to the corresponding expected value in the table. The power of data-driven testing is that you can create one test and then pass it many different values and so leverage that one test to check many things.

One thing to note about *Figure 7.1* is that the expected values do not need to be defined in the data table. For example, if you had many inputs that all have the same expected value, you could just hardcode that value into the test and then use the data table for inputs only. For example, you might want to run a set of tests that iterates over a list of product IDs and checks that they all have a price greater than 0. In fact, this is quite a common way to do data-driven testing and is the default way that Postman supports. Don't worry though; in this chapter, I will also show you how to run data-driven tests where the expected values are defined in the data table.

Data-driven testing is a powerful technique, but as with most powerful things, it can be abused. Before deciding to use data-driven testing, there are a few questions you should ask yourself. First, you need to figure out whether there is a need for multiple inputs to a test. For example, if you were testing an endpoint that returns a given resource every time, there isn't much point in trying different inputs. Another example would be if there is really no distinction between different classes of input. There is a bit of complexity involved in this, so let's dig into how to set up data-driven inputs.

Setting up data-driven inputs

Say you were testing a search endpoint. You could construct an almost infinite list of inputs to this, but is there really a meaningful distinction to be made from a functional standpoint between a search for the term "dog" and a search for the term "cat"? Unless there is specific reason to check for a term, you don't want to create inputs that are essentially equivalent. Thinking through what inputs might be equivalent can be tricky and this is where a testing technique known as **Equivalence Class Partitioning** (**ECP**) can be helpful. With ECP, you partition the inputs to your tests into various classes and then use only one input from each class in your test. The tricky part, of course, is deciding how to partition the inputs. However, thinking this through carefully can help you refine your inputs and reduce the number of iterations that you need to test. ECP is easiest to do if you are dealing with numerical or mathematical functions, but it can also be applied to text-based inputs as well. Let's use inputs to a password field as an example.

The broadest classes for a password field would be `Valid` and `Invalid`. Since a given username only has one valid option, we certainly can't break that class down any further, but what about the `Invalid` class? Are there any classes of invalid inputs that might be worth considering? If you think about where the boundaries of the field are, you can come up with two more classes: `Empty Password` and `Really Long Password`. You could also think about security concerns and come up with another class called `Injection Flaws`. I'm sure if you thought about it long enough you could come up with a few more ways to partition the input data for this password field, but the point is that by breaking this down into four or five partitions, you can check on the input for each of these partitions and know that the password field handles invalid inputs reasonably.

If you were to try and test all possible invalid inputs to the password, you would never finish. ECP gives you the ability to limit the inputs in a way that makes sense. In addition to defining the inputs for a data-driven test, you need to also think about the outputs.

Thinking about the outputs for data-driven tests

Carefully defined inputs can keep the number of iterations that you run a test for reasonable, but in order to set up useful tests, you need to also think about the outputs you are using. You can have a well-designed set of inputs, but if you don't have good outputs, you aren't going to get any useful data out of the tests. There are two sets of outputs to consider. There are the outputs generated by the test itself along with the outputs you define in your data table. Let's think about the ones defined in your data table first.

When you are creating a table for data-driven testing, you will need to know the answer to the question "what should the expected result be of this input?". This means that the outputs in your data-driven testing table need to be easily computable. This might mean that they are trivially simple, as in the example of the password field where you know that one value should allow you to log in and all others should not. They might, however, be more complex than that. You might, for example, have an API that takes in a first name and a last name and returns a username in the form of `<first initial><last name>`. In this case, the expected result is easily computable since you can manually create a username that fits the pattern based on the inputs without too much difficulty.

However, there could be other inputs that are much harder to compute the correct outputs for. For example, there is an API (`https://github.com/aunyks/newton-api`) that allows you to do some complex math such as finding the area under a curve. If you are not a mathematician, you might have trouble computing the answer for a given input. You could perhaps send a request and assume that the response you get back is correct and use that to check that things don't change going forward, but if you are testing a brand-new API, that might be a difficult assumption to make.

Figuring out what the expected value for a response should be is not unique to data-driven testing, but it is something that you should consider when constructing the data table for these tests. Knowing the expected value is only half the problem, though. You need to be able to compare it to the actual value that you get from the test. Once again, this is not unique to data-driven testing, but there are some additional considerations that can come into play with data-driven testing. The comparison of an expected value to the actual result can be done using the assertions and techniques we covered in *Chapter 6, Creating Testing Validation Scripts*. However, with data-driven testing, you have multiple inputs, which means that you won't get the exact same output for each row in the data table. When creating the comparisons in your tests, you need to be aware of this.

If you have a data-driven test that is checking through a list of user IDs, you can't set up an assertion that compares their email address to a static value. If you were only calling one user – say someone called Jane Doe – you could check that the email address was `jane.doe@something.com`, but if you are calling the same tests with multiple users, you would need to check something more generic. In this case, for example, you could check that the email address field contains an @ and a . or something like that instead.

When setting up data-driven tests, you need to think about both the inputs and outputs of your data table and the tests themselves; but now that you have a good grasp of how to effectively use data-driven testing, let's take a look at how it works in Postman.

Creating a data-driven test in Postman

Postman provides tools for running data-driven tests, but in order to use them, you will need a test. This section will show you how to create an actual input file that you can use, and it will then teach you how to create the kind of test that you need for this in Postman. It will also show you how to get data from a file and use that data to compare it to the results of your request.

I will show this all to you with a practical example. The example will use the API provided by JSON Placeholder (`http://jsonplaceholder.typicode.com`). This is a sample API that you can use to get fake data. Before creating a data-driven test, follow these steps:

1. Add a collection called `JSON API`.

2. Add a request to the collection called **Users**.

3. Set the request URL to `http://jsonplaceholder.typicode.com/users/1` and send the request. You should get back a response with a bunch of data for a user.

Now that you have a working request, let's look at how to set up a data-driven test. Since a data-driven test takes in multiple inputs, you will need some kind of variable, or something that changes with each input. That is called a **parameter**, and for this example, I want you to parameterize the user ID in the URL. You can do that by turning it into a variable with the following steps:

1. Replace the `1` in the URL with a variable called `{{userId}}`.

2. For ease of management, create an environment to save this variable in by clicking on the **New** button and choosing the **Environment** option.

3. Name the environment `JSON API Env` and create the `userId` variable with an initial value of `1`, and then click the **Add** button to create the environment.

4. Close the dialog and then choose **JSON API Env** from the environment dropdown at the top right of the Postman application.

Now, if you mouse over the `userId` parameter in the URL of your request, you should see that it has a value of `1` and if you were to send the request again, you would get back the same response as you did previously. With the input parameter defined, it's time to look at how to create the data that you will use to drive the test.

Creating the data input

Input files for data-driven tests are often created as .csv files. If you have access to Excel or another spreadsheet program, you can use that to make the file, but otherwise, you can easily create the data in any text editor. For the purposes of this demonstration, I want you to create a file that will run for the first five users in the list. The first row of the file is the header and will have the name of the parameter that you are defining. This parameter name needs to match up with the name you are using in the test, so in this case, userId. On the next line, put the first user ID of 1, and then on the next line, user ID 2, and so on until 5. Once you are done, you should have a file that looks something like this:

Figure 7.2 – Input data

Save this file and call it something such as userInputs.csv. In this case, you are only defining inputs and not outputs. I will show you how you can set up outputs later in this section. For now, I want to show you how to run a simple data-driven test. In fact, for this first run, let's keep it so simple that we won't even add an assertion to the request. Let's just run the request once for each input in the file, by following these steps:

1. Before opening the collection runner, it is important to ensure that you have saved any changes in your request. The collection runner will use the latest saved version of any requests that you run, so go to the **Users** request that you created and ensure that you have saved all changes.

2. Open the collection runner by going to the JSON API collection and clicking the **Run** button at the top right of the collection tab.

    This will open the collection runner for you. Ensure that the **Users** request is selected in the run order panel.

3. Click on the **Select File** button and browse to where you saved the `userInputs.csv` file and open it.

When you do this, you will notice that Postman sets a few things for you automatically. It detects that you have five rows of data in the file and so it sets the **Iterations** field to 5. It also detects that the file type is **text/csv** and chooses that option for you. You can also preview the data that Postman will use for each iteration by clicking on the **Preview** button.

4. Click on the **Run JSON API** button to run the request.

The collection runner will call the request once for each line in the file, passing each respective `userId` value to the request. Of course, without any tests, this is a pretty boring test run, so let's look at adding a test to the request.

Adding a test

In order to actually do something useful with the request, we are going to need at least one test so that we can verify that things are working correctly. In order to do this, close the collection runner and head back to the main Postman application.

As I discussed in detail in *Chapter 6, Creating Test Validation Scripts*, you can create a test by going to the **Tests** tab of your request. For this example, set up a check that verifies that the email address field has an @ symbol in it. You can use the **Response body: JSON value check** snippet to get started. You can then modify it to get the email address field using `jsonData.email` and check whether it contains the @ symbol. Rename the test as well, and the final code for the test should look like this:

```
pm.test("Check for @ in email", function () {
    var jsonData = pm.response.json();
    pm.expect(jsonData.email).to.contain("@");
});
```

Now, if you re-run the data-driven test in the collection runner (don't forget to save the request first!), you will see that it calls each request with the different user IDs and then checks whether the email field on each request has an @ in it. You should see something similar to the following:

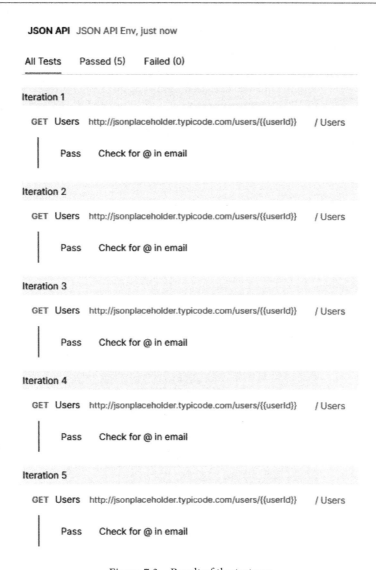

Figure 7.3 – Result of the test run

Now that we are actually checking something in the response, these tests are much more interesting, but what if we wanted to check something more specific? What if we wanted to check that certain user IDs match up to certain email addresses? We can't create an assertion in the test that checks for this because the email address will change as we run through each iteration of our dataset, so what can we do? Well, if we don't want to create a separate request for each of the users, we will need to define the expected email for each user ID in our file and then compare the emails from the API responses to those that we have defined in our file.

Comparing responses to data from a file

Comparing data from an API response to data from a file requires changing things in a few different places. You will obviously need to add some data to the file itself, but you will also need to get that data into the test assertion that does the comparison between the actual and expected values. You can set this all up with the following steps:

1. Open the `userInputs.csv` file and add a new column to it.

2. Create a header called `expectedEmail`. This will be the variable name that you will use in the test.

3. Add the email address to each row that corresponds to the user ID for that row.

    You may need to manually call the endpoint with each user ID in order to find out what the correct email address is for each row.

4. Modify one of the email addresses so that it is incorrect. It is always a good idea to check that your tests will actually fail if something goes wrong.

    Once you have modified your file, it should look similar to what is show in *Figure 7.4*. Make sure that the file is saved:

```
userId, expectedEmail
1, Sincere@april.biz
2, Shanna@melissa.tv
3, Nathan@yesenia.net
4, IncorrectEmail@kory.org
5, Lucio_Hettinger@annie.ca
```

Figure 7.4 – Data table with inputs and outputs

With the file set up with output data, you now need to use that data in your test assertion.

5. Go to the **Tests** tab of the **Users** request in Postman. Right now, it is set up to expect the email of the response to contain an @. Instead, I want you to change it so that it checks whether the email is equal to `expectedEmail`. After making those changes, the code should look like this:

```
pm.expect(jsonData.email).to.eql(expectedEmail);
```

However, the problem is the `expectedEmail` variable in this line is not yet defined. Test scripts can't directly use a variable in this way. Instead, we have to extract the variable from that place where these kinds of variables are stored. There are actually a couple of different ways to do that in Postman. One way to do it is to use a special variable called `data` that Postman uses to store variables that get passed in from a file. With this variable, you can get the `expectedEmail` value using the following code:

```
var expectedEmail = data.expectedEmail;
```

Although this works, I think it could be confusing to people looking at this test in the future. Unless you know that the data variable contains a map to variables passed in by a file, you won't understand this line of code. Postman provides a number of methods for interacting with variables in scripts, and I think it would be better to use one of those for this instead if we could. Thankfully, there is a method we can use for this – the `replaceIn` method. You can use it in this way to get `expectedEmail` into your test script:

```
var expectedEmail = pm.variables.
replaceIn("{{expectedEmail}}");
```

Now that you have the expected email variable from the file, rename the test to something such as `Validate Email Address From File` to more accurately reflect what it is doing.

If you save all changes to the request and then open the collection runner, you can select the modified file and run the JSON API collection. Once you do so, you should see results like those in the following figure, where the second-last result is failing, verifying that the check you have created is indeed working:

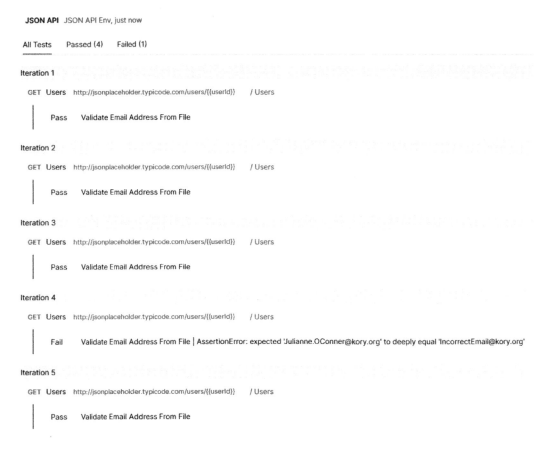

Figure 7.5 – Test result of a data-driven test run

I only have space in this book to show you this one example of using data-driven testing functionality in Postman, but I hope that it has illustrated the power of this technique. I really want to make sure that you understand how to use this technique, and so let's turn to some hands-on practice.

Challenge – data-driven testing with multiple APIs

I don't have the space to work through another full example, but I would like you to practice this a little more. I'm going to give you a challenge that I think will be, well, challenging. In this section, I will get you started with the challenge and give you a few hints to help you successfully solve it. In order to solve this challenge, you will need to use everything you have learned in this chapter about data-driven testing, but you will also need to use some of the information covered in *Chapter 6, Creating Test Validation Scripts*. In that chapter, I explained how to create tests that use multiple requests, and you are going to need that information to solve this challenge.

Challenge setup

For this challenge, I want you to use the Postman Echo API. This sample API has a number of different endpoints that you can use. In this case, you will use the **Time Addition** (`https://postman-echo.com/time/add`) and **Time Subtraction** (`https://postman-echo.com/time/subtract`) endpoints. Each of the endpoints will take in a timestamp as a query parameter and then add or subtract the given amount of time from that timestamp. You can find the documentation on how to use them here: `https://docs.postman-echo.com/#4cef08e8-75d3-2a31-e703-115cf976e75e`.

Your job is to test these two APIs using data-driven testing techniques. You will need to set up a file that has the necessary inputs and then verify that you are getting the correct outputs. There are two ways you could check the correct outputs. You could just manually figure out the answers. If you give a timestamp and you add 10 days, it's pretty easy to manually figure out the answer. However, that could be a bit tedious to create for multiple input values, so instead I want you to use a different method to validate the answers.

I want you to start with the `/time/add` endpoint. Pass it timestamps and different units of time to add to the timestamp. Then, use the `/time/subtract/` endpoint to subtract the same amount of time from the result of the first request and verify that you get back the initial timestamp. This is going to be challenging to figure out, so I'll give you a few hints to help you along the way.

Challenge hints

This challenge is going to require reading data from a file to drive the test, as well as passing data between tests. Things could get complex doing this and so here are a few hints to help you out as you try to figure this out:

- The query parameter that constructs the data time instance can be sent as `timestamp`, `locale`, `format`, or `strict`. For the purpose of this challenge, don't worry about testing all those variations. You can stick with the `format` parameter to specify the date time instance.

- The `add` and `subtract` endpoints return the dates in a fully expanded format (something like `Mon Oct 12 2020 00:00:00 GMT+0000`). Since you are going to be comparing the input dates to the dates that are output by the `/time/subtract` endpoint, you will want to create your input dates in a similar way.

- Don't forget about the order that you need to run requests in when passing data between them.

- Manually send requests to the two endpoints to make sure you understand the format of the responses that they give.

With these hints, along with what you have learned in this chapter and the previous one, you should be able to come up with a way to do this. I would recommend that you give yourself at least 30–60 minutes to work through this exercise. Experiment with different things and try to get to the point where you can run the two requests in the collection runner with several different input values that you have defined in a file.

Summary

Data-driven testing allows you to do a lot more with your tests. It allows you to create test cases in external sources and then use those test cases to drive your tests. It also lets you leverage the power of automation much more effectively. With just a few tests, you can try out many different inputs and variations and learn a lot about the system under test. Data-driven testing is one of those testing techniques that you can really only use with automation and it is techniques like this that make automation so useful.

In this chapter, I have given you a good grounding in understanding what data-driven testing is and when it makes sense to use it. I have shown you how to set up data inputs and how to think about and use outputs in data-driven testing. You have also learned how to apply this all in Postman and seen how to create data inputs that Postman can use. In addition, you have seen how to add tests that can get variables that are defined in an external file and use them to dynamically compare against various test results.

You have seen how to set up and run these kinds of tests with the collection runner. This is a great tool for running tests locally, but what if you want to run them on a schedule or in a continuous integration system? The collection runner is interactive, but in the next chapter, I will show you how to run collections and tests from the command line using a Postman tool called Newman.

8
Running API Tests in CI with Newman

The year was 2007, and I was hanging out with some friends who were techies. They always had the latest tech gear and in 2007, the latest tech gear was a new phone that Apple had put out. A phone that didn't have a physical keypad. A touch screen phone! Can you imagine that? They were showing off their new iPhones and the rest of us were gathered around to check out this crazy new phone. I remember trying it out and accidently clicking on something and struggling to figure out how to navigate on it. I thought it was all going to be a fad and we'd be back to using our Blackberries, with their physical keyboards, soon.

Fast forward a few years and along with almost everyone else in the world, I had my own smart phone. The meteoric rise of handheld computing devices has changed a lot of things in our culture. For many of us, these devices are the primary way in which we use the internet and interact with computers. These touch screen devices are handy and have allowed us to expand the reach of the internet to every corner of the globe. Who knows – you might even be reading this book on such a device! You can do almost anything on your phone now that you would have needed a computer for 10 or 15 years ago. However, there is one thing that most of us would rarely do on a mobile device, and that is to use its Command Prompt.

It's not that you can't use the Command Prompt on a mobile device, it's just that it would rarely make sense to do so. The Command Prompt has already become a less frequently used tool in computing due to better and better operating system user interfaces, but with the smart phone era, we are less likely than ever to have used it. I think that is too bad. The humble little Command Prompt has a lot to offer. If you want to be a power user in the software testing and development world, learning your way around the Command Prompt is a must. This isn't a book about the Command Prompt, but in this chapter, I am going to show you some Command Prompt tools. If you already have experience with the Command Prompt, that is great, but if not, don't worry – it is easy to pick up what you need to know to follow along. You will be able to learn everything you need to know as you go through the examples in this chapter.

The topics that we are going to cover in this chapter are as follows:

- Getting Newman set up.

- Understanding Newman run options.

- Reporting on tests in Newman.

- Integrating Newman into CI builds.

By the end of this chapter, you will know how to do the following:

- Install and set up the command-line test runner, Newman.

- Use Newman to run collections from the Command Prompt.

- Execute any Postman test in Newman.

- Generate reports in Newman, using both built-in reporters and community-created reporters.

- Create your own reporter to customize test reporting.

- Run tests in build systems.

Technical requirements

The code that will be used in this chapter can be found in at `https://github.com/PacktPublishing/API-Testing-and-Development-with-Postman/tree/master/Chapter08`.

Getting Newman set up

Newman is a tool built by the team behind Postman so that you can run Postman collections from the command line. It is also maintained by the Postman team and has feature parity with Postman, which means that you should be able to do anything in Newman that you can in Postman. However, Newman is not installed when you install Postman, so you need to install it separately. In this section, I will show you how to get started with Newman. I will go over how to install Newman, as well as how to use it at the command line. In order to do this, I will also show you how to install the Node.js JavaScript framework and how to use its package manager to install Newman and other helpful libraries.

Installing Newman

Newman is built into **Node.js**. Node.js is a JavaScript runtime environment. JavaScript generally runs in web browsers, but Node.js provides an environment for running JavaScript outside a web browser. With Node.js, you can run JavaScript code on servers or even directly on your own computer. This lets developers write applications directly in JavaScript, which is exactly what Newman is. One other major feature of Node.js is the package manager. The **Node.js package manager**, or **npm**, makes it easy for programmers to publish and share their Node.js code. This package manager makes installing and setting up things such as Newman dead simple, but in order to use it, you will need to install Node.js.

Installing Node.js

Since Node.js allows you to run JavaScript outside your browser, it has to be installed as an application on your computer, which you can easily do by performing the following steps:

1. Go to `https://nodejs.org/en/download/` and find the install package for your operating system.

    I would recommend getting the package from the **Long-Term Support** (**LTS**) section as it will have everything that you need for this book and will be a little more stable.

2. Once you have downloaded the installer, run it in the same way you would install any other program on your operating system.

    You can keep all the defaults on the install wizard.

3. Once the installer has completed, verify that it has been installed correctly by opening a Command Prompt and typing in the following command:

```
node -v
```

This will print out the current version. You should see something like this:

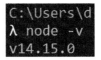

Figure 8.1 – Node version

4. Verify that npm has also been installed correctly by typing in the following command:

```
npm -v
```

This will print out the version number of npm that was installed.

Now that you have installed Node.js, you can use the package manager to install Newman.

Using npm to install Newman

npm has a few different options for installation, but the basics of it are straightforward. If you know the name of the package that you want to install, you can simply call the npm install command, followed by the package name that you want to install. npm will then install that package and any dependency packages that you need in the folder you are currently in. By default, npm installs the package so that it is only available in the current folder, but there are options that let you change the scope of where it is installed. The most used of these options is --global (or it's shortcut, -g), which will install the package globally. This means that it will be available to run no matter where your Command Prompt is currently located.

You are going to want to be able to run Newman from anywhere on your computer, so you can install it with the -g option by executing the following command in the Command Prompt:

```
npm install -g newman
```

You will see information about the different packages and dependencies that npm is installing for you flash by and in a few seconds, Newman will be installed and ready for you to use.

Running Newman

Now that you have Newman installed, let's run a command in it to make sure everything is working correctly. The easiest way to do that is by running a collection in Postman, but first, you will need a collection to run. You can create a simple collection in Postman and then export it by following these steps:

1. In Postman, create a new collection called `Newman Test` and add a request to the collection called `Test GET`.

2. Set the request URL to `https://postman-echo.com/get?test=true`.

3. Save the request and then click on the **View more actions** menu beside the collection in the navigation tree and choose the **Export** option.

4. Leave the collection version as v2.1 and click the **Export** button.

5. Choose a folder on your computer to save the collection in, set the filename to `TestCollection.json`, and click on **Save**.

Now that you have a collection, you can run that collection with Newman. To do that, you will need to navigate to the folder where you have saved the collection. You can navigate to different folders while using the Command Prompt by using the `cd` command. This command will change directories for you, and you can use it by calling the command, along with the path to the directory that you want to go to. So, in my case, I could put in the following command:

```
cd C:\API-Testing-and-Development-with-Postman\Chaptee08
```

Note that if you have a space in your directory path, you will need to enclose the path in quotation marks so that your command will look like this instead:

```
cd "C:\path with spaces\API-Testing-and-Development-with-Postman\Chapter08"
```

Once you have navigated to the directory where you have saved the collection, you can run that collection in Newman. To do that, you must call the `newman` command with the `run` option and then give it the name of file where your collection has been saved. In this case, the command would look like this:

```
newman run TestCollection.json
```

Hit *Enter* and Newman will run that collection. Once it has completed, you should see a simple report of what it ran, as shown in the following screenshot:

```
Newman Test
→ Test GET
  GET https://postman-echo.com/get?test=true [200 OK, 733B, 419ms]

                               │        executed │          failed │
  ─────────────────────────────┼─────────────────┼─────────────────┤
                    iterations │               1 │               0 │
  ─────────────────────────────┼─────────────────┼─────────────────┤
                      requests │               1 │               0 │
  ─────────────────────────────┼─────────────────┼─────────────────┤
                  test-scripts │               0 │               0 │
  ─────────────────────────────┼─────────────────┼─────────────────┤
              prerequest-scripts │             0 │               0 │
  ─────────────────────────────┼─────────────────┼─────────────────┤
                    assertions │               0 │               0 │
  ─────────────────────────────┴─────────────────┴─────────────────┤
  total run duration: 469ms
  total data received: 395B (approx)
  average response time: 419ms [min: 419ms, max: 419ms, s.d.: 0µs]
```

Figure 8.2 – Newman collection run report

This report shows what request was run, along with its status code and the time it was run. It also shows you details about the iterations, requests, and scripts that were run. Since this was a very simple collection, there isn't much here, but we can verify that Newman is indeed installed and set up correctly.

There are many other options in Newman for running more complex collections. You can see some inline help for those various options by calling the following command:

```
Newman run -h
```

This will list the various options that you have when running collections in Newman. I won't go over all of them in this book, but some of them will be helpful for you, so I will show you how use them.

Understanding Newman run options

Now that you have Newman installed and running, it's time to look at how to use it in a variety of cases. You have already seen how to run it with a simple collection, but what about if you have environment variables or data-driven tests? In this section, I will show you how to run Postman collections, including collections that contain environment variables and data-driven tests. I will also show you some of the options that you can use to control Newman's behavior.

Using environments in Newman

Often, a collection will have variables defined in an environment. Requests in that collection will need those variables when they are run, but the values don't get exported with the collection. To see this in practice, you can modify the **Test GET** request in the Newman Test collection that you made earlier by following these steps:

1. Create a new environment called `Newman Test Env`.

2. Modify the URL field of the **Test GET** request to set the `https://postman-echo.com` part to a variable called `baseUrl`.

   Save that variable in the environment that you just created.

3. **Save** the request and then export the collection to a file (you can use the same filename we used previously and just overwrite it).

If you go to the command line and run that collection with Newman, you will see an rror message similar to the following, since it can't resolve the `baseUrl` variable that you created:

```
λ newman run TestCollection.json
newman

Newman Test

→ Test GET
  GET {{baseUrl}}/get?test=true [errored]
       getaddrinfo ENOTFOUND {{baseurl}}
```

Figure 8.3 – Error resolving variable

In order to correct this error, you can manually specify the environment variable by using the --env-var flag. To do that, execute the following command:

```
newman run TestCollection.json --env-var "baseUrl=https://
postman-echo.com"
```

This tells Newman that it should set the baseUrl environment variable so that it's equal to the specified URL. With that information, the collection can run correctly. However, it is a lot of work to manually type this in. If you have multiple environment variables, you can call this flag multiple times, but you would still have to type each of them in, which would get very tedious. Instead of doing that all manually, let's see how you can save yourself some work by using an environment that's been exported from Postman. You can export an environment by following these steps:

1. Click on the **Environments** tab on the left-hand side of the navigation panel, as shown in the following screenshot:

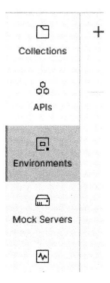

Figure 8.4 – Navigating to Environments

2. Click on **Newman Test Env** in the navigation tree.

3. From the **View more actions** menu at the top-right of the environment panel, choose the **Export** option, as shown in the following screenshot:

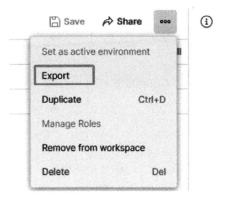

Figure 8.5 – Export environment

4. Name the file NewmanTestEnvironment.json and click **Save**.

Now that you have the environment saved, you can use it in Newman. To that, you can use the -e flag to let Newman know where to look for environment variables. Putting this all together, you should have a command that looks like this:

```
newman run TestCollection.json -e  NewmanTestEnvironment.json
```

If you run this command, you should see that it now successfully runs the collection. This is a much more scalable option than manually typing in each of the variables!

Running data-driven tests in Newman

In *Chapter 7*, *Data-Driven Testing*, I showed you how to use the powerful data-driven testing concept in Postman. In that chapter, you ran the tests with the collection runner, but what if you wanted to run them in Newman? You've already seen how you can use the -e flag to specify an environment. Similarly, you can specify data-driven inputs using the -d flag. Let's modify the Test GET request to turn it into a simple data-driven test, by changing the URL so that it has a couple of variables that you can create data for in a file. Set the query parameter and the query parameter value to both be variables. The request URL should look something like this:

```
{{baseUrl}}/get?{{queryParam}}={{queryParamVal}}
```

Now, you can create a file containing data that you will use as inputs. Create a simple .csv file containing two columns, each named after one of the variables. Create a couple of rows of input in the file. You should have a file that looks something like this:

```
queryParam,queryParamVal
test,true
query,1
```

Figure 8.6 – Data-driven input file

Save this file as DataDrivenInput.csv. Before running your collection in Newman, you will need to export it again since you have made changes to it. Make sure you save the request in Postman and then export the collection again. You can use the same name you did previously and just overwrite the old file. Now that you have all the files that you need, you can run the collection in Newman with the following command:

```
newman run TestCollection.json -e NewmanTestEnvironment.json -d
DataDrivenInputs.csv
```

After a few seconds, you should see a report showing the results. You will see that it ran the request with each of the inputs in your file, along with a table summarizing the results. Now that you can run a collection with an environment and data-driven inputs, you should be able to do most of what you need in Newman. There are a several other options that Newman has though, so let's take a closer look at some of them.

Other Newman options

The -e and -d flags inNewman will give you most of the control that you need when running collections, but there are a few other flags that I want to highlight in here as well. I won't cover every possible flag in detail, but if you want, you can find out more by looking at the documentation: https://github.com/postmanlabs/newman#command-line-options.

If you have a large collection with a lot of requests in it, there might be times when you don't want to run the whole collection. For example, you may want to only run a subset of the requests for debugging purposes. One option you can use for this is the --folder option. This option allows you to specify the name of a folder in your collection that you want to run. Newman will then only run requests that are in that folder. If you want to run several folders, you can just use the --folder option multiple times.

Another option you may want to use is the `--delay-request` option. This option allows you to specify an amount of time (in milliseconds) that Newman should wait after a request finishes before it starts the next request. You might want to use this if you have requests that depend on each other. For example, if you had a POST request that created some data and then you were running a GET request to check whether that data was there, you might want to put in a slight delay so that the server has time to fully process the POST request.

You can also specify timeout values, which will dictate how long Newman waits for certain actions to happen before it considers them to have timed out. You can specify the `--timeout` flag to set a timeout value for how long you want to wait for the entire collection to run. You will want to be careful with this value since it can be hard to figure out how long it will make sense for this to be if you have a lot of requests in the collection. A more targeted option for this is `--timeout-request`, which specifies the amount of time to wait for a request to complete before considering it to have timed out. You can get even more targeted than that if you want by specifying the `--timeout-script` option, which sets the maximum amount of time any of the scripts (such as test or pre-request scripts) can run before you consider them to have timed out. These three flags are all need you to specify a number that represents the amount of time in milliseconds.

You can also use options such as `--bail`, which lets Newman know that you want it to stop running as soon as any failure occurs. By default, it will stop the run as soon as a failure is detected, but if you want it to complete the current test script before stopping, you can specify it as `--bail failure`. You can also use the folder modifier as a way to skip running the entire collection if some of the inputs are incorrect.

Another option you may need to use occasionally is the `-k` option. This option will disable strict SSL, which is sometimes required if you are getting SSL certification errors when running your request. You can also specify the `--ignore-redirects` option to prevent the redirect links from being automatically followed.

There are several other options that Newman offers. Newman supports everything that Postman does, so if you are ever unsure of how to do something in Newman that you can do in Postman, check out the Newman documentation – you will find a way to do it.

Reporting on tests in Newman

Newman is a powerful tool for running tests, but the point of having test automation isn't just so that you can run tests. The point of test automation is to be able to improve a product's quality based on the results you get. You need to know when tests fail so that you can follow up on those failures and see if they represent issues in the product. Effective test automation also requires paying attention to the tests themselves. You want to run tests that are effective and useful, and not just keep running a test that isn't telling you anything. In order to do all of this, you need test reporting. This section will help you understand how reporting works in Newman. You will learn how to use the built-in reporters that Newman has. You will also learn how to install and use community build reporters, and I will even walk you through an example that shows you how you can build your own Newman test reporter.

Using Newman's built-in reporters

You need reports on failed tests and summaries that show you how well your tests are doing. When you ran Newman earlier, you could see some reporting that was provided at the command line. These summaries are helpful when you are running locally, and Newman has several built-in reporter options that you can use to control that report's output. You can specify which reporter you want to use with the `-r` flag. If you do not specify a reporter to use, Newman defaults to using the `cli` reporter, but there are four other built-in reporters that you can use. The other available reporters are the `json`, `junit`, `progress`, and `emojitrain` reporters.

The `json` and `junit` reporters will each save the report to a file. The `json` reporter saves the data in JSON format in a `.json` file, while the `junit` reporter saves the data in a **JUnit**-compatible `.xml` file. JUnit is a testing framework for the Java programming language. The JUnit XML format can be parsed by different programs, including build systems such as Jenkins, to display nicely formatted test results.

The `progress` reporter will give you a progress bar in the console while the tests run. Although I have mentioned it here for completeness, the `emojitrain` reporter isn't something you will ever use. It prints out the progress as an emoji, but it is hard to get an emoji to display correctly in a Command Prompt, and there isn't any added value over what you can see with the `progress` reporter.

You can use multiple reporters at once if you want. So, for example, you could use both the CLI and progress reporter at the same time by specifying them as a comma-separated list after the `-r` flag, like this:

```
-r cli,progress
```

You can also specify additional options that will be applied to some of the reporters. For example, the `cli` reporter has a `no-success-assertions` option that will turn off the output for assertions that are successful while it is running. In order to use these options, you need to specify them with the `--reporter` flag. You will then add the name of the reporter and the reporter option to the flag, turning it into one big flag. So, for example, to use the `no-success-assertions` option for the `cli` flag, you would specify the following flag:

```
--reporter-cli-no-success-assertions
```

Alternatively, to specify that you want to save the JUnit report in a folder called `reports`, you could specify the following flag:

```
--reporter-junit-export reports
```

Note that specifying the reporter's options does not enable that reporter. You will still need to specify which reporters you want to use with the `-r` flag. There are several different reporter options available for different types of reports. You can see the list of options here: `https://github.com/postmanlabs/newman#reporters`.

Using external reporters

In addition to the built-in reporters that Newman comes with, it allows you to use externally developed reporters. These reporters don't come installed with Newman, but once you have installed them, you can use them to create the reports that you want. Postman maintains an external reporter called *Newman HTML Reporter*. There are also several community-maintained reporters that you can install and use if you want. These include reporters such as the *csv* reporter (`https://github.com/matt-ball/newman-reporter-csv`), which will export your report in `.csv` format, and *htmlextra* (`https://github.com/DannyDainton/newman-reporter-htmlextra`), which gives you some more in-depth data output compared to the basic HTML reporter that Neman maintains.

There are also several reporters that can help you create reports for specific tools. For example, you could use the *TeamCity* (`https://github.com/leafle/newman-reporter-teamcity`) reporter if you're running on a TeamCity CI server, or you could use the *Confluence* (`https://github.com/OmbraDiFenice/newman-reporter-confluence`) reporter to report data to a Confluence page. There are several other tool-specific reporters listed in Newman's documentation: `https://github.com/postmanlabs/newman#using-external-reporters`.

I don't have the space to show you how to use all these reporters, but I think the *htmlextra* reporter is a useful one, so I will walk you through how to install and use it. You should be able to use what you will learn next to install any of the reporters that you need.

Generating reports with htmlextra

Similar to installing Newman, you can install htmlextra with npm. Call the following command to globally install htmlextra:

```
npm install -g newman-reporter-htmlextra
```

Once it has downloaded and installed, you can specify it by passing in `htmlextra` to the `-r` option. For example, to use it with the data-driven test mentioned earlier in this chapter, you could call the following command:

```
newman run TestCollection.json -e NewmanTestEnvironment.json -d
DataDrivenInputs.csv -r htmlextra
```

Once the requests have run, you can go to the `newman` folder in your working directory, and you will see an `.html` file in there that you can open in a web browser. This will give you a nice dashboard summarizing the results of your run. The default dashboard is useful, but if you want, you can also customize it. For example, you can change the title to `My Test Newman Report` by adding the following to your command:

```
--reporter-htmlextra-title "My Test Newman Report"
```

There are several other options that allow you to customize parts of the report. You can check those out in the documentation here: `https://github.com/DannyDainton/newman-reporter-htmlextra`.

Creating your own reporter

Even with the number of community supported reporters out there, you might not be able to find one that does exactly what you need. In that case, you could just make your own! Doing this requires some JavaScript knowledge, but let's walk through an example so that you can see how it would work. Unless you are fairly proficient with JavaScript, you will probably want to stick to reporters that others have made, but understanding how something works behind the scenes is still helpful. To make your own reporter, follow these steps:

1. On your hard drive, create a new directory called `MyReporter`.

2. Open a Command Prompt and use the `cd` command to navigate into that directory.

3. Create a blank npm package by calling `npm init`.

   You will be prompted for a few things. First, you will be asked what name you want your package to have. The default name is set to `myreporter`, but this will not work. A Newman reporter must have a name that starts with `newman-reporter-`.

4. Type in `newman-reporter-myreporter` and hit *Enter* to accept the new name.

5. Hit *Enter* again to accept the default version number.

6. Type in a short description and hit *Enter*.

7. Leave the entry point as its default of `index.js` by hitting *Enter* again.

8. We won't bother with a test command, Git repository, or keywords, so you can just hit *Enter* to skip past each of those options as they come up.

9. Put in your name as the author and hit *Enter*.

10. Since this is just a test package that you are playing around with, you don't need to worry about the license too much and can just hit *Enter* to accept the default one.

11. Once you've gone through all those options, npm will show you the `package.json` file that it is going to create for you, which has all those options in it. You can tell it to create that file by hitting *Enter* to send the default response of **yes** to the question.

    Now that you have a blank npm package, you can create a reporter.

12. Add a file called `index.js` to the folder you've created and open that file in a code or text editor.

This file is where you will put the JavaScript code that you will use to create your custom reporter. As I mentioned previously, creating a custom reporter will be difficult if you only have a beginner's understanding of JavaScript. I can't go into the depth of JavaScript that you will need for this process in this book, but I will show you a simple example so that you can see, in very broad terms, what it takes to do this. Newman emits events while it is running that the reporters can listen for and then perform actions based on receiving them. The following code shows a couple of examples of using those events:

```
function MyCustomNewmanReporter (newman, reporterOptions,
    collectionRunOptions) {
    newman.on('start', function (err) {
        if (err) { return; }
        console.log('Collection run starting')
```

```
    });
    newman.on('item', function (err,args) {
        console.log(Ran: '+args.item.name)
    });
    newman.on('done', function () {
        console.log('all done!')
    });
    };
module.exports = MyCustomNewmanReporter
```

The file needs to include a function (in this case, I have called it
MyCustomNewmanReporter) and then it needs to export that function with module.
exports at the bottom of the file. Once you have done that, you can do anything you
want to inside the function. In this case, I am showing three different examples of how you
can use Newman events.

The first event I'm looking at is the start event:

```
    newman.on('start', function (err) {
        if (err) { return; }
        console.log('Collection run starting')
    });
```

This event is sent whenever Newman starts running a new collection. You can see that I
listen for that event with the newman.on method. I then tell it what event I am listening
for ('start') and give it a callback that can take in two arguments. The first argument is
the error object and, in this case, this is the only argument I need to specify. I then check
whether there is an error and if so, stop execution. If there isn't one, I merely log out the
fact that the collection run has started.

The second example in my code is listening for the item event:

```
newman.on('item', function (err,args) {
        console.log(Ran: '+args.item.name)
    });
```

In this case, I have specified both arguments in the callback. The first one, as shown previously, is the error object, which will only happen if there is an error. The second argument is an object that contains summary information about the event that I am listening for. In this case, that object is the item object since this is an item event. This object has several properties, but in this example, I am accessing the name property and printing that out. The item event is emitted when a test has completed.

The final example in my code is listening for the done event, which is emitted when a collection run has completed:

```
newman.on('done', function () {
        console.log('all done!')
    });
```

This example shows how the callback arguments are optional. In this case, I am not accessing any of the properties of the summary object and I'm not worrying about the errors, so I don't bother specifying those things.

One other thing that should be noted in this example is that the MyCustomNewmanReporter function takes in three arguments. The newman argument is the class that emits the events and these examples have shown how to use it, but I did not show you how to use the other two inputs to that function. The reporterOptions argument will include things such as the silent option or other reporter options that you might want to support. collectionRunOptions includes information about all the command-line options that were passed in.

This example is obviously very simple and there is a lot more complexity to creating your own reporter. If you want to figure out more, I would suggest that you go to the Newman GitHub repository (https://github.com/postmanlabs/newman) and look through the documentation there. While you are there, you can also check out how the built-in reporters work. They use the same approach that you would need to use to create your own reporter. You can see the code for them here: https://github.com/postmanlabs/newman/tree/develop/lib/reporters. Another great example can be found in Deepak Pathania's neman-reporter-debug GitHub repository. If you look at the DebugReporter.js file (https://github.com/deepakpathania/newman-reporter-debug/blob/master/lib/DebugReporter.js), you will see a number of different examples showing how to use many of the Newman events and options.

Now that you know how to create your own custom reporters, we will take a look at how to use Newman in **Continuous Integration** (**CI**) builds in more detail.

Integrating Newman into CI builds

Running your collection via the command line with Newman can help you quickly and easily run tests locally, but the real power of it comes in being able to automatically kick off and schedule runs. Many software companies now use **CI** systems that automate how builds and tests are continuously run every time a change is made to the code. Newman allows you to easily integrate into these CI build systems. This section will walk you through some general principles of using Newman in CI systems. I will then show you a specific example of applying those principles to integrate Newman into a Travis CI build.

General principles for using Newman in CI builds

There are many different CI systems and integrating with each one requires knowledge about how that system works. In broad terms, though, there are a few things you will need to do, regardless of the system you are working with:

- You will need to make sure the build system has access to the collection, environment, and any other data files that the run needs. Usually, the easiest way to do this is to include the tests in a folder in your version control system, alongside the code. Your build system will have access to the code to build it, so if you include your tests in there, it will also have access to them.

- You will need to install Newman on the CI system. If your build system has a node, this can easily be accomplished with npm.

- You will need to specify the command that will run the collections that you want. This works the same as running Newman in the command line locally. You just might have to be careful when it comes to figuring out where the path to the tests is on the CI server.

- You will need to set up a schedule for the tests. Do you want them to run on every pull request? Or maybe only when code is merged into the main branch? Or perhaps you only want them to run if some other build steps have succeeded?

The exact implementation of each of these steps is going to vary, depending on the integration system you are working with, but you will need to think about each of them to run your collections in a CI system.

Example of using Travis CI

I will show you an example of this using Travis CI, a popular CI system that integrates with GitHub. If you have a GitHub account, you can follow the Travis CI Getting Started guide at `https://docs.travis-ci.com/user/tutorial/` to get started with using it. Let's get started:

1. Once you have that set up, you will need to make sure that Travis CI has access to the collection and environment files. Upload them into a directory in your GitHub repository. I would suggest putting them into a directory called `tests`.

2. You will now need to install Newman on the CI system.

   In Travis CI, you can do this in a file called `.travis.yml`, so create that file if it is not there already. Note that the filename starts with a period. Inside this file, you can specify that you want to install Newman on your system by including the following commands:

   ```
   install:
   - npm install newman
   ```

   For this to work, Travis CI will need to have node available, so you will want to add `language: node_js` to the top of the `.travis.yml` file so that it knows that it will need to use an environment that has a node available for these runs.

3. Now, you will need to give Travis CI the command that you want it to run. You can do this in the `script:` section, like this:

   ```
   script:
   - node_modules/.bin/newman run tests/TestCollection.
   json -e tests/NewmanTestEnvironment.json -d tests/
   DataDrivenInputs.csv
   ```

   Notice that that you will probably have to specify the full path to Newman. Since you usually can't install packages globally on a build system, you need to install them locally. In that case, the Newman command will be in the `node_moules/.bin/` folder, as shown in the preceding example. You can also see that I specified the path to the `tests` folder, which is where each of the files are located.

4. Travis CI will default to running scripts every time you trigger a build. You can set up your build triggers in GitHub, and I will leave that as an exercise for you to do on your own if you want.

This is, of course, just one example of how to apply the general steps, but for any build system that you use, you will need to follow similar steps if you want to run your Postman collection via Newman. The exact setup and commands needed for each step will differ from platform to platform, but the general ideas will hold true.

Summary

I don't know about you, but I just love it when you can use a tool from the command line. Newman enables you to run Postman collections from the command line, and this opens up many possibilities. In this chapter, we have learned how to use Newman to run collections on the command line and how to leverage this to integrate API testing into build systems. Of course, to do this, you needed to learn how to install Newman, as well as Node.js, so that you can install it with npm.

We then walked through some of the options for running Newman and saw how to run a collection in Newman, as well as how to include an environment and event data file for data-driven testing. We also saw some of the powerful reporting capabilities in Newman. This included the options for using the built-in reporters that come with it, as well as installing and using external reporters that others have shared. We walked through an example of using the htmlextra reporter. There, we showed you how to install and use it. In addition, you learned how to create your own reporter.

In this chapter, you have acquired the skills to use a powerful API testing tool. Put it to good use! Now that you can run tests in CI builds, it is time to look at the next step: what happens to your APIs once your clients start using them? In the next chapter, we will explore how to use Postman to monitor what is happening with our APIs as they are being used.

9
Monitoring APIs with Postman

I remember taking a class on time management. One of the topics we discussed in that course was how to manage your email. As students, we shared how we each approached our email. I can still distinctly remember one of my fellow students being completely shocked and almost bewildered that I didn't empty my email inbox every day. For me, all email stays in my inbox. If it is unread, I still need to deal with it, and if it is marked as read, I don't need to look at it again, but I don't bother to archive it or put it into another folder. This student thought it was totally bonkers that I wouldn't archive and label everything. And then there is the other side of the spectrum. I know people who have literally thousands of unread emails in their inbox. If they get an email that they don't want to read, they just leave it.

When I see an inbox like that, I become kind of like the student in the time management class. I can't even understand how anyone can work like that. But somehow, they do. We all have different approaches to how we think about and handle our email, and sometimes, seeing how someone else does it can be a bit shocking to us. It's hard not to think of our way as the one that everyone uses. The reality, though, is that even with something as simple as email, there are many different ways of using the tool.

This is one of the great challenges of testing. It is really hard to think of ways of doing things that are different from the way you do it. To use the phrase popularized by Donald Rumsfeld, there are known unknowns. We know that people will use the system in unknown ways but don't know what those ways are. There are techniques we can use as testers to come up with new ideas and reduce the uncertainty, but with any significant user base, we will never be able to predict all of the ways that clients will use our system. As the saying goes, if users can do it, at least one of them will. I have seen that played out again and again in my years as a software tester.

You design a system to work in a certain way, but a client wants to do something the system doesn't allow for yet, so they figure out some way to get it to do what they want even if that means using a feature in a way that you never intended. Of course, then later on, when you change that feature, you end up breaking things for your client. As testers, we want to prevent that, but how do we go about predicting all of the ways that our customer will use our system? The truth is, we can't. No matter how good we get at figuring out the unknowns, we will never be able to understand and predict everything those that interact with our software will do.

This is why software developers and testers have increasingly turned to monitoring to help them out. Monitoring allows you to see some details of what your customers are doing with your product and hence allows you to respond to issues that they hit quickly and effectively. It also allows you to better understand usage patterns before making changes to the system.

In this chapter, I will show you how to use monitoring in Postman. We will cover the following topics:

- Setting up monitors in Postman
- Viewing monitor results

Technical requirements

The code used in this chapter can be found at `https://github.com/PacktPub-lishing/API-Testing-and-Development-with-Postman/tree/master/Chapter09`.

Setting up a monitor in Postman

Monitoring in Postman allows you to stay up to date with how your API is working. Normally, when you create tests in Postman, you will run them against a local build or perhaps as part of a continuous integration build. With monitors, you can run tests using staging or even production builds to make sure that certain aspects of your API are working as expected.

In this section, I will show you how to get started with creating monitors in Postman and I'll explain some of the different options that you have and when you should use them. This section will also show you how to add tests to a monitor so that you can check for exactly what you are interested in.

Creating a monitor

To create a monitor in Postman, click on the **New** button and then select the **Monitor** option on the wizard. You can then set up the monitor with the following steps:

1. For the first step of the process, you can choose to either add new requests to a collection and monitor those, or you can pick an existing collection to monitor. For now, let's just create a new collection explicitly designed for monitoring:

Figure 9.1 – Monitor a new collection

2. In the **Request URL** field, enter https://swapi.dev/api/people.

3. Ensure that the **Check Status Code** field has a value of 200 and that the **Check Response Time** field has a value of 400.

4. Click on the **Next** button to go to the configuration page. On that page, you can create a name for the monitor and choose which environment to use if the collection needs one. In this case, name the monitor SWAPI Test Monitor and leave the environment unspecified.

   The configuration page also has options to specify the frequency with which you want to run the monitor. Note that a free Postman account, at the time of writing this, only has 1,000 monitoring calls per month. You will want to keep that in mind when setting up the frequency of your monitor. Also, in this case, we will just be doing this for demonstration purposes, and so you should delete the monitor after working through this example. We don't want to be unnecessarily running requests against a service.

5. By default, Postman will automatically select which region to run the monitor from, but if you have specific regions that you want to run from (for example, if you wanted to see the latency from a region), you can manually select one from the list. For now, leave the **Automatically Select Region** option selected.

6. There are also additional preferences that you could set. Click on **Show additional preferences** to see them. Postman will automatically send email notifications to the email address you used to log in to your Postman account, but if you want to add additional email addresses to receive notifications, you can do so here. You can also specify options such as whether you want it to retry when it fails, or if you want to set a timeout or a delay between requests. For this example, just leave all of the options unchecked. At this point, the configuration page should look like this:

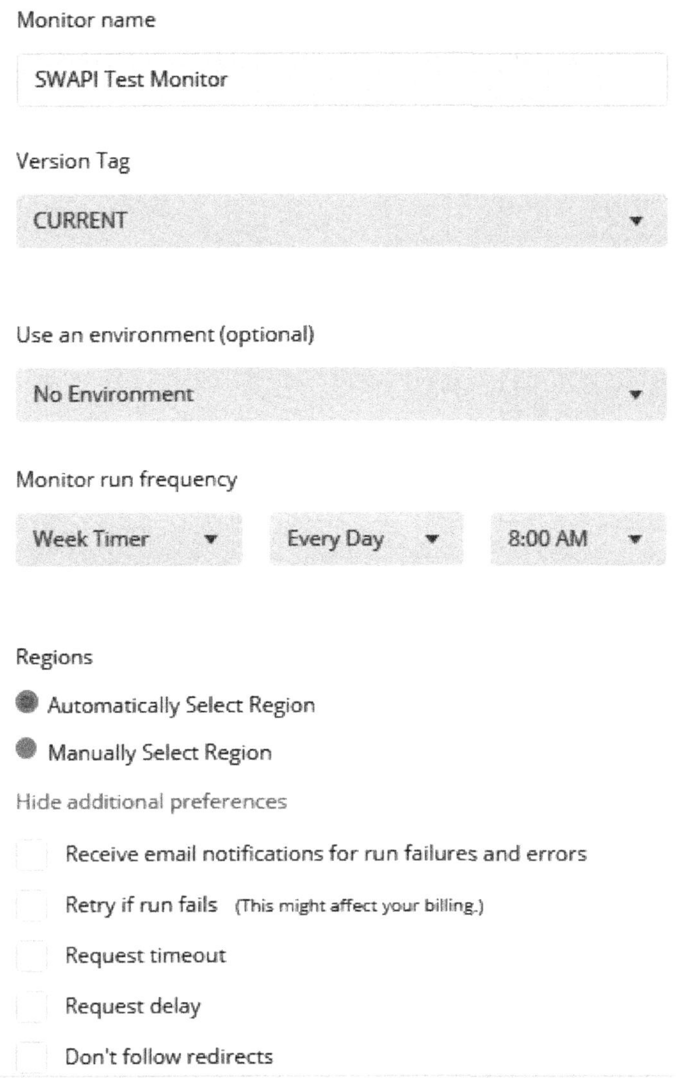

Monitor name

> SWAPI Test Monitor

Version Tag

> CURRENT   ▼

Use an environment (optional)

> No Environment   ▼

Monitor run frequency

> Week Timer   ▼   Every Day   ▼   8:00 AM   ▼

Regions

⦿ Automatically Select Region

◉ Manually Select Region

Hide additional preferences

☐   Receive email notifications for run failures and errors

☐   Retry if run fails   (This might affect your billing.)

☐   Request timeout

☐   Request delay

☐   Don't follow redirects

Figure 9.2 – Monitor configuration

7. Click on the **Create** button to create the monitor. After a few seconds, the monitor will be created.

Monitors that you have set up can be viewed by clicking on the **Monitors** tab to the left of the navigation pane. If you go there and click on the monitor, you will see that you can manually kick off a run of the monitor if you want. You can also make changes to the monitor by going to the **View more actions** menu at the top-right of the page and choosing the **Edit** option:

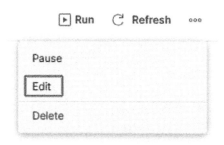

Figure 9.3 – Edit a monitor

Click on the **Run** button to run the monitor and you will see a report of the run, showing whether any of the tests failed and how long it took to run the monitors. If you go to the **Collections** tab, you will see that a new collection called SWAPI Test Monitor has been added to the collection list. The request in that collection will call the endpoint you specified and has a test that checks that the status code is 200 and the response time is below 400 milliseconds.

These steps will get you started with creating a monitor, but there are several other options that we didn't use. When initially setting up the monitor, we left most of the additional preferences blank. These options are available for a reason though, and so I want to take a moment to look at what they do and why they are there.

Using additional monitor settings

You can see the additional monitor settings if you edit the monitor and expand the **Additional Preferences** section. There are different settings here as you can see in the following screenshot:

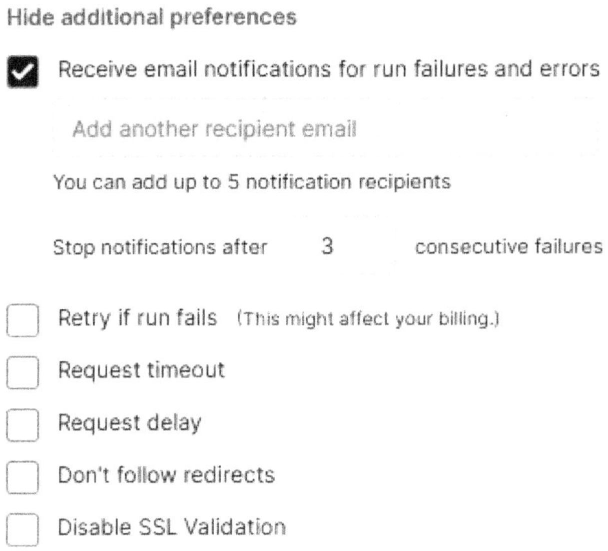

Hide additional preferences

☑ Receive email notifications for run failures and errors

  Add another recipient email

  You can add up to 5 notification recipients

  Stop notifications after   3   consecutive failures

☐ Retry if run fails   (This might affect your billing.)

☐ Request timeout

☐ Request delay

☐ Don't follow redirects

☐ Disable SSL Validation

Figure 9.4 – Additional preferences for monitors

Let's look at each of them in turn.

Receiving email notifications

The email notification setting is pretty self-explanatory. Whichever email addresses you specify will get notified of any monitor failures. By default, Postman will have the email address associated with your account in there, but you can easily add more.

You can also control how much Postman will bug you about this. If you have a monitor that is running quite frequently and it starts to fail, you might get an email every 10 minutes about this failure. If you are already investigating the failure, you might find this annoying. Postman allows you to control this by specifying how many times you want to be notified about a failure that is happening every time. By default, it will stop notifying you once the same monitor has failed three times in a row, but you can change that number to be higher or lower based on your workflows.

Retry on failure

Sometimes, there are minor glitches in our systems that we can't do anything about. If you are monitoring a part of the system where you might occasionally get this kind of glitch, you might not want to have to investigate every single one. In that case, you can use the **Retry if run fails** option. If this option is specified and a run fails, Postman will immediately run it again before notifying you of the failure. You can specify how many times it will retry (either once or twice). However, if the previous time the monitor was run, it failed, Postman will assume that this current failure is legitimate, and it will not try to re-run it for you.

Since the number of monitor calls is limited depending on which plan you are using, you will want to be aware of how this option could affect that. Automatically rerunning a monitor in this way will count against your monitor limit.

Request timeout

The request timeout option is used to determine how long Postman will wait for a request to return data before moving on to the next request. By default, it does not specify any timeout value. Postman does limit the total time that a monitor can run for to 5 minutes, but if you had a monitor with a few requests and one of them was hanging, it could prevent the other requests from running. To avoid this, you can use the request timeout option. When you choose that option, you will need to specify how long Postman should wait before it considers the request to have timed out. Of course, the amount of time that you specify here cannot exceed 5 minutes as, at that point, the total run time available for the monitor will be exceeded.

Delay between requests

Some services need a short pause between requests to allow data to be fully synchronized. If you need to do something like this in a monitor, you can use the **Delay between requests** option to specify the time in milliseconds that you want to Postman wait after a request has finished before sending a new one.

The maximum amount of time a monitor can run for is 5 minutes, so be aware that adding delays between requests contributes to this. If you make the delay too long, you won't be able to run very many requests in your monitor.

Don't follow redirects

Some API responses return a **redirect response**. These are responses that have a status code starting with 3. They tell the browser that it should immediately load a new URL, which is provided in the location header of the initial response. You may want to have a monitor that checks that an API endpoint is giving back the correct redirect but not want the monitor to actually follow that redirect. If this is the case, you can use the **Don't follow redirects** option to tell Postman that you do not want it to load the redirect URL.

Disable SSL validation

During development of a new API, it may not make sense to purchase a signed SSL certificate. However, if your server does not have one yet, monitors that you run against it will probably error. To work around this situation, you can specify the **Disable SSL validation**. This will tell Postman that you do not want to check for an SSL security certificate and so will prevent your monitors from failing due to missing certificates.

Although there certainly are times when you would need to use this option, if you are monitoring a production server, I would recommend against using this option. I have seen it happen where a company forgets to update its security certificate and this ends up causing errors for end users. The point of monitors is that you will know whether your end users are seeing errors and so, generally speaking, you want your monitors to fail for SSL validation errors.

Understanding these options will help you to choose the settings that will allow you to create monitors that do what you need them to. However, another very important aspect of a good monitor is ensuring that you have tests in place that check the things that matter.

Adding tests to a monitor

When you created the monitor, it automatically added a request for you, but what if you want to check some additional stuff? To add additional checks to your monitors, go to the collection in the Postman app and add a new request to that collection. Let's monitor a second endpoint in this API. Set the endpoint of the new request to `https://swapi.dev/api/films` and then go to the **Tests** tab.

You can add a check to this request that checks for a `200` response with the following code:

```
pm.test('check status code', function () {
    pm.response.to.have.status(200);
})
```

Another check you might want to add to a monitor is to check the size of the request. You could just add a check that verifies the data, but then, every time even just a minor thing changes in the request, you would need to update your monitor. Instead, you could use a check directly against the size of the request. You can check that the size of the request is bigger than a given value as a rough estimate of it still working correctly with the following code:

```
pm.test('check response time', function() {
    pm.expect(pm.response.responseSize).to.be.above(18000);
})
```

You can of course add any other checks you want to your monitors in the same way you would add a test to a request normally. However, it is a good idea with monitors to make the checks more generic. Usually, a monitor is meant to be a quick check indicator that something might be going wrong. You want to get that feedback without running all of the detailed regression checks that you would usually run and so you will want to design the monitors to be quite simple.

Any monitor failures should be pretty good indicators that something has gone wrong with the system in production. That can come from code changes although, hopefully, issues introduced in that way would be caught by tests run in your build pipeline. Often, monitors will catch things that went wrong with a deployment or perhaps with some hardware or software breaking in the production environment itself. You want to be able to trust your monitors and so you should make them fairly generic so that you can be sure that if they report a failure, it is something important to follow up on.

If you have monitors that fail for minor things, it is easy to end up with alert fatigue. In that case, you get so many alerts about failures that aren't really failures at all, and you end up ignoring the failures. You remember the story of the boy who cried wolf? He thought it was funny to say there was a wolf when there wasn't and after a while, the villagers started to ignore him. They assumed that he was just trying to trick them again and when a real wolf came, they didn't respond to his cries for help. The same thing can happen with monitors. If they fail too often, you will stop trusting them. Think carefully about how you set them up.

As with all automated tests, I think it is important to *"test the tests."* You don't want your tests to fail unnecessarily, but you do need to make sure that they actually will fail if something goes wrong. Let's set the expected response size to 19000 instead and then send the request. You should see a failure in the test results as shown in the following screenshot:

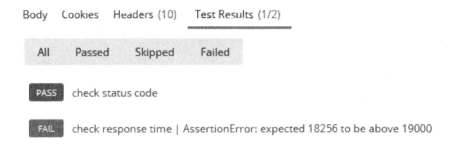

Figure 9.5 – Failed check

You could modify the other check as well to be sure and then put them back to the correct values. Postman will now run the two requests in this collection on the schedule you have set up.

We've seen how to create monitors in Postman. I've also shown you how to set up a monitor so that it does what you need it to. You've learned about the various settings that are available and seen how to add tests to monitors. With all of that under your belt, it is now time to look at how to view the results of monitor runs.

Viewing monitor results

Once you have created your monitors, they will run on the schedule you specified. In this section, I will show you how to view and understand the results of these runs. I'll also show you how to delete a monitor that you no longer need.

If a monitor fails, Postman will send you an email letting you know that there is a problem. This email will let you know about the failure and give you a link that will take you to the monitor. Postman will also send you a weekly summary of your monitors so that you can see how they are doing overall.

Although monitors usually run on the specified schedule, you don't have to wait for the scheduled run time. If you suspect there might be an issue, or you just want to check something out, you can manually run your monitor outside the specified schedule.

To see the monitor results, you will need to go to the **Monitors** tab and select you monitor from the list.

If your monitor has not yet run, you will see a notification to that effect, and you can click on the **Run** button to kick off a run. Once the monitor has run, you will see a chart showing some information about that monitor. The chart is split into two parts. The bottom of the chart (labeled 1 in the following screenshot) shows you how many of the checks have failed:

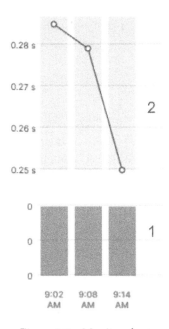

Figure 9.6 – Monitor chart

In the example shown in this screenshot, there are no failures so everything is at 0, but if some of the checks had failed, you would see that displayed here.

The top part of the chart (labeled 2 in the figure) shows how long the requests took to resolve. This can be a good indicator to look at as well. You might have monitors that are not failing, but if over time things are getting slower, that might also indicate a problem.

> **Important note**
>
> If you are running multiple requests in your monitor, the time shown in the monitor plot is the average of the times taken by each of the requests. If you want to see the individual request times, you can click on the **Request Split** option at the top of the chart.

If the monitor has only been run a couple of times, as shown in the previous screenshot, it is pretty easy to look through the results, but if you have a monitor that is running on a regular schedule, the number of results on this plot will start to get quite large. However, you can still view the results by using the filtering options. These options are available at the top of the chart and they can be used to narrow down the results that you see. You could, for example, look at the results from just one specific request if you want, or you could set the filters to look at only the results for failed or errored runs, as shown in the following screenshot:

Figure 9.7 – Monitor result filters

One other thing that can be helpful if you are trying to figure out why a monitor is failing is to look at the test results for that monitor. If you click on one of the bars in the graph, you can scroll down on the page to see a summary of the results that show what requests were run and what checks each test did. Additionally, you can look at some results in the console log by clicking on the **Console Log** tab. This tab is also available after clicking on a run in the chart. Some details are not shown in here for security reasons, but it can give you a bit of additional information.

Now that you have had the chance to set up and run a monitor as well as look at the results, I want to show you how to clean them up. Not all monitors need to stay around forever and since the free version of Postman comes with a limited number of monitor calls, you may want to remove monitors that you don't need. Let's look at how to do that in the next section.

Cleaning up the monitors

Since you don't need to worry about the status of the SWAPI service, I would suggest that you don't leave these monitors running. They will count against your monitor run quota and will create unnecessary load on the SWAPI service. You can remove the monitor with the following steps:

1. Go to the **Monitors** tab and select **SWAPI Test Monitor**.

2. Click on the **View more actions** menu beside the monitor and select the **Delete** option:

Figure 9.8 – Delete monitor option

3. Click **Delete** on the confirmation dialog.

This will remove the monitor for you, and it will no longer run. In this section, you have learned how to do the final steps in the life cycle of a monitor. You can view the results and make decisions based on what you see. In addition, you have learned how to clean up old monitors that you no longer need.

Summary

Monitoring is an important strategy in the world of modern API development. It is impossible to fully predict everything that will happen in the real-world usage of our applications. No matter how well we have tested our APIs, there will always be surprises in the real world. Monitors are a way to mitigate the risk of these surprises. With monitors, we can see what is going on with our APIs and quickly respond to issues.

In this chapter, I have shown you how to get started with using this tool in Postman. You have seen how to create a monitor and how to add requests and tests to that monitor. You have also learned about the various options that Postman has for creating monitors and learned when to use those options. In addition, I have shown you how to view and understand the result that Postman gives when monitors are run.

Monitoring allows you to get a glimpse into how an API is working when your clients are using it, but it is no replacement for having a good understanding of how your API works. If you want to create useful monitors, you will need to know what kinds of things to look for and have a good understanding of the risks that exist in your API. In the next chapter, we will take a closer look at testing an existing API and see what lessons we can use from there to help us to create better APIs.

10
Testing an Existing API

APIs come in all shapes and sizes. I have tried to give you a few different APIs to practice on as you've worked your way through this book. If you have worked through the various examples and challenges in this book, you should have a pretty good idea of how to use Postman with various types of APIs. In this chapter, though, I want to get you thinking about how you can use Postman to test an existing API.

Although new APIs are being created every day, the reality is that there are a lot of APIs out there that do not have adequate tests. You might be working on one of those APIs. Perhaps you are even working on an API that has been around for some time. I was recently working on a project that was under a tight deadline and, to meet this deadline, we had to leave some of the API tests until later. It can be a bit overwhelming to have to go back and add tests to an API that already exists and so, in this chapter, I want to walk you through a case study where you can see examples and practice testing existing APIs. These are the topics that we are going to cover in this chapter:

- Finding bugs in an API
- Automating API tests
- An example of automated API tests
- Sharing your work

Technical requirements

The code used in this chapter can be found at `https://github.com/PacktPublishing/API-Testing-and-Development-with-Postman/tree/master/Chapter10`.

Finding bugs in an API

Finding bugs can be easy. Sometimes they just jump right out at you. However, the easy-to-find bugs aren't usually the ones that matter. Good testers are those who can find the hidden bugs that matter. Doing this is often difficult and takes some practice. In this chapter, I will help you to get started with creating good automated tests, but before going deep into that, I want to give you some practice at the skill of looking for bugs. In this section, I will help you to set up an API locally that you can use for testing.

I will then show you how to do some testing and exploration of this API and help you to find some bugs in it. I will also show you how to reset the service. This API is meant to break sometimes and so you may need to reset it back to its original state. I will also show you the steps to find one of the bugs in the system so that you can get a bit of an idea of how to go about doing this. Let's dive into this by setting up the API that you are going to test.

Setting up a local API for testing

There are a lot of sites that you can practice calling an API on. However, many of them do not give you the ability to practice POST, DELETE, and PUT calls. This is understandable since those calls can change things for other users in the system, but it would still be nice to be able to test on a full-fledged application. To help you out with that, I have created an application that you can use to practice your API testing with. To get started with using this application, you will need to make sure you have a few things in place.

If you have already done some of the other examples in this book, you should have Node.js installed, but if not, you will need to download and install it. You can get it from here: `https://nodejs.org/en/download/`. Once you have that installed, you can set up the application for local use with the following steps:

1. Download the application from the GitHub repository for this course (`https://github.com/PacktPublishing/API-Testing-and-Development-with-Postman/Chapter10`).

2. To install the application, ensure that the downloaded files are in the folder you want them to be in, and then open Command Prompt and navigate to that folder.

3. Once you are in the correct folder, call `npm install` to install the application. This will install all of the dependencies that you need and get everything ready for you.

4. After the npm install has completed, you can start the application by calling `node application_server.js`.

   This will start the server for you and you should see a message saying **JSON Server is running. Requests can be accessed at http://localhost:3000/**, as shown in the following screenshot:

```
C:\APIBook\API-Testing-and-Development-with-Postman\Chapter10 (master -> origin)
λ node application_server.js
JSON Server is running. Requests can be accessed at http://localhost:3000/
```

Figure 10.1 – Server running correctly

You can now start making requests to the server using that as the base URL. This application provides a basic API for a blog with the following endpoints:

- `/blogposts`
- `/blogposts/<id>`
- `/comments`
- `/comments/<id>`
- `/profiles`
- `/profiles/<id>`

These endpoints have relationships with each other. For example, comments are children of blog posts. You can include children resources in an API response by using the `_embed` query parameter. An example of that would be to get the list of all blog posts with the comments embedded in the response with the following call: `GET /blogposts?_embed=comments`.

You can also look at the relationship from the opposite direction where you are requesting a child resource, but you want the response to also include information of the parents. To do this, you can use the `_expand` query parameter. This parameter will cause the API to return the requested resource along with information about its parent. For example, if you want to see the first comment in the system along with the information about the blog post that it belongs to, you can do so with the following call: `GET /comments/1?_expand=blogpost`.

This API is a full CRUD API, so you can use `GET`, `POST`, `PUT`, and `DELETE` with it. We will use this API throughout this chapter as we learn more about testing an existing API.

Testing the API

The first thing I want you to use this API for is to practice finding bugs. Later in this chapter, we will look at using it to practice setting up automation in Postman. To get started with exploring, though, you will need to first have some familiarity with how this API works:

1. Ensure that you have the server running and then create a new collection in Postman called something like `ExampleBlogAPI`.

2. Add a request to this collection called `blogposts` and set the URL of the request to `http://localhost:3000/blogposts`. Make sure the request method is set to `GET`.

3. Send the request and you should get back a list with one blog post in the list.

   In the blog post data, you will see that there is a `profileId` variable. Let's check on the profile of the author of this blog post.

4. Add a new request and set the endpoint of the request to `http://localhost:3000/profiles/1` and the method to `GET`. **Send** the request.

   This gives you the name of the person who wrote the blog post, but notice that it does not give you any information about what posts this user wrote. On the other hand, if you add another request that looks at the response of the `/comments/1` endpoint, you can see that it includes an entry with the `blogpostId` variable of the blog post it is associated with. This means that you can use the `_expand` parameter on the comments but not on the profiles.

As I said before, this API is a full CRUD API, which means that you can also create, update, and delete data. For example, if you want to create a new blog post entry, you can use the following steps:

1. Set the action to `POST` and the endpoint to `http://localhost:3000/blogposts`.

2. In the **Body** tab, set the type selection to **raw**, as shown in the following screenshot:

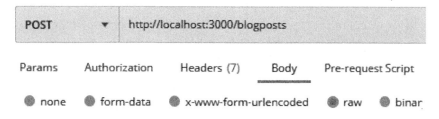

Figure 10.2 – Setting the raw body type

3. Choose **JSON** from the drop-down menu, as shown in the next screenshot:

Figure 10.3 – Set the body type to JSON

You can then fill out the actual body of the request. You don't need to specify the ID since the server will automatically create it with the next available ID, but you can set the `title`, `body`, and `profileId` fields by specifying JSON similar to that shown in the following code snippet:

```
{
    "title": "The second blog post",
    "body": "This is my second blog post",
    "profileId": 1
}
```

4. Send the request and you should see that a new blog post has been created.

You can also check that it has been created by changing the action to GET and sending the request again to see the full list of blog posts in the system.

Similarly, to create a new post, you can use PUT to modify an existing blog post. To do that, you can use the following steps:

1. Go back to the request that gets the blogpost information and change the endpoint to /blogposts/1.

   When you are modifying a resource, you need to let the server know exactly which resource you are modifying and so you need to specify the blog post ID in the endpoint. The blog post ID (1 in our example) is the resource identifier that tells the server which blogpost we are interested in.

2. Set the API action to PUT.

   As with creating a new resource, you need to specify the data that you want to modify. You do that in the body of the request.

3. Set the **Body** type to **raw** and choose **JSON** from the drop-down menu.

4. Specify which fields you want to modify. For example, to modify the body of the blog post, you could specify JSON as shown in the following snippet:

```json
{
    "name": "The first blog post",
    "body": "This is my first blog post. Look I
        modified it!",
    "profileId": 1
}
```

Notice that, although you are only modifying the data in the body field, you need to specify all of the other fields as well. This service is very simple, and so it will blindly apply whatever you give it in a PUT call. It will not just update the fields that you request but rather will replace the entire resource with the data you have given it. This service does not support it, but if you are interested in only changing one property (as we are doing here), you can sometimes use the PATCH method instead of PUT. PUT generally updates a resource by replacing it while PATCH is intended to only modify the specified fields and leave everything else the same. For this book, we will continue to use PUT, but if you see PATCH used in production, just think of it as something similar to PUT but that does a partial update of the resource instead of completely updating it.

Deleting data is simple with this API. Just call the endpoint for the resource that you want to remove and specify the action as DELETE. Now that you know how to call this API, it's time to look at what bugs you can find in it.

Finding bugs in the API

This API is not very robust. It doesn't do much error checking and so it should be pretty easy to break it. Before moving on with this chapter, I want you to do just that. Spend some time exploring how this API works and trying to break it. There are several possible ways to do that, and I would strongly encourage you to spend a few minutes thinking about the kinds of inputs and configurations you could use that might cause problems for this API. See if you can get the server to give you a 500 error!

Note that this is meant to be a challenge, which means that it is OK if you find it a bit tough to do. Stick to it for a while and you might just be surprised at what you can do. It's OK to feel a bit frustrated and lost sometimes as that is often when the most learning is happening! I will share with you one of the ways that you might see an error later on in this chapter, but first, see what you can find on your own.

As a reminder, when you are looking for bugs, don't just try the things that you expect to work. Think about what things you could try that might show you places where the API doesn't work. For example, you could think of things like the following:

- What would happen if I used the _embed and _expand parameters in places where it wouldn't be able to do anything?

- What kinds of inputs to the system might break things?

- Could I create links between different parts of the system that might break stuff?

- Could I remove links between different parts of the system that should be there?

Add your own thoughts to a list like this. What kind of things can you think of that might make this API break? This API is meant to be broken in various ways, so see what you can do to find those broken spots. Since this API is meant to break, let's look at how you can reset it if it does break.

Resetting the service

As you try things out in this API, you might end up causing corruption that the API can't recover from. If you do that, don't worry—it's part of what you are trying to do. However, it could mean that you can't do other exploration and testing that you want, so you may want to reset the service. You can do that with the following steps:

1. Go to Command Prompt that the service is running from.

2. Hit *Ctrl + C* to stop the service.

3. Call `node reset_db.js` to reset the data.

4. Restart the service by calling `node application_server.js`.

This will reset all of the data back to this initial state for you.

Now that you have had the chance to do some exploring and find some bugs on your own, it's time to look at an example of the kinds of bugs you can find in this API.

Example bug

There are several bugs that you might have found in this API. I will share the steps to reproduce one of them here so that you can get a better feeling for how to find a bug like this. Finding this bug comes down to combining two ideas. To understand them, let's look at some steps of how you might figure this out.

Let's start with exploring the `_expand` and `_embed` query parameters. If you call the `/blogposts/1` endpoint with `?_embed=comments`, you will get back a response that has the comments for that blog post embedded in it. If you instead call it with `?_expand=comments`, it will tell you that you have a bad request.

Comments are children of blogposts and not their parents, so it makes sense that we are not allowed to expand it as if it is a parent. We sent an incorrect request and the server correctly responded to that by giving you an error message and a `400` response. Everything is good so far, but we should keep this in mind. Just because the server was able to handle the error properly here, doesn't mean it will be able to do so everywhere. What would happen if we tried to do this same expansion, but this time, instead of doing it on an individual endpoint, we did it on the blog posts list?

Try calling `/blogposts?_expand=comments` and you should see a `500` error from the server. It turns out that it doesn't handle the incorrect input correctly in this place. There are other ways to trigger server errors in here as well, but hopefully, this example helps you with thinking about how to search for bugs in an API.

Exploring an API and trying to find bugs interactively is an important testing skill, but often when you are looking at an existing API, you will be interested in adding test automation. It is often important to be able to run a suite of tests against an API every time changes are made, so let's turn our attention to the process of creating automated tests.

Automating API tests

API test automation is often valuable, and in this section, I want to help you to think about how to get started with creating it for an existing API. However, I'm not going to walk you through a step-by-step process of doing this since I want you to practice doing this on your own. You will learn more if you try some things out on your own. I won't just throw you in the deep end though. In this section, I will give you a quick review of some concepts that will help you with creating API test automation. I will then give you a challenge that I want you to try, and I'll also give you some guidance on how you might break down your approach to solving this challenge. If you work through this challenge, you will find that you have learned a lot about how to create good API test automation. So, let's start with a review of some important concepts for API test automation and think about how they could play out in creating tests for this API.

Reviewing API automation ideas

We have already looked at exploring this API and so you should have a pretty good feeling for how it works and what the various pieces of it are. Use that information to help you to put together a well-organized collection of tests. Think about how you are going to organize the tests and how you can set things up to test the various endpoints and available actions for each one.

This API does not have any authorization, so you don't need to worry about that, but you will want to think about how to create test validation. What kind of things do you want to check for each API call? What kind of inputs might you want to use to check these things? It is a bit more difficult to come up with great test cases when you are testing an application that isn't dealing with real situations but try to imagine that this API is for a real blog posting service. What kinds of things would you want to check for something like this?

In this section, I want to challenge you to take this existing API and create a suite of tests for it. That is a pretty big task, so let's take it on one piece at a time. I want to strongly encourage you to do each of these pieces for yourself. Save all of your work into a collection and at the end of this chapter, I will show you how you can share it so that others can see what you have been learning. I will work through examples showing how I approached these challenges, but you will gain much more out of it if you first try to work through this on your own.

This is a big challenge, and so I have a few hints and ideas for you in the next sections that will help you to break down your work and approach it systematically.

Setting up a collection in Postman

I would suggest that you don't just start adding tests right away. First, take a bit of time to think about how you want to set up the collection in Postman that you can use for your testing. Careful consideration of how you are going to organize your collection and set up the tests will help you out a lot later on when you are adding tests. It is also a good practice to think this stuff through as it can have a big impact on how easy it is to run and maintain tests later on.

Here are some things that you might want to consider when defining the structure of your collection:

- What are the various endpoints for this API?
- How does the testing of the different parameters fit into the way I would set up the tests for this collection?
- How am I going to test the various types of actions that are available?
- In what way do the different pieces of this API relate to each other and how might I want to check those relationships in my tests?

You may want to think through these ideas and map out some ideas on a piece of paper first so that you get a good idea of how you are going to approach this. This might feel like it is overkill for this API, and it probably is, but it is a good skill to practice. Real-life APIs will often be much more complex than this and being able to break them down and think carefully about how you will structure the automation is a crucial skill to have. This structure will be helpful when you start adding tests to the requests.

Creating the tests

Once you have the structure in place, you can start to flesh it out and create the tests themselves. You will want to fill in the appropriate URLs for each request, being sure to create parameters wherever it makes sense to do so. You will also want to consider whether there are any places where you could use data-driven testing to simplify your tests. As you create the tests, here are a few questions you might want to consider:

- What kind of things do I want to check for each request?
- How can I reduce the number of inputs to the test while still getting good coverage?
- Am I using variables and environments efficiently?
- Will these checks be stable and consistent?
- Will these checks actually fail if something goes wrong?
- What will happen when this test is run multiple times?

Creating tests for each of the requests is a big job, but it is a critical part of any test automation work. The things that we check for inside each test will, to a large extent, determine how useful the tests are. Take a bit of time to work through this challenge. You will find that as you try to balance out the need for coverage with the need for some degree of efficiency, you will learn a lot. Make sure you also take the time to think about how you can share data between tests. Environments and variables are powerful tools in real-life API testing so be sure to use this challenge as an opportunity to test your skills on these things.

Don't rush through this challenge. There is a lot that you can do with this, and by spending time working through it, you will be learning a lot. I keep repeating this throughout this book, but that's because it is true; the best way to learn this kind of thing is by practicing. Take your time and think about how you are approaching test creation. Try different things until you are comfortable with the structure of your request and with the tests that you've added to them. Once you have put in the effort to do this yourself, it will be helpful to compare what you came up with to another solution. I worked through this challenge myself and I have shared my approach in the next section.

An example of automated API tests

I've laid out a challenge for you around creating test automation for a simple API. I hope you have worked through that challenge on your own and have a robust suite of tests that you can run against this API. In this section, I will show you one possible way that you could go about doing this. This is by no means the only way to do this and perhaps is not even the best possible way. If what you have looks quite different than this, that is no problem at all. There is a lot of benefit to seeing how other people approach their work, and so take this section as a place where you can see the work of someone else and perhaps even learn something from it.

In this section, I will walk you through the process of designing the collection layout, and then I will show you the various tests that I made and how I set things up to share data between them and make them easy to run and maintain. I will also explain my thought process and why I decided to do things the way I did. This will allow you to see what considerations I was using and help you to think about the kind of trade-offs that go into designing API test automation.

Setting up a collection in Postman

The first thing you needed to do was to figure out how you wanted to set up your collection in Postman. I approached this by first creating a collection called `ExampleBlogAPITests` to store my tests in. Before I started creating any requests in there, though, I decided to diagram out how the API worked and how the various pieces of it related to one another. To do this, I explored how the various endpoints worked and drew out a diagram showing how they are related to each other. The following shows what this diagram looks like:

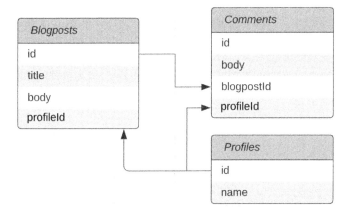

Figure 10.4 – API layout

This diagram shows what data is stored in each endpoint and shows how they relate to each other. So, for example, in this diagram, you can see that comments are children of blog posts. This means that you can use the _embed query for them. Profiles, on the other hand, are parents of blog posts and so if you are looking at blog posts, you would need to use _expand to include them in the response. Of course, inverse relationships exist if you are going in the opposite direction. This is an important consideration that I will keep in mind while designing the test structure.

Now that I have a good grasp of the API structure and relationships, I can look at the actions available on each endpoint. I put together a small table to help me to map that all out, as you can see in the next screenshot:

Endpoint	Actions
/blogposts	GET, POST
/blogposts/<id>	GET, PUT, DELETE
/comments	GET, POST
/comments/<id>	GET, PUT, DELETE
/profiles	GET, POST
/profiles/<id>	GET, PUT, DELETE

Figure 10.5 – API actions

Understanding the structure of the API is a good place to start, but it is certainly not the only thing I want to consider when designing my test layout. An API serves a purpose and although this is a fake API, I can imagine that the purpose it serves is to support a blog site. When thinking about that, I want to consider what workflows might be important to consider. For example, when a user posts a comment, maybe we would want the middleware using this API to check whether their profile ID exists, and if not, prompt them to create a profile. At the API level, this workflow might look like making the following calls:

- POST /comments: Giving a profileId that is not yet in the system

- GET /profiles/<profileId>: Where profileId is the one given in the first step

- POST /profiles : Creates a new profile using the next available profileId variable

- POST /comments: The same comment as before, but now the profile ID exists

- GET /blogpost/<blogpostId>?_embed=comments: To refresh the page with the new comment

If I set up each of the endpoints in their own folders and then create tests for this kind of workflow as well, I might end up duplicating some things that I'm checking. After some consideration, I decided that I would still create a folder for each endpoint. I would use those checks as **smoke tests** to let me know that at least the basic functionality of the API was still working. Smoke tests are a set of tests that can run quickly and give you an early indicator of any potential problems. Much like the saying "where there is smoke, there is fire," smoke tests let you make sure that everything is reasonably stable before you go on with more complex testing. This is a good automation strategy to take so that is how I've decided to implement these tests.

Once I pulled all of these pieces together, I ended up with a folder structure that looked something like this:

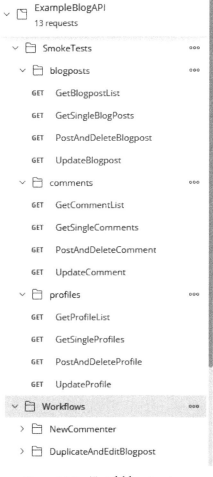

Figure 10.6 – Test folder structure

Let's zoom in and take note of a couple of things in this screenshot. You can see that I chose to combine the POST and DELETE tests:

Figure 10.7 – Post and delete combined

This is because I decided that I wanted to try to make it so that tests leave the system in the same state it was in when the test started. This makes it much easier to manage the tests since you don't need to worry about what order tests run in. It can also make debugging much easier since you don't need to do much to get the system into the same state that it was in when the test failed. To maintain the system state when creating new items, I would have to delete them afterward. Since I need to do this anyway, I just combined them both into one test. I should note, though, that a Postman request can only use one action type, and so to do this, I will need to use some background calls. I will show you how I did that in the *Creating the tests* section.

I also have not included separate requests for each of the query parameters. Instead, I plan to use data-driven testing to exercise those different options. I will, once again, get into that in more detail later in this section.

I included a couple of examples of the kinds of workflows you might check with something like this. In real-life applications, these would be built out based on conversations with project managers and others in the business along with the developers and testers. I included a couple here as examples, but I'll be focusing on the other parts of this collection in more detail and include those just as examples of the kinds of things you might think of when doing this kind of testing. A collection with a bunch of requests is a good start, but it isn't worth much without some tests.

Creating the tests

Now that I have the structure of my requests in place, I'm ready to start creating them. The first thing to do is to fill in the endpoints for each of the requests that I've made. I'm going to need to go through each one and add the URL, but I want to be forward-thinking as well. I'm working on a local build here. What if, in the future, I was to need to test this on a production server somewhere or even just on a different port number? I don't want to have to go through and update every single URL in this test suite. This is where environments are helpful.

Updating the environment

To make future maintenance reasonable, I will make a variable to store the base URL for this collection. I anticipate that I'm going to need other variables as well, so I will go ahead and create an environment that I can use to store the variables, as shown in the following screenshot:

Figure 10.8 – Creating an environment

As you can see in the screenshot, I have also created a variable called `base_url` that I will use in the URL for each of the requests.

> **Important note**
>
> As shown in the previous screenshot, environment variables have an initial value and a current value. With a newly created environment variable, those values will both be the same, but if you modify the value later, Postman will set that in the current value while keeping the initial value there for your reference.

Once I have added the environment and made sure that it is the active environment, I can enter the request URL for each of the requests. For example, the URL for the GetBlogpostList request would look like this:

Figure 10.9 – Request URL

Using a similar pattern, I can quickly add the URL to each of the requests. I also add a variable to the environment for the id of each object type, as shown in the following screenshot:

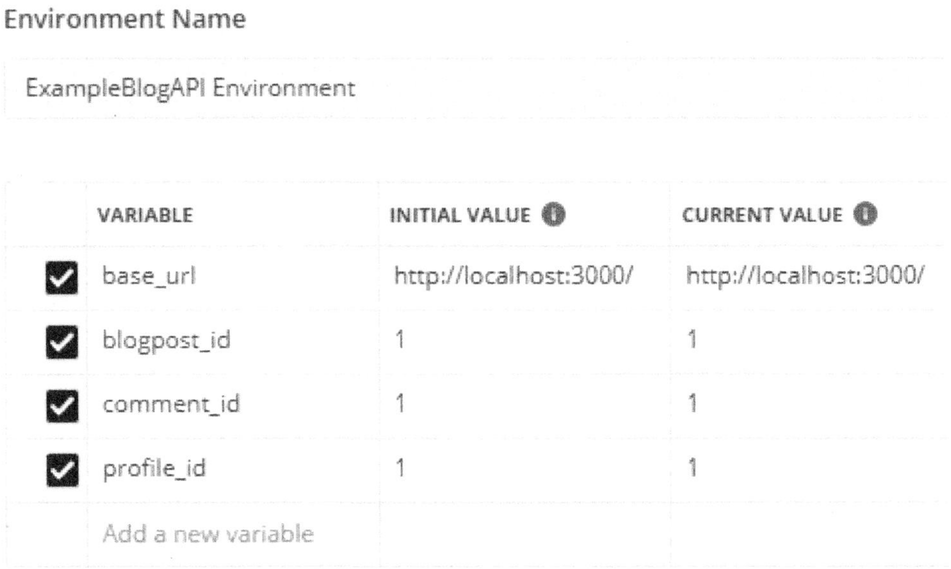

Environment Name

ExampleBlogAPI Environment

VARIABLE	INITIAL VALUE ⓘ	CURRENT VALUE ⓘ
☑ base_url	http://localhost:3000/	http://localhost:3000/
☑ blogpost_id	1	1
☑ comment_id	1	1
☑ profile_id	1	1
Add a new variable		

Figure 10.10 – Object IDs in the environment

This will allow me to use the same request to potentially call more than one of each object. While going through and adding the URLs, I also updated the call methods so that they are using the correct one for each request. Now that this is all filled out, I'm ready to start adding tests to these requests.

Adding tests to the first request

I know that I will most likely want to share some of the tests and scripts that I make across multiple tests. However, a common mistake that automation engineers (and developers in general) make is to over-generalize. They can often spend too much time making a general solution that will work in a wide variety of contexts. This is great, except that it can take a lot of time to make a generalizable solution like this, which can lead to wasted time and effort. To avoid that, I will first add a test to one of my requests and then as I start adding more tests after that, hopefully, I will be able to see which things make sense to generalize and share between tests.

The first place where I will add tests is to the `GetBlogpostList` request. At this point, there is only one blog post in the list. I could just check that the entire response body does not change. This is an acceptable thing to check if you are pretty sure that the data will be stable. However, if you expect that it might change, you will want to be more careful with checking something this specific. In this case, since this is a list of requests, I fully expect that it will change over time, so I don't want to just blindly check it.

Instead, I set up a test that ensures that the first blog post in the list doesn't change. This check is based on a few assumptions about the system, but we must make assumptions at some point, so I will go ahead with it. I want to create a couple of tests that will all use the response data, so I will create a variable for that and one that stores the first blog post data that I do not expect to change. These variable definitions look like this:

```
var jsonData = pm.response.json();
var firstBlogPost = {
    "id": 1,
    "title": "The FIRST blog post",
    "body": "This is my first blog post",
    "profileId": 1
}
```

I can then create a test that will check that the first blog post data stays consistent:

```
pm.test("Check first Blogpost Data", function () {
    //assume that the first blogpost won't change
    pm.expect(jsonData[0]).to.eql(firstBlogPost);
});
```

Now, this is a good start, but if I am checking the list of blog posts, I want to do more than just look at the first item in the list. I also want to check that any other items in the list are correct. I will try to set up my tests so that they don't change the system, but I like to be as careful as possible when creating tests. I don't like having to go and update tests multiple times just because of some small change elsewhere in the system. To create a robust check, I will create a test that checks that all of the blog posts in the list have the correct fields in them. I can do that with a test like this:

```
pm.test("Check that each blogpost has required fields",
function () {
    var x;
    for (x in jsonData) {
        var postKeys = Object.keys(jsonData[x]);
        pm.expect(postKeys).to.have.members(['id','title',
            'body','profileId']);
    }
});
```

So, now that I have a couple of tests in place for this first request, let's look at some of the other requests and see whether there is anything we can do to share data between the tests.

Adding tests to the second request

The second request I will add a test to is the GetSingleBlogPosts request. This request will get the information about a given blog post, but don't forget that I've parameterized the blog post ID for this, so I don't know exactly what blog post I'm going to get. I can't use the test that checks the first blog post, but I should be able to do a similar test to the one where I check that each blog post has the required fields. In fact, I should be able to directly use that same test in both requests.

Instead of having the same test exist in two different requests, I will move it out of the `GetBlogpostList` request and into the `blogposts` folder so that both requests can use it. This can be done with the following steps:

1. Highlight the text for that test in the **Tests** panel of the `GetBlogpostList` request and cut it, as shown in the following screenshot:

Figure 10.11 – Cut the test out of the first request

2. Click on the **Edit** option on the menu beside the **blogpost** folder, as shown in the following screenshot:

```
 ∨  ☐  blogposts                                              ○○○

     GET   GetBlogpostList                  ┌─────────────────────────────┐
                                            │  A͟I   Rename        Ctrl+E  │
     GET   GetSingleBlogPosts               │                             │
                                            │  ✎    Edit                  │
     POST  PostAndDeleteBlogpost            │                             │
                                            │  GET  Add Request           │
                                            └─────────────────────────────┘
```

Figure 10.12 – Editing a folder

3. Go to the **Tests** panel for the folder and paste in the copied test.

4. Click on the **Save** icon at the top-right of the panel to save this test into the folder.

The test is now saved in the folder instead of the request, but if you go to the original `GetBlogpostList` request and run it, you will see that the test fails with a *ReferenceError* since the `jsonData` variable is not defined. To fix this, I will need to copy the line where I defined that variable from the test into the folder. At this point, the code in the folder looks like this:

```
var jsonData = pm.response.json();
pm.test("Check that each blogpost has required fields",
function () {
    var x;
```

```
    for (x in jsonData) {
        var postKeys = Object.keys(jsonData[x]);
        pm.expect(postKeys).to.have.members(['id','title',
            'body','profileId']);
    }
});
```

This test will now run against all of the requests in the `blogposts` folder. For example, if you go to the `GetSingleBlogPosts` request and run it, you will see that the test is run too. In fact, if you go and do this, you will see that the test fails with an assertion that looks like this:

FAIL Check that each blogpost has required fields | AssertionError: expected [] to deeply equal ['id', 'title', 'body', 'profileId']

Figure 10.13 – Failing test

At first glance, this seems odd until you remember that the test is looping over all of the blog posts in the list and checking each of them. However, when we call the endpoint for an individual blog post, we don't get a list. We just get back that blog post. Does this mean that it won't work after all to share the code? Well, not so fast. We should still be able to share some of it. We know that for any given blog post, the code inside the loop should be valid. I just need to factor that out into its own method and we should be able to use it.

Unfortunately, that is a bit tricky to do with Postman. You can just write a function in a folder and then call it in all tests in that folder. There are some ways to work around this though. I used the following steps to create a function that I could then call in the tests:

1. Go to the **Test** tab of the **blogposts** folder and create a function called `check_blogpost_keys`.

2. Copy the part of the code that checks the blog post keys into that function.

3. Modify the code so that it checks the object that gets passed into the function. The code looks like this:

```
function check_blogpost_keys (blogpostData){
    var postKeys = Object.keys(blogpostData);
    pm.expect(postKeys).to.have.members(['id','title',
        'body','profileId']);
}
```

4. Call the function from inside the `for` loop. The `for` loop now looks like this:

```
for (x in jsonData) {
        check_blogpost_keys(jsonData[x]);
    }
```

5. Save the folder, and go to the `GetBlogpostList` request and run it to make sure that everything still works.

So far, this seems great, but I need to be able to access this function from a request and not just from the folder.

6. Edit the folder again and save the function inside of an object. The code for doing this looks like this:

```
utils = {check_blogpost_keys: function (blogpostData) {
        var postKeys = Object.keys(blogpostData);
        pm.expect(postKeys).to.have.members(['id','title',
          'body','profileId']);
        }
    }
```

What this code is doing is creating an object called `utils`. This object maps the name of the function to the definition of the function, which means that I can call this function by calling that key from the function. In other words, calling `utils.check_blogpost_keys(<input object>)` will call the function. However, the `utils` object that I am creating here still needs to be made available for the requests in this folder.

Objects defined in the **Tests** tab of the folder will not be available until too late in the process, but by moving this to the **Pre-request Scripts**, I can make it available for all of the tests in the folder.

Once the `utils` object has been moved to the pre-request scripts, I can copy the `Check that each blogpost has required fields` test back into the **Tests** tab of the `GetBlogpostList` request and change it so that it is using the `utils.check_blogpost_keys()` call to check the results. The test should now look like this:

```
pm.test("Check that each blogpost has required fields",
function () {
    var x;
    for (x in jsonData) {
        utils.check_blogpost_keys(jsonData[x])
```

```
    }
});
```

That was a lot of complexity to just make it possible to share a couple of code lines between tests. Given how small this API is, it probably wouldn't make sense to do this normally, but I think that being able to share code like this is important if you want to make good test automation and so I wanted to spend a bit of time explaining how to do this.

Now that we have this shareable code, I can use it when adding tests to the other requests in this folder. The test that I add to the GetSingleBlogPosts request looks like this:

```
var jsonData = pm.response.json();
pm.test("Check that the blogpost has required fields", function
() {
        utils.check_blogpost_keys(jsonData);
});
```

This test also uses the shared function from the util object. A nice thing about this is that if the expected keys in the blogposts responses were to ever change in the future, we would only need to update them in one place. There are more requests to add tests to though, so let's look at the next request.

Adding tests to the POST request

The next request I want to add tests to is the PostAndDeleteBlogpost request. Before I can add tests though, I need to fill the body of the request that will be sent during the POST call. On the **Body** tab of the request, I will set the type to **raw** and then select **JSON** from the drop-down menu and add the following body:

```
{
    "title": "New Blog Post Title",
    "body": "This is a blog post that I created with the
        API",
    "profileId": 1
}
```

I will then add the same test code to this that I was using in the previous requests.

When I set up the structure for this collection, I wanted this test to POST and then DELETE the newly created blog post so that it wouldn't change the state of the system. Postman allows you to send API calls directly from a script, so you can do that in the **Tests** tab using the following code:

```
var post_id = jsonData.id;
var base_url = pm.environment.get("base_url")

pm.sendRequest({url:`${base_url}blogposts/${post_id}`,method:
'DELETE'}, function (err, response) {
    pm.test("Delete Response is OK", function () {
        pm.expect(response.status).to.eql('OK');
    });
    pm.test("Delete Response body is empty", function () {
        pm.expect(response.json()).to.eql({});
    });
});
```

The pm.sendRequest function allows you to send API calls. You need to specify the endpoint you are calling, the request method that you want to use, and a callback function. You can see that I have defined variables for base_url and post_id. I wanted to ensure that the base URL would automatically update if I ever change it for the collection, so I made sure to use the variable from the environment. I also needed to get the id of the blog post that was just created and use that in assembling the URL. Obviously, I need to set the method to DELETE and then in the callback I've defined the tests that I want to run.

I have defined the tests right inside the callback to the sendRequest function. The first test checks that the DELETE response returns a response status of OK. The second test checks that the body of the response is empty since I do not expect a delete call to return anything.

This gives us tests for the POST and DELETE call, but we aren't done yet. Now, let's look at the UpdateBlogpost request and see how to test a PUT call.

Adding tests to the PUT request

To test the UpdateBlogpost request, I first need to put something in the body of the request so that it will actually update correctly. Once again, I can do so using the **raw** and **JSON** options. I decide to set the body to this value:

```
{
    "title": "modified Blog Post Title",
    "body": "This is a blog post that I modified ",
    "profileId": 1
}
```

As I am doing this, I realize something. When I mouse over the `blogpost_id` variable in the URL, I can see that I have set it to 1. However, if you remember, I have a test in the `GetBlogpostList` request that assumes that the first request will not change. If I change that blog post with the PUT request, the next time I run the request getting the list of blog posts, it will fail. I have a couple of options available to me:

- Remove that test from the POST request—the test probably isn't strictly necessary there, so this is an option.

- Create a new blog post before doing the PUT call—if I did this, I would want to also delete it afterward.

- Get rid of this request and include the PUT call in the `PostAndDeleteBlogpost` request— this is probably a better choice than turning the PUT request into a POST, PUT, or DELETE request, but it would make that test hard to debug if something went wrong.

- Make sure I set the request back to its initial state after modifying it—I think this is probably the best choice.

I wanted to share this list with you so that you can get a bit of an idea of what kind of thought process goes into designing good test automation. You need to consider things like making one test too big to easily debug and what assumptions your tests might be making.

I think this thought process also highlights why I wanted to make tests that leave the system in the same state it was in when the test started. In this case, I remembered that I had this assumption in one of my other tests, but if multiple people were working on the automation or if it had been a long time since I created that test, I might have accidentally caused another test to fail due to my actions in this test.

So, how do I go about creating this test so that it will not change the system? I used the following steps to set up this test:

1. On the **Pre-request script** tab, I create a request that will GET the data for the blog post and store that response in a variable. The code looks like this:

```
//get original value
var base_url = pm.environment.get("base_url");
var post_id = pm.environment.get("blogpost_id");
pm.sendRequest({url:`${base_url}blogposts/${post_
id}`,method: 'GET'}, function (err, response) {
    pm.environment.set("original_get_response",
      response.json());
});
```

2. Moving over to the **Tests** tab, I create the same test as the one on the other requests where I am checking that the blog post has the required fields.

3. I can then use the `original_get_response` variable that I made in the **Pre-request scripts** to reset the post back to its original state. I will once again use the `sendRequest` function. Since this time I need to send body data, I need to specify a few more things, as you can see in the following code:

```
//reset the blogpost back to its original state
var base_url = pm.environment.get("base_url");
var post_id = pm.environment.get("blogpost_id");
var original_response = pm.environment.get("original_get_
response")
pm.sendRequest({url:`${base_url}blogposts/${post_id}`,
    method: 'PUT',
    header:{'Content-Type': 'application/json'},
    body:{mode: 'raw', raw: original_response}},
    function (err, response) {
        console.log(response.json());
});
```

You can see that I had to specify the Content-Type header and specify that the mode of the body data I was sending was raw. This finishes up this test. So far, I have created a good suite of tests for the requests that I have. These tests should check the things I care about and not fail unnecessarily. They give reasonable coverage of the endpoints, but I still need to think about how to test the query parameters.

Adding tests for query parameters

None of the tests so far are checking what happens when I use the _embed and _expand query parameters. When I initially designed the test layout, I had thought that I could test these using data-driven testing on the existing endpoints. However, after trying a few things, I have discovered that it would be very difficult to do this due to the way the values of the query parameters are named. I have decided that instead, I will need to add new requests to check each of the query parameters.

This is a very common thing in designing test automation. Much like other development work, you can't plan everything accurately upfront. You will almost always need to have some iteration on what you do. It is still very valuable to spend some of that up-front time planning, but don't let the plan exert too much control on what you do. As you discover new things during the process of creating the tests, it is OK to change the plan.

Based on the diagram that I made for the way the different pieces of the API interact, I've decided to add two more requests to the **blogposts** folder, as shown in the following screenshot:

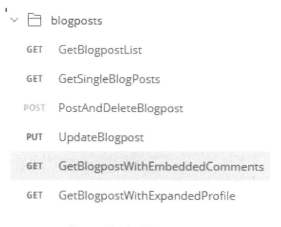

Figure 10.14 – New requests

I also decided to make the tests for these requests simple. I will just assume
that the first blog post, comment, and profile will not change and then
hardcode in the expected values for each of those in the tests. For example, the
GetBlogpostWithEmbeddedComments request looks like this:

Figure 10.15 – Embedded comments request tests

GetBlogpostWithExpandedProfile takes a similar approach to testing this. Now
that I have this in place, I can run all of the tests in that folder. I would then need to work
through similar steps to set up tests in the comments and profiles folders, but at this point,
you should have a pretty good idea of how to go about that, so I won't walk through it in
detail.

We have covered a lot in this section, and you have done a lot of work in thinking through this challenge. You've learned how to create automated API tests including a review of some automation test ideas along with how to set up collections and tests in Postman. You then learned how to create several different tests for different kinds of GET requests as well as tests for POST and PUT requests, tests that use query parameters. Along the way, you've learned a lot of tips and tricks for organizing tests, including how to effectively share code between requests and how to use environments. That's a lot of material and this kind of work should be celebrated and shared so, in the next section, I want to show you how you can do just that.

Sharing your work

If you went through this exercise and built a suite of tests, you will have learned a lot about API test automation. One thing that is important in the modern economy is being able to showcase your work. There are millions of testers and developers working in the industry and you want to be able to stand out from the crowd by showing that you really know your stuff. One great way to do that is by sharing examples of the work you have done and the things you have learned.

I have had a blog for years and have found that to be a helpful way to stand out. I personally love blogging, but it does take time and certainly isn't for everyone. If you want something simpler, there are still ways that you can share your work. You can create a GitHub account, for example, and create public repositories that showcase what you have done and learned.

Within Postman, you can also share what you have done. These features are mostly intended for helping with collaboration between team members, but you can also use them to showcase the work that you have done.

Sharing a collection in Postman

You can share a specific collection in Postman with the following steps:

1. Click on the **View More Action** button beside the collection that you created when doing the previous exercise in this chapter.

2. Choose the **Share Collection** option from that menu:

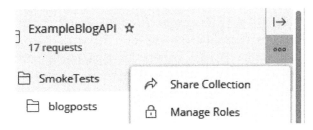

Figure 10.16 – Share Collection menu option

3. If you were trying to share with teammates, you could share the collection to a shared workspace, but in this case, you are trying to share with the public, so choose the **Embed** tab.

4. On this tab, you can click on the **Generate Code** button to create HTML that you can embed onto a web page. You can also choose the **Static** button option if you want to generate Markdown code that you can use in something like a GitHub repository.

5. Make sure to also pick the appropriate environment from the environment drop-down menu.

You can then copy the code and use it on whatever site or resume you want. If you just want the link, you can go to the **Get public link** tab as well and get a shareable link from there.

Summary

This chapter has mostly been about working through an example of creating automated tests for a simple service, but it has taught a lot of lessons along the way. After learning about how to set up the testing site, you learned how to explore the API and find bugs in it. Once you were able to do that, we started to look at how you can automate tests. I gave you a challenge: creating a test automation suite for the test API. I hope you took the time to work through the challenge on your own and were able to learn a lot about what API test automation would look like.

I also walked you through an example of how I would have gone about solving the challenge. While going through my solution, you learned about how to set up collections in Postman in a way that organizes the requests so that they will be maintainable. You then learned some more about using environments to set up and share variables. I then walked you through creating tests for the different requests.

The tests that I created for the first request were straightforward although I did show you how to check the properties of multiple items in a list. The tests for the next request built on that and you learned how to set up a test in a folder so that it could be shared across multiple requests. As part of this, you learned how to define a function and save it into an object so that you can call the function from multiple tests.

After that, you learned how to create tests for a POST call. In this section, you learned to use the sendRequest method to send an API call from within a test so that you could clean up the test and leave the state of the system unchanged. The tests for the PUT request then showed you how to get some data in a pre-request script that you could then use while cleaning up after the test completed. The final tests that we looked at showed how test design is an iterative process, and you learned how to update and change your plans based on new information that you learned while creating the other tests.

The last thing you learned in this chapter was how to share your work so that you can show others what you have done. You have learned a lot in this book, so don't be scared to share what you have learned with others!

This chapter has taught you a lot about how to create tests for existing APIs, but sometimes you will be working with brand new APIs. When you get to this, it is exciting because you can follow some design-driven approaches, and so in the next chapter, we will look at how you can design an API specification for new APIs.

Section 3:
Using Postman to Develop an API

This section will give you information on how to use Postman to help you with creating an API from scratch.

This section includes the following chapters:

11
Designing an API Specification

Magic shows are a lot of fun. The magician does something that seems impossible and it thrills and excites us. How can they possibly do that? I could never do that!

From the outside, software development can seem a lot like that. The developer types out some code and, like magic, something happens in the application. How can they possibly do that? I could never do that!

Of course, if you look on the internet, you can find videos that show you some of the tricks magicians use. It turns out that many magic tricks involve a few simple rules. Similarly, with a bit of time, you can understand how software development works. For those of us who have made it through the frustration of learning to code, we realize that actually, we can do that. It's not so complicated after all. It's just the application of a few simple rules.

I kind of felt that way about API specifications and schemas. I'd heard the term before, and I had seen errors come up in my code editor saying that I had a schema validation error. As far as I could tell, though, all this came about by some sort of magic. I did not understand how they worked and how to use them. Well, it turns out that much like magic tricks, this kind of thing can also be learned.

The next couple of chapters in this book will revolve around helping you learn how to use Postman when you design a new API from scratch. The first step in that process will be to use an API specification language to set up an API definition. In *Chapter 3*, *OpenAPI and API Specifications*, I introduced you to the concept of API specification languages and how to use them. This chapter will build on those concepts and help you work through much more complex examples of this. If you have not yet read *Chapter 3*, *OpenAPI and API Specification*, you may want to go back and review the material in that chapter.

The topics that we are going to cover are as follows:

- Creating an API specification

- Adding the API to Postman

- Understanding API versioning

Technical requirements

The code used in this chapter can be found at `https://github.com/ PacktPublishing/API-Testing-and-Development-with-Postman/tree/ master/Chapter11`.

Creating an API specification

I want to keep this practical for you, so in this chapter we are going to walk through the process of creating an API specification from scratch. In order to do this, we will create a specification for the API of an imaginary to-do list application. I want you to imagine that you are going to create the API for an application that can create and display items on a to-do list. This application will allow users to create new to-do items. It will also allow users to mark those items as complete and to make changes to the item after they have created it. They can also delete an item that they no longer want to track.

Our job in this chapter will be to create an API specification that lays out exactly what this API is going to look like. We will then look at how we can use this specification in Postman to create an API and set up tests for it. For the work we are doing here, you don't need to worry about what the user interface will look like.

The approach we will use is the design-first methodology. You will first design the API specification and then once that is laid out, we will look at how to use it to create the API itself. There are several different API specification languages out there, but the most common one is the **OpenAPI Specification**, so that is what we will use in this chapter.

In this section, I will show you how to set up an API definition file that uses the OpenAPI Specification to define the rules for what that API can do. I will show you how to define the endpoints and the parameters for those endpoints. I'll also show you what a schema is and how to use it with the OpenAPI Specification. In addition, I will walk you through some of the complexity of defining the behavior of request bodies and responses, as well as showing you how to create examples in the specification.

> **Important note**
>
> Although I will show a lot of detail about using the OpenAPI Specification in this chapter, I can't cover everything here. If you need more information on any of this, you can check out the documentation for this specification here: `https://swagger.io/docs/specification/about/`.

In order to do all that, you are going to need to define an OpenAPI Specification file. Let's look at how to do that next.

Starting the file

OpenAPI Specification files start with some general information about the API. There can be a lot of detail that goes into this, but let's keep it simple for this API. We will define what version of the OpenAPI Specification we are using and then include a few details about the API itself, as shown in the following code:

```
openapi: 3.0.1
info:
   title: ToDo List API
   description: Manages ToDo list tasks
   version: '1.0'
servers:
   - url: http://localhost:5000/todolist/api
```

I've decided to set the server URL as running on the localhost for now. That can always be changed in the future if you want.

An API specification needs to be saved into a file. There are some different editors and tools available for editing these files, but I suggest that you just use your favorite code or text editor. It can get overwhelming to learn too many things at once. Instead of trying to figure out which editor to use and what features it has, stick with one you know.

OpenAPI Specification files can be saved as either **JSON** or **YAML**. **JSON, or JavaScript Object Notation**, is a common coding format, but it is a bit less readable than YAML, so I prefer to use YAML format for this kind of file. If you have created code similar to what was shown previously, you can save it to a file called `todoList.yaml`.

With this starting point in place, you are now ready to start filling out the details of the API in this file. The easiest place to start is with defining what endpoints the API needs, so that is where we will turn our attention next.

Defining the endpoints

Endpoint definition is one of the key parts of designing an API. In this case, we know that the API needs to supply a list of tasks for the to-do list. A logical thing to do, then, would be to have an endpoint called `/tasks` that will give us information about all the tasks in the system.

However, just getting a full list of tasks isn't going to be enough. We are also going to need to be able to get and modify information about individual tasks. In order to do this, we will need another endpoint called `/tasks/{taskdId}`, where `taskId` is a number representing the task that we are looking at.

If you think about the different actions that this API supports, we can then start to build out the methods for each of these endpoints. We are going to need to be able to `GET` the full list of tasks and we will also want to be able to `GET` individual tasks. We also know that we need to be able to create new tasks, and the best way to do that is by doing a `POST` on the `/tasks` endpoint. In addition, we need to be able to modify and delete individual tasks, so we will need `PUT` and `DELETE` calls on the `/tasks/{taskId}` endpoint. If you put all this information into the `.yaml` file, you should have a section in there that looks like this:

```
/tasks:
  get:
  post:
/tasks/{taskId}:
  get:
  put:
  delete:
```

Now that you have this skeleton in place, you can start to fill out the details of each of these requests. There are several different fields that you can add to each request. You don't need to add all of them, but I would suggest including the `description` and `responses` fields. The `description` field is just a text description of what the endpoint does, but the `responses` field can contain a lot of information about what you expect the response to look like when that endpoint is called.

For example, if you fill out the GET request for the `/tasks/{taskId}` endpoint, you might make something that looks like this:

```
/tasks/{taskId}:
  get:
    description: Gets the information for the specified task
    responses:
      <200':
        content:
          application/json:
```

This response is defined as having a response code of 200. It also defines the content type as `application/json`. This means that an acceptable response from a call to this endpoint is one that has a code of 200 and one in which the data is in JSON format. This is a start, but it doesn't say anything at all about what that data should look like, so it isn't really that helpful in helping you design the endpoint.

In order to do that, you are going to need to define a schema for what you expect these requests to respond with when they are called. Wrapping your mind around what a schema is and how to use it can be a bit intimidating, but like anything else it is something that you can learn, so let's dig into it and see what it is all about.

Understanding the API schema

We can define rules that dictate what the response should look like by defining the **schema**. At its most basic, a schema is just a set of rules that you can apply to the data of the response. These rules include things like what fields are supposed to be there and what kinds of data are allowed to be in each of those fields. There are many different rules that can be applied to a response with the OpenAPI schema. This schema is based on the JSON Schema specification, which is a widely used description of rules that can be applied to structured data.

Although it can take a bit to wrap your head around, a schema is actually a very important design tool. When we take the time to think carefully about what rules should apply to the data we are sending and receiving, we are working on a design problem. By using a schema to lay out the specific rules for what things an API is allowed to do, we are engaging in a design process.

In real-life application development, you would want to talk to those designing the user interface to see what information they would need. You would have a discussion about what data is needed, what data might be optional, and what data you want to make sure you never get. All of these things can be defined with schema rules. Since we aren't actually developing a user interface for this API, we can just make some reasonable assumptions about what this data should look like.

For example, we can assume that each task will need to have some text—let's call it a title—that defines what the task is. It will also need a way to represent the status that lets the users know what state a task is in. For our purposes, let's say that the status can be either New, In Progress, or Completed. We could get more complex and say that it needs something like a due date, but let's keep it simple for the first pass at this API and just define those two properties. So, now that we know what properties we want each task to have, how do we set up a schema that defines this?

You can define a schema entry under application/json. At this point, you could create the schema directly under that object. However, since most of the responses that we define in this application are going to have similar data in their responses, it would make much more sense to have this schema defined in a place where we can reference it from multiple endpoints. You can do this in OpenAPI by creating a new section in the file called components and then specifying a schemas entry where you will create each type of schema that you need:

```
components:
  schemas:
```

You can now go ahead and create a schema for what response we should get back when calling the endpoint for an individual task. You know that the content is going to be a JSON object, so you can start with that and define the type as object. We've already decided that it will need to have two properties, a title and a status. The title will need to be a string so we can define its type as string. The status will also need to be a string, but it can't be just any arbitrary string. It is only allowed to have a certain set of values. Specifying that set of values is called enumeration. Pulling this all together, you can create a schema for the task response that looks like this:

```
components:
  schemas:
```

```
task:
    type: object
    required:
        - title
        - status
    properties:
        title:
            type: string
        status:
            type: string
            enum: [New, In Progress, Completed]
```

Note the `required` entry in there. By default, all properties are considered to be optional, so in this case, we will only consider it to be a valid response if it includes the `title` and `status` properties. Now that you have defined this schema, you need to reference it from the endpoint. You can do this using `$ref`, making the `content` portion of your endpoint definition look like this:

```
content:
    application/json:
    $ref: '#/components/schemas/task'
```

This defines the response for a GET call on the /tasks/{taskId} endpoint, but we would expect to get back the exact same schema when doing a PUT or POST call as well, so we can define those in a very similar way. However, for a DELETE call we would expect things to be a bit different. This call does not return the object that is deleted. Instead, it returns an empty object, so you can set the schema for that to be `type: object`.

Another endpoint that should give back a different response is when we get the full task list using the /tasks endpoint. Each item in the list will be a task object and can thus use the task schema, but they will all be wrapped in a list so you can't just directly reference the task schema. Instead, you can define a new schema called `tasks`. The type of this item will be `array` since we expect it to be an array of items. You can specify the items as a reference to the task schema since each item in the array should have that schema. In the `.yaml` file, it would look like this:

```
tasks:
    type: array
    items:
        $ref: '#/components/schemas/task'
```

With that, you have defined the schema for these API responses. We aren't quite ready to import this specification file into Postman, but when you do, you will be able to use these schema rules to validate that you are getting the correct responses from the API calls that you send.

With the schema defined, it's time to take a step back and look again at the endpoints. You've defined the different endpoints along with the methods that they support, but one of them has a path parameter in it. This parameter needs to be defined in the specification as well, so that's the next thing we will look at.

Defining parameters

In the /tasks/{taskId} endpoint, you have specified a path parameter (taskId) but have not yet defined it. The OpenAPI Specification requires that parameters like this are defined for each request on this endpoint. You can do this by adding the parameters key and then specifying the schema for that parameter. Since this parameter needs to be defined for multiple call types, you can create a new entry for it in the schemas section and define the schema there:

```
taskId:
  type: integer
  minimum: 1
```

This specifies that the taskId must be an integer and that it cannot be less than one. You can then reference this schema from the parameter along with specifying the name of the parameter and the fact that it is a required path parameter. Pulling that all together, the code for it would look like this:

```
parameters:
  - in: path
    schema:
      $ref: '#/components/schemas/taskId'
    name: taskId
    description: Id of the task
    required: true
```

This specifies the details for this parameter and is placed under the GET, PUT, and DELETE definitions for the endpoint. Note that the – in parameter has the – in front of it. This is because parameters is considered to be an array object and in YAML, arrays are specified with a dash.

Now that you have a definition in place for the parameter, it's time to look at ways that we can flesh out the endpoint definitions that we have. You have added a response to each endpoint, but most APIs don't just have one response code, so let's take a look at how you can add additional responses to the API definition.

Adding additional responses

So far, all the responses that we have set up in the specification have been about what happens when everything goes OK. But we all know that not everyone uses an API in exactly the way it was meant to be used. What happens if someone sends data in the wrong format? What should the API do then?

The `responses` object is plural, which indicates that we can add more responses to it. Each response definition that you add starts with a status code. Let's look at adding a `400` response to the `/tasks/{taskId}` GET call. Just like with the `200` response, we can add a description and then specify what the content of that response should look like. Since a `400` means that the user has specified the data in the wrong format, the API won't be sending back a `task` object. Instead, you could define the schema as an error string:

```
'400':
  content:
    application/json:
      schema:
        type: string
```

Since you will probably want all of the endpoints to have a `400` response, it would be a good idea to create an entry in the `schema` section that you could then reference from all of the endpoints. You could also add responses for other response codes that you want the API to give. We didn't talk about authentication in the API, but if it was authenticated, you might want to put in `401` and `403` responses. We want to walk through creating these responses as they are all very similar to what you have done already. If you want, you can look at the `ToDoList.yaml` file in the GitHub repo for the book to see this all laid out in one place.

Every API call should have a response of some sort. Not all API calls require data in the body of the request, but some of them do. Let's take a look at how you define that kind of data in the definition file that we are working on.

Describing request bodies

When sending a POST or PUT request, you need to specify some data in the body of the request. In a similar way to defining the responses, you can define the content of a request body for these requests. The request body for the POST response in the to-do list API might look like this:

```
requestBody:
  required: true
  content:
    application/json:
      schema:
        $ref: '#/components/schemas/task'
```

The required: true item means that you must specify a body when sending this request in order for it to be a valid request. The rest of the definition is the same as that for a response. You specify the content type that is allowed (and you can specify multiple content types if the API supports more than one), and then you specify the schema that dictates what rules the body needs to follow. In this case you can use the same task schema that was defined earlier since that same data format is what you will need to specify when creating a new task.

The PUT request body definition is the same as the one we just defined for the POST request. You could directly copy the entry from the POST request into the PUT request. In this case, that would be a fine thing to do, but if you were using the same body definition in a few places, it could get cumbersome to copy and paste it to multiple places. It would also be a pain to update if the requirements of the body ever changed. Instead of pasting the same definition into multiple places, you can create a reusable body definition and reference it from each place. You can do so with the following steps:

1. Go to the components section of the specification file and add a requestBodies entry.

2. Under the requestBodies entry, create a name for the shared body definition – maybe something like taskBody.

3. Cut the requestBody definition out of the POST endpoint section and paste it into the new location. The code should look like this:

```
components:
  requestBodies:
    taskBody:
```

```
        required: true
      content:
        application/json:
          schema:
            $ref: '#/components/schemas/task'
```

4. Add a reference to the `requestBody` entry in both the POST and PUT requests. These entries should look like this:

```
requestBody:
  $ref: '#/components/requestBodies/taskBody'
```

These definitions will allow validation of the requests that are being sent, and setting them up in this way makes them easy to maintain if the API was ever to change.

We have now covered most of the parts of the OpenAPI Specification, but one other commonly used item is examples. They are not required for an API definition, but they are nice to have, so let's look at how to use them.

Using examples

So far, we have defined the behavior and schema of the API, but it is also nice to give some examples so that API users can understand a bit better how the API works. Examples are just illustrations of possible ways to use the API. They are not rules that must be followed, but they can be really helpful to have in place. They can help human users understand how to use the API, and they can also be used as a basis for creating automated tests.

Examples can be added to a `requestBody` or to a response. Let's add one to the `requestBody` that we defined in the previous section. You can do that by adding an `example` key to the `application/json` content type item and then specifying examples of the properties that need to be sent. The code for that would look like this:

```
content:
  application/json:
    schema:
      $ref: '#/components/schemas/task'
    example:
      title: 'Learn API Testing'
      status: 'New'
```

This example shows you one way to specify the body of the request. In this case, we only added one example, but what if we wanted more—say, one for each different status type? You can do that by changing the key to `examples` (with an s) and then giving each example a name and value, which would look like this:

```
examples:
  New:
    value:
      title: Learn API Testing
      status: New
  InProgress:
    value:
      title: Learn API Testing
      status: In Progress
  Completed:
    value:
      title: Learn API Testing
      status: Completed
```

Examples can also be defined for responses as well as in a few other places in the definition. They are all defined in a similar way, so you should be able to figure out how to do them.

With that, we have covered most of the main features of the OpenAPI Specification. There are, of course, additional details that I haven't been able to show you here, but by using what you've learned in this chapter, you should be able to create your own API definition file. Creating a file like this is helpful for thinking through the API design and for documenting what your API should do, but it can also be used for a lot more than that. In the rest of this chapter, we'll look at how you can use this kind of file in Postman to help you with your testing work.

Adding the API to Postman

Now that you have created a specification file, it's time to see how you can use it in Postman. In this section, I'll show you how to use the OpenAPI Specification to create an API and collection in Postman. You will also learn about the automatic testing that Postman does with this and some of the different ways that you can use the specification file to verify that things are working correctly.

In order to do all this, you will need to import the file into Postman. You can do that with the following steps:

1. Click on the **Import** button and, on the **File** tab, click on the **Upload Files** button:

Figure 11.1 – Uploading an OpenAPI file to Postman

2. Browse to where you have saved the `.yaml` file and import it.

3. Leave the **Generate collection from imported APIs** option selected but change the **Link this collection as** option to **Test Suite**:

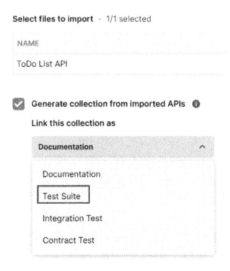

Figure 11.2 – Link imported specification to a test suite

4. Click on **Import**.

Postman will automatically add a collection for you with the title you specified in the specification file. In that collection, it will add requests for each of the endpoints that you've defined. If you edit the collection and look at the **Variables** tab, you will see that it has also added a variable for **baseUrl**.

Postman has also automatically created an API from the imported specification file. If you go to the **APIs** tab in the navigation panel, you can click on the **ToDo List API** to see what Postman has added for you. The **Overview** tab shows you a summary of the API, but if you go to the **Define** tab, you can see the imported API definition.

You may see some errors in there. Although I suggested starting with a simple text or code editor when working with an OpenAPI file, there are certainly some benefits to having an editor that understands more about how the specification works and can give you some feedback. For example, when I imported the file, I got some warnings like these letting me know that `description` is a required field for some of the entries:

Figure 11.3 – Missing required property

You can make any necessary tweaks to the definition in Postman. Once you have addressed any errors, you can go to the **Test** tab. You will see the test suite that Postman created for you there, and you can click on the **Validate** button beside this test suite to validate that everything you need has been specified in the definition.

Postman uses the specification for a couple of different kinds of validation. This particular validation is just to ensure that the collection and specification match each other. It lets you check that you've created the specification correctly and that it is ready to use for creating tests. You may want to re-run this validation if you make changes to your collection or if you update the specification. Although this is a useful check, it is not the only one that Postman does for you. It will also run contract tests for you.

Contract testing

When you import an OpenAPI Specification and create a collection from it, Postman will automatically run schema validation checks every time you make an API for one of those requests. If the API responds with data that is incorrectly formatted, you will get a warning letting you know that there are discrepancies between the specification and the current response. This kind of testing is known as **contract testing**.

With contract testing, you are essentially ensuring that the data from running your requests matches what is specified in the current contract. In this case, that contract comes from the definition files that you've created. Essentially, the definition file says that if you do a certain action you will get back a response that follows the rules you laid out in the schema for that action. This is a contract that you are providing and when you run the actual requests, Postman will check and see if they are matching that contract and give you a warning if you are not. You can create explicit contract tests in Postman as well, where you manually specify the schema, but since you created this schema in OpenAPI there is no need for that.

You can, however, add some tests of your own if you want. I've covered how to create tests in several other chapters in this book, so I won't go through the details of this again. The point that I want to make here is that you automatically get an entire suite of tests defined for you when you set up an API in Postman using an OpenAPI Specification file.

The enabling of tests like this is an important and powerful part of using an API specification, but there are other ways that it is helpful as well. One of the things that can help you with it is API versioning. This is an important topic in its own right, and so we will dig into it in more detail in the next section.

Understanding API versioning

Contract testing is a powerful concept that allows very fast and robust test automation. However, we shouldn't forget that contract tests are still tests. Sometimes tests fail because of bugs in the code, but sometimes they fail due to expected changes in the code. There are times when we need to update an API so that it invalidates the contract that we have laid out in the specification file. In those cases, we need to update the API definition. However, what if there are people who are still relying on the functionality to work in the way that it used to?

One common way to deal with this problem is by versioning the API. In this section, you will learn about API versioning and when it makes sense to use it.

When you define API versions, you can pick which version of the API you are using when you call the endpoints and it will give back responses that match the specified version. But how do you set that up in Postman? Well, you can create a new version of your API in Postman with the following steps:

1. Select the **ToDo List API** from the APIs list.

2. At the top of the page, you will see a tag showing you what version of the API is currently active. The API that was created from the OpenAPI import will be tagged as **draft**, as shown in the following figure:

Figure 11.4 – Draft API status

3. Click on the **Show All Versions** link beside that tag.

4. On the resulting flyout, click on **Create another version**.

5. Call this `v1`, leave the **Schema** option selected, and click on **Create Version**.

Postman will create a new version of your API and make it active. If you look at the **Define** tab you will see that it includes the API definition, but if you go to the **Test** tab, you will see that it no longer has a test suite defined since you did not choose to add the element to this version of the API.

If you return to the **Define** tab, you can update `url` to append `v1` to the end of it so that it looks like this:

```
servers:
  - url: http://localhost:5000/todolist/api/v1
```

This means that if you include `/v1` in any API calls to this service, you will get back responses that match the specification defined in version 1 of your API. If you click on **Show All Versions again** and pick **draft** from the list, you can go back to that version of the specification. Any changes that you make to this version of the API will not be reflected in version 1.

API versioning usually only needs to happen for breaking changes to an API, meaning changes that will alter the responses or input parameters in such a way that calls that rely on things being that way will break. You can usually make small changes to your API, such as adding a new error response code, without creating a new version. If you are significantly modifying the structure of an API response, though, you will probably want to create a new version of your API.

Thinking through when to create a new API version

API versioning can add complexity to managing and testing, so let's take a minute to reflect on when you would want to version an API. We will use the to-do list API that we've been working with throughout this chapter to think this through.

Imagine that you need to add in a due date field to the API. The field will be optional when creating or updating tasks and will be returned if it is there when getting tasks. The API is currently at v1. Do you need to create a new version of the API or not?

Well, let's look at how we can modify the definition to accommodate this change. First of all, you will need to add a new property to the task schema called `dueDate`. The type of this property will be `string` and it will have the `date-time` format. You can add an entry like this to the properties of the `task` schema to define this:

```
dueDate:
  type: string
  format: date-time
```

Since properties are considered to be optional by default, this is all that we need to do to specify that this is an allowable option for any calls that create, modify, or get tasks. So, now that you have updated the specification, what do you think? Should you create a new version of this API?

I would suggest that in this case you do not. This new property is optional, and so any previous calls or tests using this API will not have their contract broken since they can continue to use the API as they were before. In this case, you do not need to create a new version of the API.

Of course, if this was made to be a required field, you would need to create a new version of the API since in that case old calls that did not send that field would fail. This would then be considered a breaking change, which would necessitate an API version change.

API versioning and the ideas around when and how to deprecate old versions is a long and complex topic in its own right. I won't get into the details of it all in this book, but it is something to think about as your API continues to grow and evolve. API versions add complexity, as you can see here. The different versions will have different contracts and will need different tests. You will also sometimes need to update things in multiple places when making a bug fix or other holistic changes. Thankfully, Postman can help you out a lot with managing this on the testing front.

Summary

In this chapter, we explored what it looks like to use an API specification file to drive the design of an API. We saw how to get started with creating files like that and dug into the details of defining the different endpoints for an API. You also learned what a schema is in the context of an API test and learned a lot about how to set one up in an OpenAPI Specification file.

We also covered a lot of examples showing how to define the different parts of an API. You learned how to define parameters and how to create the definitions for request bodies and for the responses that a request returns. In addition, you learned how to use examples in the OpenAPI Specification.

Once we had gone over all of this, you learned how to use the file to help you out with defining an API in Postman. You saw how you can get Postman to automatically create collections and APIs for you, and you used Postman to edit and change the definition. We also went over how Postman uses the specification to automatically run contract tests for you. You also learned how to use API versioning in Postman.

In the next chapter, we will be looking at practical examples of creating and using mocks in an API. We will build on the things that we have covered in this chapter and show you some additional ways that you can use the power of an API specification file to help you with API design and testing.

12
Creating and Using a Mock Server in Postman

Mock servers are used to help solve many different testing problems. They can help you control what inputs the UI gets, and they can be used to help drive better designs and to better understand how an API works. In many ways, the ability to create and use mock data is essential to good API testing and development. However, creating and using mock servers can also seem a bit intimidating if you are new to API testing concepts. It seems like a big and difficult thing to understand, let alone create and use.

I remember when I first started learning about mock servers and I thought that it was going to be a difficult and complex thing to use. I was expecting I would need to learn a whole bunch of new and different concepts in order to be able to use them. In some ways I did have to learn a lot of new stuff, but in other ways it turns out that if you have the right tools, creating and using mock servers is actually pretty easy to do. Postman is one of the tools that makes it simple to set up and use mock servers, and so in the rest of this chapter I will walk you through how to do this in Postman.

In this chapter, you will learn about the following:

- Different approaches to testing with mocks
- Setting up a mock server in Postman
- Creating useful mock responses
- Using a mock server

Technical requirements

The code used in this chapter can be found at `https://github.com/`
`PacktPublishing/API-Testing-and-Development-with-Postman/tree/`
`master/Chapter12`.

Different approaches to testing with mocks

There are a lot of different ways to test things. In this book, we are obviously looking at how to test APIs, but APIs exist as part of a larger ecosystem. Some APIs are used to support external workflows, and some are built to support internal UIs and workflows. When you think about the ways that we use and test APIs, there are two main things that we are doing.

Sometimes, we are the *producers* of the API. When we are working in this way, we are looking at how to verify that an API works the way it should, but even in this domain there are different ways to approach testing. Although APIs work below the UI, they still can include a lot of the development stack. An API call will be sent via the internet to a server and then the server will do some processing, including in many cases querying databases. It will then package up the information into the correct format and send it back over the network to the client that sent the API request.

One way to test this is at the integration level where you send a request and see what you get back. This kind of testing is great because it lets you see that all the different pieces are working well together. However, it also means that there are many points of failure. If something goes wrong in the network, or if there is a bug in the database query, or if there is a problem in formatting the response, the test will fail. This can make it harder to figure out where the issue is. It can also make each test take some time to run.

Although you should always have some integration tests, it is often more efficient to break up the different parts of the service and test them on their own. So, instead of just doing one call that sends a request through the network, does work on the server, and then sends back a response, you could test the different pieces of it separately. You could create tests on the server that verify that the SQL queries work correctly, tests that check that the server can handle different kinds of API requests, and tests that check that everything gets properly packaged up again.

Other times, we are the *consumers* of the API. This might be an API that another team at our company has made, or an API that provides information from another company altogether. In this scenario, the API is a black box to you, and you are not able to test the underlying pieces of it. The testing that you do in this situation is often more targeted at making sure that the API gives you the information that you need in the format you need it. These kinds of tests are less about helping you find where bugs are in the API and more about ensuring that any changes to the API won't break your downstream workflows.

In this realm, a full integration test would be doing something like clicking in a UI and ensuring that things go correctly through the system and that the UI responds correctly. There is still further test decomposition that can happen here as well. We could have a set of tests that checks whether the API continues to give back the responses we want, and then another set of tests that checks that the UI works correctly with those responses.

In fact, I need to go on a short rant here if you will indulge me. As testers, we often approach UI test automation in a very foolish way. We act as if it is a good way to test the functionality of a system. The reality is, UI automation is a very slow and error-prone way to check the functionality of a system. It is much better to check low-level functionality in a unit test. However, this does not mean that UI automation is not valuable. It really is. It's just that it needs to be used to test the UI. We shouldn't be trying to verify business logic or database behavior or stuff like that in UI automation. We should be trying to verify UI behavior. UI tests are for testing the UI. OK, I won't rant about this anymore, but it leads nicely into why mocking is such an important part of a good API testing strategy.

As a reminder, a **mock** is some code that substitutes for some real code and directly returns certain values given a certain input. As a concrete example, imagine an online store that uses a credit card service by calling the API. When testing that store, you might not want to send the credit card details to the credit card service, so you could instead create a mock server that you send these details to. This server could be set up so that it responds with a message that says it was processed, or maybe some different error states. Doing this allows you to test the application without needing to call the actual credit card service and perhaps rack up charges. It also allows you to try out some tests that would otherwise be difficult to do. Now that we understand some of the importance and reasoning behind creating mock servers, let's take a look at how to do it in Postman.

Setting up a mock server

There are a couple of different ways in which you can create mock servers in Postman. In this section, I will show you how to set one up that is based on a specification file. This will be the primary use case that I cover in this chapter, but I will also make sure that you understand some of the other ways that you create mock servers as well.

Creating a mock server from a specification file

In the previous chapter, I walked you through how to set up an API specification for a to-do list API. You may want to go back to that chapter and see how that was done, or you can download the specification from the GitHub repository (`https://github.com/PacktPublishing/API-Testing-and-Development-with-Postman`) for this book and import it into Postman as a starting point. If you do create the API from the imported OpenAPI definition file, ensure that the **Generate collection from imported APIs** option is selected and set the **Link this collection as** option to **Test Suite**, as shown in the following screenshot:

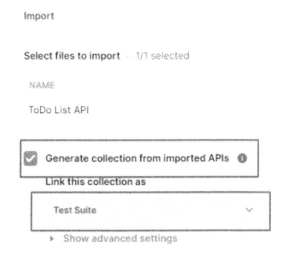

Figure 12.1 – Imported API specification options

Call the collection **ToDo List API**. You will also need an environment later on in this chapter, so let's go ahead and make it now using the following steps:

1. Click on the **New** button and choose the **Environment** option.

2. Name the environment `ToDoList Mock Env`.

This creates an empty environment. Later on, we will add values to this environment, but for now we just need to have one available. Once you've created an environment, you should be ready to create a mock server. You can do so with the following steps:

1. Go to the navigation pane and on the **API** tab, click on **ToDo List API**.

2. Go to the **Develop** tab, click on the **Add Mock Server** dropdown and choose the **Create new mock server** option, as shown in the following screenshot:

Figure 12.2 – Creating a mock server

3. From the resulting dialog, choose the **Use an existing collection** option and then select the **ToDo List API** collection from the dropdown.

4. Click on **Select Collection and Continue** to proceed.

5. Give your mock server a name like ToDo List Mock and choose the **ToDo List Mock Env** environment from the dropdown.

6. Click on **Create Mock Server** to create the server.

7. Once it has created the server, Postman will show you some information about it, including a mock server URL. Click on that URL to load it into a request.

8. The request will currently be called untitled request. We are going to use this request to do some tests, so click on the **Save** button to the right of the request.

9. From the resulting dialog, name it something like ToDo List Mock Request.

10. At the bottom of the dialog, find the **ToDo List API** collection and click on it so that this request will be saved in that collection.

11. Click on the **Save to ToDo List API** button to save the request.

12. The mock server URL can now be used as the base URL for requests to the to-do list service. If you add **/tasks** to the end of it, you can send the request and get back a response.

You will notice that it gives you back some values. Depending on the order in which Postman execution happens on your machine, you may see something that says "Bad data sent" or you may see a list of tasks. Either way, where are those values coming from? In this case, Postman has made some assumptions based on the information in the specification file. You can create or modify these values in Postman. I will show you how to do that in the next section when we discuss creating good mock responses, but first I want to take a minute to reflect on what we are doing here.

At this point, we have an API specification file that tells us how the API should behave, and we have this mock server that we can use. However, we don't yet have any code that actually stores or creates to-do items. If we were trying to develop an application, we would still need to develop a UI for it. In order to do that, we would need the API calls to return some data for us. We have not yet created code that passes data through an API interface and so it might seem that we are stuck in the water.

However, this is where a mock server can be very helpful. Once we flesh out what this server is doing, we can use it to give us data to use during the development of the UI. This opens up the possibility of working on the UI and the backend at the same time. In order to do that though, you are going to need to have this mock API send back responses that you can use. Before looking at that, I want to make sure you can create mock servers in other ways as well.

Creating a mock server from a collection

Before showing you how to use examples to customize the responses of your mock server, I want to mention a couple of other ways in which you can create mock servers in Postman. You don't need to go through these steps at this time, but the reality is you won't always have a specification to use when creating a mock server. In that case, you can still create mock servers in a few different ways. One way you can do that is to directly create it from a collection. You can do so with the following steps:

1. Go to a collection in the `Collections` navigation panel and click on the **View more actions** menu button:

Figure 12.3 – View more actions menu button

2. From the resulting menu, choose the **Mock Collection** option.

    This will bring up a panel where you can fill in a name and select an environment for your mock server to use.

3. You can then click on the **Create Mock Server** button to create the server.

At this point, you will have a mock server and could follow through with a lot of the same steps as I've outlined previously. One other common way to create a mock server is with the **New** button.

Creating a new mock server from scratch

Perhaps the most obvious way to create a mock server is by using the **New** button in Postman. There is a lot of similarity to things I've already covered, but I will just take you quickly through this so that you are aware of the details of this method as well. You can create a new mock server by using the following steps:

1. Click on the **New** button at the top of the Postman application and choose the **Mock Server** option.

2. On the resulting panel, ensure that the **Create a new collection** option is selected:

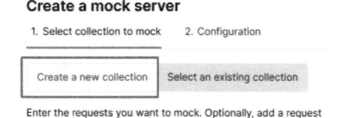

Figure 12.4 – Create a new collection option

3. Add a request URL (perhaps something like /test) and a response body (maybe something like "Hello!").

4. Click on **Next** and name the server.

5. Click on **Create Mock Server**.

Postman will create the server for you, but it will also create a collection that the server is using. We will learn more about how these collections work and how Postman uses them to give you the mock server responses in the next section, so let's look at how do that now.

Creating good mock responses

When we created the API specification as shown in the previous chapter, we added a few examples. Postman will attempt to use those examples along with the default values in the specification to create responses for your mock calls. However, the default stuff that Postman sets up will need to be customized a bit to our specific needs.

In this section, I will show you how to use Postman to create good mock responses. We will look at the following topics:

- Using default examples

- Creating your own custom examples

- How to use dynamic variables in your examples

- How to give different responses based on different path parameters

- How Postman picks which example to return to you

This sounds like a lot, but we will work through it one step at a time and by the end of this section, you will have a good grasp of how to use examples in Postman to create useful mock responses. Let's start by looking at some of the default examples that Postman has generated.

Using default examples

Let's return to the question I posed earlier in this chapter: how does Postman know what data to return when we send a request to a mock server? When we created the mock server, we didn't explicitly define what responses it should give back for various requests, so how does Postman know what kind of response is correct? Well, let's take a look and see.

In the `Collections` navigation tree, go to the `GET` request on the `/tasks` endpoint of the **ToDo List API** collection. This request has two examples. You can find the examples in the navigation panel, as shown in the following screenshot:

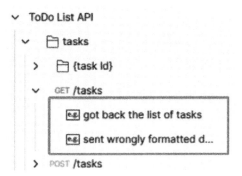

Figure 12.5 – Request examples

If you click on the example called **got back the list of tasks**, you will see that the body of it has a list of tasks. If you click on the **sent wrongly formatted data** example, you will see that the body of it is just set to the string `"Bad data sent"`.

Mock servers will return responses based on examples defined in the requests in this collection, and so you will have seen one of these responses in the request that you sent. You can modify these examples if you want and then save the changes. If you then send another request to the mock server, you will then get back the new data in the response. How did this initial data get generated though? Well, to answer that we have to go all the way back to the API specification that you imported.

You can look at the API specification in Postman by going to the API and clicking on the **Define** tab. If you look at the /tasks path and then the description of the 200 response under that path, you will see that it is called **got back the list of tasks**. This is the same as the title for the example on the request in Postman, so clearly that is where Postman is getting the data for the response from. But if you look closely you will see that we haven't defined the rest of the data you see in the example, here in the spec, so where is the data in the body of the response coming from?

The answer lies in the schema for this response. If you scroll down to the /components/ schemas/task section of the specification, you can see the properties of a task response defined. Postman has used those properties to generate some representative values. So, the title property is defined as a string, and Postman has generated a simple string to use there. The status property, on the other hand, is defined as an enumeration of some specific values and so Postman has picked one of those values to be used in the response. Since the dueDate property is defined as a date-time string, Postman has generated a sample data for that field. Postman has also automatically generated two items for this, since the /tasks field is an array.

All of this adds up to a nice simple example, set up automatically for you. Pretty cool, right?

As you've noticed, there are two different example responses. One of them specifies a 400 response and one of them a 200 response. This is helpful for testing out how an application will respond to different API response codes, but how can you get the mock server to respond with the data for the response code that you are interested in?

In order to do this, you can use the following steps to specify the x-mock-response-code header when sending the mock request:

1. Go to the mock request and click on the **Headers** tab.

2. Below the headers that have already been added is a spot to add a key and a value. Type in x-mock-response-code in the **Key** field and put 400 in the **Value** field.

3. Send the response.

This will ensure that you get back a message that says **Bad data sent**. By specifying 400 in the x-mock-response-code header, you have told the mock server that you want it to return data for an example that has a 400 response code. Since an example with a 400 response code is defined on this endpoint, the mock server is able to give back that response.

If you change the value of the x-mock-response-code header to be 200, and send it again, you will get back the data from the example with the 200 response code. This header is one way to specify which example you want to use in the response, but there are other headers that Postman provides as well. For example, you could use the x-mock-response-name header to specify a response that you want by name. Postman has a number of x-mock headers that you can use. We'll see a couple more examples of them in this book, but if you want to see more of them, you can see details in the Postman documentation (https://learning.postman.com/docs/designing-and-developing-your-api/mocking-data/mock-with-api/).

These default examples are a good place to get started and are helpful, but there is a lot more that we can do with examples in Postman. Let's look at how you can customize examples next.

Creating custom examples

Although default examples are a great way to leverage the power of your API specification, for some mock responses you will want to do more than what you have defined in the specification. Postman offers a lot of flexibility with how you can set up mock responses. Let's look at some of those options and see how to use them.

We will use the same mock request that we already created, so first of all, make sure that the x-mock-response-code header is set to 200. We are now going to take a look at how to mock a POST call, so go ahead and change the method on the mock request to POST. Before sending this request, you will want to specify a body for it which you can do with the following steps:

1. Click on the **Body** tab.

2. Change the type to **raw** and select **JSON** from the dropdown.

3. Set the body to have something like the following value:

```
{
    "title": "{{title}}",
    "status": "{{InProgress}}",
    "dueDate": "{{dueDate}}"
}
```

4. You will notice that the values have been defined as variables. These variables need to be added to the environment. Ensure that the **ToDo List Mock Env** environment is selected.

5. Click on the **Environment quick look** icon and then edit the environment.

6. Add the three variables (`title`, `InProgress`, and `dueDate`) to the environment and give them the values shown in the following figure:

	VARIABLE	INITIAL VALUE ⓘ
✓	title	Learn Postman
✓	InProgress	In Progress
✓	dueDate	2021-01-01T01:01:00.001Z

Figure 12.6 – Variable values

7. Click on **Save** and close the environment tab.

Return to the **ToDo List Mock Request** and **Send** it. When you do that, you should see that you get back a response, but you should also see a little warning icon saying there are two issues as shown in the following screenshot:

Figure 12.7 – Issues with sending the mock request

Postman is highlighting these issues because it is comparing the data you sent and received to the schema specified in the API specification. If you click on the **2 issues** link, you will see a flyout that shows you what those issues are. In this case, it tells you that there are some issues with the data returned. This is because when you send the POST request, it expects to get the data back in a way that matches the schema settings, but the data is instead a more generic type.

This can be corrected by updating the example to send back the same data that we are creating. You can modify the saved example to do that using the following steps:

1. In the **Collections** navigation panel, go to the **POST /tasks** request and choose the **created a new task** example from the **Examples** dropdown.

2. Modify the example response to use the variables in the same way you set them up in the mock request body. It should look something like this screenshot:

Figure 12.8 – Body of the POST response

3. This example is creating a task that is already in progress, so rename it to `Create an In Progress Task`.

4. Click on **Save**.

If you now return to the mock request and send it, you should see that the body matches what you sent and Postman is no longer reporting any issues with this request.

As you can see, this is a powerful feature. However, if you were to call this mock API from outside of Postman, it would only return data that reflects the current value of the variables. This means that if you are developing something and you want to create new objects, you will not get back an object based on the data you created, but will rather get back an object that is based on these variables that have been defined in Postman. Many mock services have to do this, where they essentially have hardcoded responses for the POST requests that you make, and it is important to note that this is a limitation with this mock server as well. However, you can add a little more flexibility into mock server responses by using dynamic variables in your examples, which we will look at in more detail next.

Using dynamic variables in examples

We've already seen how to use environment variables in request examples, but Postman also has a number of built-in variables that support returning dynamic responses. These variables will generate different kinds of dummy data for you. For example, if you use the `{{$randomCity}}` variable, you will get back a random city. There is a large list of these variables that you can find at `https://learning.postman.com/docs/writing-scripts/script-references/variables-list/`. These variables are generated using the faker.js library (`https://github.com/marak/Faker.js/`) and so will have the same limitations and abilities that this library has. Let's look at how to use them in one of the examples in the to-do list API by using the following steps:

1. Go to the `GET` request for `/tasks/:taskId` and open the **Got back the specified task** example.

2. In the example response, set **title** to `"{{$randomVerb}} {{$randomNoun}}"`

3. Set **status** to `"New"` and **dueDate** to `"{{dueDate}}"`.

4. Make sure to save the example.

   At this point, the example response should look like this:

   ```
   {
       "title": "{{$randomVerb}} {{$randomNoun}}",
       "status": "New",
       "dueDate": "{{dueDate}}"
   }
   ```

Postman does have dynamic variables for generating random dates, but they are not in the format that our specification requires and so using them would cause validation errors. Instead, I've just set it up to use the `dueDate` variables that we created for our last request.

If you go back to the mock request, set the method to `GET`, and change the endpoint to end with `/tasks/1` and hit **Send**, you will get back a response that includes a random verb and noun in the title. If you hit **Send** again, you will see that you get back a response that includes a different title.

> **Important note**
> Since Postman has created multiple examples for each request, you might not get back the example that you expect. If you are getting back the `400` response instead of `200`, don't forget that you can set the `x-mock-response-code` header to `200` to force Postman to respond with the correct example.

Dynamic variables are a great way to inject some randomness into your mock responses; however, you will notice that I still had to hardcode in the status. Since the status only has three allowed values, we can't just generate a random string for it. Instead, we need to hardcode it to one of those acceptable values. But what if you wanted to be able to get back a response with a certain status code? Maybe you want a response that is the same as this example, but that has an **In Progress** status instead. In order to do that, you can set up multiple responses based on the path variable.

Responding based on parameters

You may want to create several different responses for a mock server that all return a 200 status code. In this case, you can't use the x-mock-response-code header to pick which response you will get back. Instead, it often makes sense to create different responses based on query parameters or path variables. In order to do this, you will need to create two additional examples, one for the New status and one for the Completed status. You can set that up on the GET /tasks/:taskId request with the following steps:

1. Go to the **Got back the specified task** example.

2. Ensure that you are on the **Params** tab in the example request and in the **Path Variables** section give the taskId a value of 1.

3. Click on the **Save** button.

4. Go to the example response body and copy it.

5. Go back to the /tasks/:taskId request, click on the **View more actions** menu, and choose the **Add Example** option.

6. Paste your clipboard into the example response body.

7. Change the status in the data you pasted to be "In Progress".

8. Set the **Status Code** value of the example response to 200 OK.

9. Set the value of the taskId path variable to 2. At this point, the request should look like this:

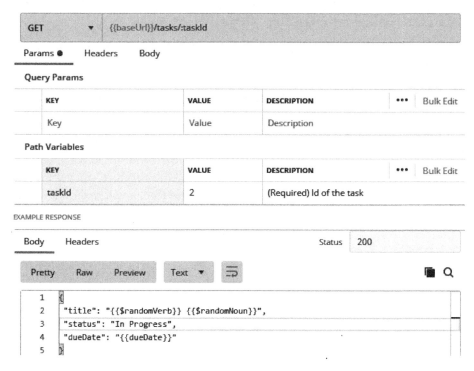

Figure 12.9 – A new example setup

10. In the example response, go to the **Headers** tab and create a key called `Content-Type` with a value of `application/json`.

11. Set the name of the example to `In Progress example` and click on **Save**.

12. Go back to the `/tasks/:taskId` request and create another example.

13. Once again, paste in the copied body, but this time set the status in the body response to `"Completed"`.

14. Set `taskId` to 3 and **Status** for the request to `200 OK`.

15. Set the `Content-Type` header to `application/json` and name this example `Completed task example`, then save it.

You now have an example for each status type and each of those examples is mapped to a particular task ID. You can try it out with your mock request. If you call `/tasks/1`, you will get back a response with a status of **New**, while if you call `/tasks/2` or `/tasks/3` you will get back responses with statuses of **In Progress** and **Completed** respectively.

You've now learned a number of different strategies that you can use when creating examples for mock servers, but it is important to understand how Postman goes about picking which example to respond with when you make a request to the mock server. In order to this, we will need to look at how example matching works in Postman.

Understanding example matching

You have seen how you can back different responses depending on the ID you call, but what happens for other task IDs? What if you call /tasks/4? If you make that request against your mock server, you will notice that it gives back an incorrectly formatted response. Why is this? Well, it comes down to the way that Postman does example matching. When you make a request to the mock server, Postman has to figure out which of the examples it will return to you. It uses a set of internal rules for this.

After applying some obvious filters such as improperly formatted responses and which kind of request method has been specified, Postman will look at the URL and try to find a match. It first looks for an exact match, and if it can't find that, it will make a few guesses at what you might be looking for. One of the things it will try is to remove alphanumeric IDs from the path. So, in the case of the /tasks/4 example, since Postman can't find an exact match for that, it will remove the /4 from the end and try again. In this case, it finds the example for the /tasks endpoint and returns that, which is why you are getting a response that is a list of tasks instead of a single task.

You don't want to have to explicitly specify every ID that you might call though, so what can we do? Well, Postman will also do what is called **wildcard matching**. With wildcard matching, you can have Postman return the same response regardless of which ID you have specified. You can take a look at a concrete example of what this is like with the following steps:

1. Go back to the GET /tasks/:taskId request and choose **Add Example** from the **View more actions** menu.

2. Fill out the body with an appropriate response, like the ones I showed you when you were creating other examples in this chapter.

3. Set the **Status** response code to 200 and create a Content-Type header that is set to application/json.

4. Replace :taskId in the sample request URL with {{taskId}}. It is important that the new {{taskId}} variable be undefined.

5. Name the example something like Generic task id Response and save it.

Now, any requests that you send to the /tasks/{{taskId}} endpoint that are not for resources 1, 2, or 3 will give you back that generic response. Hopefully, the examples give you a good understanding of how Postman goes about doing example matching. If you want to see this in more detail, you can check out the documentation on example mapping in Postman at the following URL:

https://learning.postman.com/docs/designing-and-developing-your-api/mocking-data/matching-algorithm/

You should now have everything you need to create a mock server that gives back useful responses, but there is more to it than this. You will want to use that mock server to help you create a good-quality application. I'll show you how to do that in the next section.

Using mock servers

You've now created a mock server that gives back different responses for various situations. The whole point of having a mock server, though, is so that you can use it for testing and development purposes. In this section, I want to show you how you can use a mock server to help out with those things. I will show you how to use mock servers in both frontend and backend development. I will also show you how to use them to help you with continuous planning and give a brief introduction on how to use them for testing purposes.

Let's dive right in by looking at how to develop code against a mock server.

Developing against a mock server

One of the reasons you would create a mock server is so that you can use it to provide data for you while you are creating a UI. This book isn't about UI development, so I won't spend too much time talking about how to develop UIs. However, there are a few things to keep in mind when developing against a mock server.

APIs act as a kind of glue or pipeline between different parts of an application. We've been looking at an example of a to-do list application and if we were developing it in the real world, we would need to have a backend that could store the data about our tasks and that could process the API requests to do what the client wants. We would also want to have a UI where customers could type in their task and set status and due dates. The API is the pipeline between these two things, and you can use a mock server to help out with both of those things.

Developing a UI using a mock

At first glance, using a mock for UI development is straightforward. You should be able to set the base URL that your application will use to the mock server URL and then develop the UI as you normally would. However, there are a few things to consider. At a basic level, once you start using the mock server, you may discover that there are some changes that you need to make to the responses. This is where the API pipeline concept can help you. If you make changes to the mock server and the specification that it is built from, you will be letting everyone else who is using that server know what your needs on the frontend are.

Another thing you will have to take into account is that you might need to add the x-mock-response-code header to some of your calls as well, so that you are sure to get back the response that you are interested in. If you think about it, this means that you will need to do some kind of hardcoding of that in the calls your UI is making. This might not seem like a big deal, but it is important not to gloss over it. Putting in temporary hardcoding of stuff like this can lead to bugs in the future if you do not take care, so you need to make sure that you remember to remove those headers afterward. In this particular case, it is unlikely that they will cause trouble, but it is still good development practice to have some kind of reminder for yourself to ensure that you clean up these kinds of things before the code gets released.

If you were to develop against the mock server that you've built in this chapter, you would also discover that POST and PUT calls are challenging. If you were sending calls to a real server, a POST call would create the resource you send to it. In our mock server, Postman will just send back a static response. You remember that when you created the example for the POST response, you set it up to use variables. When you called the request from within Postman, you could specify the body of your POST request to use those variables. However, when you are developing from an external application, you can't directly control the Postman variables and so you will get back the current values of those variables as defined in Postman.

Since the mock responses are largely static, you will generally need to create quite a few different responses for the different scenarios that you are interested in. For example, if you want to be able to code against a POST response that uses each of the different status values, you would need to create an example in your collection for each of those responses. In fact, let's look at how you could do that with the following steps:

1. Go the **POST /tasks** request and add an example.

2. Set the response code to 201 and create a body as you did with the other examples you've made in the chapter.

3. Ensure that the status field in the example response body is set to "New".

4. Set the Content-Type header in the example response to application/json.

5. Name the example Create a New Task and click on **Save**.

You now have two examples for this request, which is great since it gives you the ability to see how your UI will react to creating these different kinds of tasks, but there is still a problem. How do you tell the server which response to give you? You can't use the x-mock-response-code header since both of them have the same response. You also can't get it to respond based on parameters since this POST call uses the same endpoint for all calls. So, what can you do?

Well, as mentioned earlier, there are a number of other possible mock request headers that you can use. You can see the **Run the mock service** section of this page in the Postman documentation:

```
https://learning.postman.com/docs/designing-and-developing-
your-api/mocking-data/mock-with-api/
```

One header that should work well for our purposes is the x-mock-response-name header. You can go to the mock request in Postman and add the header giving it a value of **Create a New Task**. You will want to make sure that the method is set to **POST** and that the URL is calling the /tasks endpoint as well as ensuring that the x-mock-response-code header is set to 201. If all that is in place, you can send the request and you should see that you get back the response that you just created.

Developing a backend when using a mock server

When you are developing a backend, you won't use the mock server. The mock is meant to be a replacement for the backend server and so you won't directly use it when creating the backend code, but there are still some things that you should keep in mind when working with a mock during backend development.

When a mock is being used to work on the frontend while development is concurrently happening on the backend, it is important to keep everything in sync with each other. While you will not be using the mock server to code the backend against, you will need to make sure that your backend is producing the same kind of data that the mock server is. If you find that you need to make changes to the way the backend provides data in the API, you need to make sure that the mock server gets updated to reflect that. This will generally be done by updating the specification file and making sure that any examples used in the mock server are updated correctly. It is very important to keep everything in sync when multiple people are working on something at the same time as each other.

Another thing to keep in mind is that although you won't be coding against what the mock server does, you still might be able to use it to help you. It is helpful to break down your code into distinct modules and so you may want to develop one part of the API at a time. There may be times when you are developing one part of the API that has some dependencies on another part. Rather than trying to work on both of them at once, you could use the mock server to replace the dependency and keep working on just the one part you are interested in. This allows you to isolate your work, but don't forget to remove any calls to mock servers and actually implement them once you are done with the part you are working on.

Continuous planning with a mock server

Mock servers help you keep everything in sync, and that is a powerful design tool. It is often hard to know exactly how an application is going to look and what it all needs when you start developing it. However, if you are using a mock server, you can start working on the frontend and backend at the same time. As you learn more and try things out, you will find that you need to make changes. You may also have inputs from clients or other stakeholders that influence what you need to do.

A mock server is very helpful in this situation as it gives you a place that you can update as plans change. If you find that you need to add or remove endpoints to your API, you can do that in the mock server and quickly see how that will influence your application. In Agile development, you want to be able to shift and change as new requirements come up and having a mock server lets you do just that.

Testing with a mock server

In a way, being able to code against a mock server enables testing as it allows you to test out a lot of things in your frontend. You can also use a mock server to create edge cases that would otherwise be very hard to test. There is a lot more that you can do with testing when using a mock server. In the next chapter, we will look at more details around contract testing and how you can use that to drive API quality, so I won't go into that topic here. There certainly is a lot that you can do from a testing perspective when using a mock server.

Summary

In this chapter, I have walked you through a lot of details related to using mock servers in Postman. You saw how to set up a mock server in Postman, but we didn't stop there. I then showed you how to create useful mock responses using examples. I walked you through how to use the default examples that Postman creates for you when you create a mock server from a specification file. I also helped you to learn how to create custom examples that do exactly what you need them to do. I then showed you some powerful options that you can use in these examples including things such as dynamic variables and responses that are specific to URL parameters. I also made sure that you understood how Postman finds the examples that it will respond with so that you can be sure that you will get back the response you are looking for when you make a request to a mock server.

After showing you how to create a mock server that gives back good responses, I dove into the different ways that you can use mock servers. I showed how to use them to help you with developing new code. You learned how to use them when creating UIs or frontends. I also explained some of the things that you should consider when working on a backend while using mock servers. I also walked you through how to use a mock server to help you be flexible and dynamic in the planning process and gave you a quick introduction to testing with a mock server.

In the next chapter, I will show you how you can contract testing in Postman, and you will also get more details on how that kind of testing ties in to mock servers.

13
Using Contract Testing to Verify an API

We've all had to sign a contract before. Maybe it was when you were buying a house, starting a new job, opening a bank account, and so on. There are a number of other reasons that we sign contracts. I have a filing cabinet where I keep important paperwork and I suspect that about half of the documents in there are contracts of some sort. Why do we use contracts so much? What exactly is a contract?

Contracts help simplify the way we do things. I've been talking about formal signed contracts so far, but there are many other kinds of contracts as well. Philosophers will talk about a social contract, for example. At its heart, a contract is just an agreement between two (or more) parties that outlines what they will do. They are so widespread because they make things much more efficient.

Think about it in terms of me buying your house. In broad terms, the way it would usually work is that once we had agreed on a price, we would draw up a contract that says that I will buy your house for a certain number of dollars and get possession of it on a certain day. This contract outlines what I will do (give you a certain amount of money) and what you will do (leave the house and give me the key). If we didn't have a contract, the selling process would be much more complicated. I would have to show up with the money in hand and wait while you moved all your stuff out of the house, and then we could trade the money for the key.

The contract is a way of establishing trust. Of course, not all contracts are explicit. If I wanted a load of gravel for my driveway, I could call up a gravel company and ask them to deliver it. They would do so under the implicit contract assumption that I would pay them for the gravel once they'd delivered it and given me an invoice. Implicit contracts like this work well when everyone is clear on the terms of the contract and when there is a high degree of trust. Some implicit contracts are based on cultural understanding, and there may be times when things get confused or forgotten. In general, you will see formal contracts for bigger and longer-term things such as buying a house or starting a new job, while implicit contracts will suffice for many of the ordinary things of life.

But what does all this have to do with API testing? Well, one powerful API testing concept is called **contract testing**. In contract testing, we create a document that works as a contract that we can test against. Much like the contracts we see in everyday life, they set out the things that each party must do. In the case of API testing, the two parties involved in the contract are two different pieces of code. An example would be the frontend and the backend of a system or two services that communicate with each other. The contract establishes the way that those two parts of the system will communicate with each other. In this chapter, you will learn all about what contract testing is, how to set up contract tests in Postman, and how to create shared contract tests that can be run and fixed by all the affected teams. We will cover the following topics in this chapter:

- Understanding contract testing
- Setting up contract tests in Postman
- Running and fixing contract tests

Understanding contract testing

In this chapter, we will learn how to set up and use contract tests in Postman, but before we do that, I want to make sure that you understand what they are and why you would use them. So, in this section, we will learn what contract testing is. We will also learn how to use contract testing and then discuss approaches to contract testing; that is, both consumer-driven and provider-driven contracts. To kick all this off, we are going to need to know what contract testing is. So, let's dive into that.

What is contract testing?

I have already talked about what contract testing means at a basic level. Contract testing is a way to make sure that two different software services can communicate with each other. Often, contracts are made between a client and a server. This is the typical place where an API sits, and in many ways, an API is a contract. It specifies the rules that the client must follow in order to use the underlying service. As I've mentioned already, contracts help make things run more smoothly. It's one of the reasons we use APIs. We can expose data in a consistent way that we have contractually bound ourselves to. By doing this, we don't need to deal with each user of our API on an individual basis and everyone gets a consistent experience.

However, one of the issues with an API being a contract is that we have to change things. APIs will usually change and evolve over time, but if the API is the contract, you need to make sure that you are holding up your end of the contract. Users of your API will come to rely on it working in the way that you say it will, so you need to check that it continues to do so.

When I bought my home, I took the contract to a lawyer to have them check it over and make sure that everything was OK and that there would be no surprises. In a somewhat similar way, an API should have some checks to ensure that there are no surprises. We call these kinds of checks contract testing. An API is a contract, and contract testing is how we ensure that the contract is valid, but how exactly do you do that?

How to use contract testing

We will learn how to create and run contract tests in Postman shortly, but first, let's look at how the process works. There are a couple of different ways that you could approach contract testing. One possible way to do it is to create a collection of tests that exercise the API in all its configuration. You would then run that set of tests every time a change was made to the API to ensure that nothing has changed. Technically, when you are doing this, you are checking the contract, but this is not what we would call contract testing.

With contract testing, you want to check just the contract itself. You don't want to run a full regression suite. Part of the value of contract testing is that it allows you to just verify that the contract is correct without needing to include full API calls. However, in order to do that, you need to be able to check the contract somehow. How do you do that?

The best way to do this is by having the contract documented somewhere. This is usually done with some kind of specification. In the previous couple of chapters, I've been showing you how to work with an OpenAPI Specification file. If you have a specification that defines all the actions that the API can perform, it will work well as the basis for your contract tests. In fact, in the previous chapter, you learned how to do one half of a contract test.

Mock servers are, in essence, contracts. They provide the frontend, or **API consumer**, with a contract that they can use. However, as we saw in the previous chapter, there are some limitations to this. Although the mock server tells the consumer what they can do, it doesn't get used when you are working on the backend code. This means that the API might change without the API consumer knowing about it. This is because those who are working on the backend code don't know what things the users or their API are relying on. They could read through various examples in the mock server and try and figure it out, but that would be a time-consuming and low-value process.

What contract testing does is create a set of tests that the API producer can run to verify that any changes they've made are not breaking any of the consumer's needs. These contract tests give the API producer something they can run, without needing to worry about the details of the consumer implementations. Well, this has been a lot of words and might seem a bit abstract, so let's take a look at a more concrete example of what this might look like. In *Chapter 10, Testing an Existing API*, we worked through creating tests for a simple API. Those tests were not contract tests, but let's consider one of the endpoints from that API and think about what it would look like to have contract tests for it.

As you may recall, one of the endpoints was the /blogposts/<id> endpoint. This endpoint would give back information about a specified blogpost. When you call that endpoint, you get back something that looks like this:

```
{
    "id": 1,
    "title": "The FIRST blog post",
    "body": "This is my first blog post",
    "profileId": 1
}
```

In *Chapter 10, Testing an Existing API*, we added tests that checked some of the values in here, but a contract test would be quite different. A contract test would check things such as which fields were available and the data types they have. So, in this example, a contract test would verify that this endpoint has the `id`, `title`, `body`, and `profileId` fields. It would also confirm that the two `id` fields return integers and that the other two return strings. Any time changes are made to the backend, these tests can be run to verify that those rules still apply. This gives the users of the API the ability to confidently make assumptions about those fields when they are using them.

There are always at least two parties involved in a contract, but which one of them gets to define what the contract looks like in the first place? Let's take a look at that next.

Who creates the contracts?

Before we get into the details of setting this all up in Postman, there is one more thing we need to discuss. Who creates these contracts? Should the consumer of the API be the one creating the contract, or should it be the provider? Much like a real-life contract, there is probably going to be some need for negotiation and the ability to reject a contract proposal, but somebody has to put the contract forward in the first place. There are two main approaches to this: you can either have consumer-driven contracts or you can have the provider be the one driving them. Let's look at each one in more detail.

Consumer-driven contracts

Consumer-driven contracts are contracts that the consumer makes. In this case, the consumer defines what their needs are from the API and provides contract tests that show the ways in which they will be using this API. These can be defined directly up-front in a design-driven manner, where the consumer needs to define the details of how the API gets designed in the first place. Alternatively, they can be provided for existing APIs by showing them which part of it this particular consumer relies on.

There are several advantages to consumer-driven contracts. The whole point of an API is to provide value to those who consume it. By letting the consumers define what the API does, you are helping to ensure that you are delivering information that is valuable to the users of your API. Another advantage is that it can help the API provider understand the different ways that consumers are using the API.

There is a "law" known as **Hyrum's Law**, which observes the following:

> *"With a sufficient number of users of an API, it does not matter what you promise in the contract: all observable behaviors of your system will be depended on by somebody."*

> *- https://www.hyrumslaw.com/*

This means that your system will get used in ways that you did not anticipate it would when you were designing it. However, if the users provide you with contracts that show you how they are using it, you can learn from that and not make changes that break workflows in unintended ways.

There are some downsides to this, though. If you have a lot of people consuming your API, you will have to run contract tests for each of them every time you make changes. There will probably be a lot of overlap between these tests, which leads to redundancy and inefficiency in your testing. Another concern is that, sometimes, the consumers tend to do some unexpected things that can really constrain future development. For example, I recently saw a case where a client was using an API that contained some information about another domain in it. The client wanted this information, so they got it from the API we had provided. However, we wanted to change the API so that it no longer returned the data, and instead returned it from the correct domain. The problem was that the client had come to depend on the data being in the "wrong" spot, which made it much harder for us to change the API to work the way we wanted it to. If you have some feature in your API that you did not put there by design, it might be a lot harder to change in the future, should consumers come to rely on it. You don't want to be in a situation where one client's use case prevents you from creating useful value for others.

Provider-driven contracts

Instead of having the contract primarily driven by the consumers, you could have the API producer be the one providing the contract. In this case, the team creating the API would create a contract that defines what data that API provides and what format that data will be in when clients request it. Consumers could then use that contract to build mock servers that they could use for testing and development.

This approach has some benefits. First, it allows API providers to set out a standard set of actions and data that are supported. According to Hyrum's Law, users will still end up using things in ways that are not defined by the contract, but then at least the API provider can explicitly say that those are not the supported ways to use this API, and they don't have to worry too much about breaking those workflows. Another benefit of this is that it is much more scalable. It doesn't really matter if you have two users or 2 million users. You have the same number of contract tests to run as the API provider.

The biggest downside to provider-driven contracts is the missing feedback loop. In this case, it is much harder for API providers to discover the interesting or unusual ways in which clients are using their APIs. This also means that since those configurations are less understood, they will be easier to break. Even if the provider can point to the contract and let the consumer know that they were using unsupported functionality, it is still never nice to break things that your customers depend on.

Now that you have a good grasp of what contract testing is and how it works, let's look at how to set up contract tests in Postman.

Setting up contract tests in Postman

Creating contract tests is similar to creating any API test: you need to create a collection and then make requests in that collection with tests in them. But what kind of tests do you create when you perform contract testing?

In *Chapter 10, Testing an Existing API*, I talked about smoke tests. These are a targeted set of tests that you can run quickly to get a good idea of how your API is doing. A contract collection is a similar idea, but with a bit more comprehensive coverage. The idea of contract tests is to describe all the different parts of the API that you need, but not to do things such as look at how to use them in a workflow or other aspects of testing. Contract tests are a good way to set the minimum bar for what needs to be working, but you will need to do additional testing beyond them for it to be effective. Of course, as with any other testing that's done in Postman, you will need to create a collection for your contract tests.

Creating a contract testing collection

Any collection can be used for contract testing, but if you have created an API specification, as I showed you in *Chapter 11, Designing an API Specification*, Postman provides some nice shortcuts for you. If you have not gone through the exercises in that chapter, you can import the API specification after getting it from the GitHub repository for this book (`https://github.com/PacktPublishing/API-Testing-and-Development-with-Postman/tree/master/Chapter11`). Once you have imported the specification, you can set up a contract testing collection by following these steps:

1. Go to the API by clicking on it in the **APIs** tab in the navigation pane.

2. Go to the **Test** tab. Then, in the **Contract Tests** section, click on the **Add Contract Test** link.

3. Choose the **Create new contract test** option.

4. On the resulting dialog, name your contract test something like `ToDo List Contract Tests`.

There are several options under **Advanced settings**. These settings are used by Postman when it's creating the collection for you. Since Postman will be programmatically generating a collection with requests in it for you, it needs to make some assumptions. These advanced options let you control how Postman makes those assumptions:

- **Naming requests**: By default, Postman names requests according to the path name, but if you choose the **URL** option, it will add the base URL to the request names as well. If you want to have your request name be something different, you can modify the OpenAPI schema. You can do that by going to the schema and setting a unique value called the `operationId` option under the path you are interested in. Once you've done that, you can choose the **Fallback** option here.

- **Set indent character**: With this option, you can choose whether indented lines in the created collection will have **Tab** or **Space** indentation.

- **Collapse redundant folders**: This option determines whether Postman should attempt to collapse redundant folders into one. Folders are redundant if they have only one child element and don't have any folder-level data to persist.

- **Optimize conversion**: Leaving this option on will help with performance, so there is little or no reason to ever turn it off.

- **Request parameter generation**: When generating values for the parameters that the requests will use, Postman can either get those values from a **schema** or from defined **examples**. If you have examples defined, I would recommend using that option, since that will put actual values into the parameter fields instead of just giving you the data type.

- **Response parameter generation**: This option works like the request parameter generation option. You can choose to either get the response parameters from a **schema** or from defined **examples**. I would recommend using examples when possible.

- **Folder organization**: By default, Postman will create the folder structure in a collection by looking at the way that the **paths** in the specification have been defined. You can, however, have it generated in the folder structure using **tags** if you have defined them in the spec file.

- **Include auth info in example requests**: If this option is on, the created requests will include authentication parameters in any created examples.

Now that you understand these options, you can choose the ones you want and then click on **Create Contract Test** to tell Postman to create a collection with requests in place for you. Once you've done that and looked at the **Collection** tab in the navigation pane, you will see that there is a collection available for you.

This is a great start, but we are not trying to create a contract collection; we are trying to create a contract test, so you still have some more work to do.

Adding tests to a contract test collection

You now have a collection that you can use for contract testing, but you aren't quite done yet. Postman has automatically created the structure and details of the request, but you need to define the actual tests that you want this collection to run. This is the point at which understanding the theory of contract testing becomes helpful. What kind of tests should you add to this collection?

With contract tests, we want to make sure that the API is fulfilling the needs that we have as a consumer. We don't want to create a comprehensive set of tests that checks everything this API can do. We just want to add tests that verify that it provides the data we are interested in. In this case, we are pretending that we have a to-do list application, so we would only want to add tests that verify data for the kinds of requests that our application is running. We would then create tests that check that those specific calls give us back the data that we need.

I covered how to create tests in detail in *Chapter 6, Creating Test Validation Scripts*, so I won't go through it again in this chapter. However, one thing that can be helpful when creating contract tests is the Postman Interceptor.

Using the Postman Interceptor

Postman can dynamically capture requests for you with its Interceptor. When creating contract tests, you want to create tests that demonstrate the actual needs of your application. The Interceptor allows you to do this. When it is running, it will capture all the requests that your application makes, allowing you to see the actual requests that you need for your contract test. Since we don't have a to-do list application to test against, I will use the **swapi.dev** API as an example. You can set up the Interceptor in Postman by following these steps:

1. First, you will need to have Chrome installed on your computer. I would also recommend that you close all tabs except one so that you don't get too much unwanted data. You can then install the Postman Interceptor by downloading it from the Chrome web store. You can download it directly from this link: `https://go.pstmn.io/interceptor-download`.

2. Click on **Add to Chrome** and choose **Add extension** on the verification prompt to install the extension.

3. Once the extension has been installed, return to the Postman app and click on the **Capture request and cookies with Postman** icon, as shown in the following screenshot:

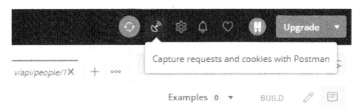

Figure 13.1 – Capture requests and cookies with Postman

4. On the **Requests** tab on the resulting flyout, set **Source** to **Interceptor** and enable the **Capture Requests** option.

5. If you want, you can also capture cookies by going to the **Cookies** tab and enabling the **Capture Cookies** option.

6. Select the **Install Interceptor Bridge** option to set up the bridge that will facilitate communication between the Postman app and the Interceptor extension that you just installed.

7. Once it has completed the setup, you will see that the **INTERCEPTOR CONNECTED** status is green, as shown in the following screenshot:

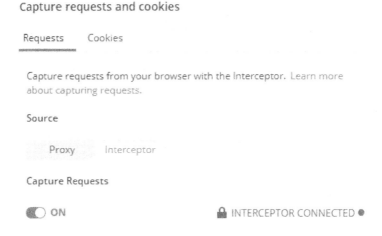

Figure 13.2 – Interceptor connected

8. Ensure that the **Save Requests to** option is set to **History**. You can save the requests directly to a collection, but there will usually be a lot of requests that you don't need in there as well, so I would recommend saving it to your history.

With that, you have the Interceptor set up and running. You can now go to a website such as swapi.dev and perform some actions there. As you do so, Postman will save all the API requests in the **History** tab. You can go to the tab in the navigation pane and find the requests that you are interested in and add them to your collection. To do so, you can click on the **Add request to Collection** icon, as shown in the following screenshot:

Figure 13.3 – Adding an intercepted request to a collection

This allows you to easily add the requests that your application sends to your contract testing collection. You will still need to create tests to check that the data and data structures are correct, but this can help you figure out what requests to send for contract tests.

As I've already said, I'm not going to walk you through a step-by-step process for creating tests for these requests, but now that you know what requests to include and what kinds of parameters they need to have, you should be able to go through this and fill in the test's details. However, in order to understand this a bit better, let's take a look at what you would do in broad terms.

You would want to use the Interceptor in situations where you do not have an already defined schema for the API that you can create contract tests against. In that situation, you can use the Interceptor to help you "reverse-engineer" how the API works and what things it provides. So, in this example, we could look at the results given back by a couple of different people and, from there, figure out which fields are required (for example, the "name" and "height" fields).

Using that information, we could build out a schema that describes the rules for these fields and then use that to create contract tests. However, even after that is done, you will still need to ensure that these tests are available for everyone who has agreed to use this contract. Everyone involved needs to be able to run and fix these tests; otherwise, they are just ordinary API tests.

Running and fixing contract tests

In many ways, contract tests aren't that different from other tests that you create in Postman. The main difference is in how they are run and what the expectations around them are. Contract tests are meant to establish a contract for how the API should work, so they need to be run primarily by the API provider. Consumers will sometimes run them to double-check the work that the provider is doing, but the main purpose of them is for the API provider to check that they are not violating the contract as they make changes to the API.

Since these tests are meant to verify things as code changes are made, these tests should be run as part of the build pipeline for the API development team. I covered how to run tests in a build pipeline in *Chapter 8*, *Running API Tests in CI with Newman*, so you can check that chapter out for more details on how to do this.

On the consumer side, you don't need to run the tests every time you make changes. Changes to the user interface do not affect the way that the API works. However, you might want to occasionally check that the API is still meeting the contract. One way that you can do that in Postman is with monitors. You can check out more details on how to use monitors by going back to *Chapter 9*, *Monitoring APIs with Postman*. Setting up a monitor to periodically check that the API is meeting the contract allows you to develop the application frontend with confidence, without needing to concern yourself with what the API development team is doing.

We all know that things need to change in software development. So, what do you do when things break? If you are doing consumer-driven contract testing, what do you do as the API provider when the contract tests fail?

Fixing contract test failures

As with any test, contract tests will fail sometimes. They will fail for the same two main categories of reasons that other tests fail: a bug was introduced or the requirements changed. In the case of a bug, the code just needs to be corrected so that it does what the contract says that it should. In this case, fixing the test failure is straightforward: you just need to change the code so that it does the correct thing.

The other case is more difficult to navigate. Try as we might, the initial design of an API won't always be able to predict the needs of the customer in the long run. There may be times when an API needs to change in ways that break the contract. There may also be times when an API consumer needs the API to do something that is not in the contract yet. In both these cases, contract tests are valuable as they make it very clear that the API contract has changed. They help ensure that the necessary conversations happen. However, this highlights the fact that the contract tests will probably have to change over time, and also that there are two (or more) different groups that might be interested in updating them. How do you go about making those changes to a shared source of truth like this?

This is where collection sharing becomes important.

Sharing contract tests

For contract tests to work well, they need to be accessible by both the provider and the consumers. This applies both from the standpoint of running the tests and from the standpoint of maintaining them. I would suggest that contract tests are shared in their own workspace, so that it is very clear that this is the location for storing those contracts. You can create and share a workspace by following these steps:

1. Click on the **Workspaces** dropdown at the top-right of the application, as shown in the following screenshot:

Figure 13.4 – Creating a new workspace

2. Click on the **+ New Workspace** link.

3. Name the workspace something like `Contract Test Workspace`.

4. Since the purpose of this workspace is to have people working together as a team, ensure its visibility is set to **Team**.

5. If you wanted to, you could insert the email addresses of the people that you want to invite to join this workspace; then, you can click on **Create Workspace**.

Once you have this shared workspace, you can easily share your contract test collection to that workspace by following these steps:

1. Click on the **View more actions** menu beside the contract test collection that you want to share.

2. Choose the **Share collection** option.

3. Select the shared workspace that you created and click on the **Share and Continue** button.

4. If you wanted to assign different people on the team different roles (for example, to administer, view, or edit) for this collection, you can do this on the next panel and then click on **Save Roles**.

This shared collection can now be viewed and edited and run by anyone you give the proper permissions to. Setting things up in this way allows you to treat this test as a contract. The shared collection establishes a contract between all the users in this workspace. Anyone in that workspace can run the tests to verify that the API is doing what it should be doing. Also, if you want, you can allow people to make changes to the contract so that things can update and change as the requirements change over time.

> **Important Note**
>
> The free Postman account has limits on how many requests you can share. If your team is doing a lot of contract tests and needs to share a lot of requests in this way, you might need to upgrade to a paid plan.

Contract testing is a powerful concept when put into practice correctly. This chapter should have given you a good foundation of how to do that, but don't forget that the most important thing is good communication. One of the main benefits of contract testing is that it makes it obvious when those conversations need to happen. When a contract test fails and needs to be updated, be sure to engage all stakeholders in a conversation about it. Software development is a very collaborative process and the real power of contract tests comes in its ability to foster that collaboration.

Summary

In this chapter, we did a deep dive into contract testing. You learned about what a contract is and how you can use it. You then learned about the two different approaches to contract testing, where it can either be consumer-driven or provider-driven. In addition to coming to a thorough understanding of the theory of contract testing, you learned how to use Postman to set up these kinds of tests. You also learned how to create a collection designed for contract testing.

I also showed you how to think about the tests that you add to a contract testing request and how to set up and use the Postman Interceptor, which lets you figure out which requests and inputs it makes sense to include in a contract test suite. I also showed you how to share contract tests in Postman so that they can be run and fixed in ways that embrace the usefulness of this testing technique.

With this under your belt, in the next chapter, we are going to put everything you have learned together into one big project that will help you put your Postman skills into practice in the real world!

14
Design and Create an API

A few times in this book, I've told you that I think it is important for you to not just read this material, but to actually try it out. I've tried to show you examples that you can follow along with and given you challenges along the way to try out. I want to end this book with a large-scale, hands-on challenge. This challenge will pull together concepts from this entire book, so if you have been following along the entire time, you should have everything you need to be successful with it.

I know, however, that not everyone reads a book linearly from start to finish, and even for those of us that do, we may read it over the course of a few weeks, or perhaps even months, and so forget some of the stuff that we've learned along the way. I will be sure to include references to other chapters in this book that you can refer to along the way as we do this. Go back and re-read them whenever necessary.

I'm going to lay this chapter out as a series of challenges that you can do. I will show solutions along the way and will also have a full end-to-end solution showing my work available on GitHub, but I would strongly encourage you to try and solve this on your own as much as possible. The best learning comes from doing. Don't just read my solution. Try these things out for yourself.

This challenge will involve going through the entire API creation life cycle from start to finish. We will need to design the API and create a specification to encode that design. We will also need to create the API and implement all the organization, tests, and documentation for it in Postman. We will then use that information to help us create a very simple version of the API. The final step will be to share what you have done so that you can show the world what you have learned!

Some of the material that you will see in this chapter is material that you have already covered in this book. This chapter will help to cement it all in your mind so that it is available when you need it. We will cover the following topics in this chapter:

- Designing an API

- Setting up the API in Postman

- Creating tests and documentation for the API

- Sharing what you have done

By the end of this chapter, you will be able to design an API, create an open API specification, set up an API in Postman, create mock servers in Postman, create tests in Postman, add documentation to API and collections, and share your progress with others.

Working through this chapter will give you a broad overview of a variety of concepts in this book and can serve as a self-assessment. I will help you ensure that you have indeed learned the concepts in this book and are able to put them into practice and use them on your own. I have been able to walk with you throughout this book, but as it comes to an end, I want to make sure that you are ready to head out and do your own API testing!

Technical requirements

The code used in this chapter can be found at `https://github.com/ PacktPublishing/API-Testing-and-Development-with-Postman/tree/ master/Chapter14`.

Designing an API

Not everyone starts with the API design, but I think it is the most logical place to start. You could dive right into making the API and let the design emerge organically. Some would argue that this is a more agile approach, but I think that there is some amount of planning required even in the most agile of organizations. I want you to start this challenge by thinking about the API design. Of course, to do that, you are going to need some information on what exactly we are designing!

In order to better understand what we are doing in this chapter, let's look at the application we are going to design an API for.

Setting up the challenge

I have worked through a few examples earlier in this book using an imaginary to-do list application, but for this challenge, we are going to try something a bit more complicated. We are going to design, test, document, and create a simple e-commerce store.

The store will have a list of items displayed on a web page. Customers should be able to filter the results based on categories (for example, men's clothes or women's clothes). The site will also need cart functionality so that items can be added to a cart (and removed from it). Of course, it will also need checkout functionality so that customers can purchase items from the cart, and lastly, it will also need a way for users to view their order history.

There is a lot to this application. Some of the functionality will be related to other objects, and so you will need to consider all the different endpoints and how they all fit together. In *Chapter 11, Designing an API Specification*, we dove right into creating the API specification. That chapter was looking at an API that was much simpler than this one is going to be. With the e-commerce API we are considering in this chapter, we could go right to making the specification, but with a more complex API like this, I want to break down the design process even more than that.

Instead of starting with the specification, I want to start with the even more basic design principles that I covered in *Chapter 2, Principles of API Design*. You may want to start with a review of the material in that chapter, where I discussed some of the principles and practices that will work well for designing an API. In that chapter, I outlined a three-step process for the design phase:

1. Start with the purpose.

2. Create usable APIs.

3. Document the design.

In this challenge, we will gloss over the first step. In a real-life scenario, it would be very important, and you would want to do research with various stakeholders to understand what the user needs were for the API. However, we can't really do that when working through a challenge in a book, so for now you can just assume the purpose is for the API to provide data that can be used to create a web page for selling items.

The second step in the process is very important, though. The first challenge I will give you in this chapter will be to design a usable API.

Challenge – Design a usable API

The first challenge I want you to work through is to design a usable API. This means that you will need to figure out things such as what endpoints it should provide so that it can meet its intended purpose and how the different endpoints relate to each other. I want you to put together a diagram or drawing that shows the various endpoints. The diagram should include all the following information:

- A list of the endpoints you will need
- Information about how various endpoints will relate to each other
- Information about parameters (including query parameters) that you might need
- A list of methods that each endpoint will need to support
- Explanations of the kinds of data that each endpoint will provide

You can think of this step in the design process as creating a lot of data that you will use in a specification, but with less demanding rigor around how it is defined. You don't need to follow any particular structure or syntax when creating this, but you will be working through a lot of the same kind of information that you will later put into a specification file.

One thing to keep in mind while doing this is that the design process will be a little bit messy. As you figure out different endpoints and how they relate to each other, you will find that you need to modify or change things that you've already done. This is part of the reason I don't want you to put it into a specification file yet. First, get a good idea of what the API needs to look like before doing that. It can be a bit tedious to update specification files when you need to make changes, so it's nice to have a good idea of what you are going to do before you start encoding it into a formal specification.

Try this challenge out. Spend some time on it. I would suggest that you give yourself 30-40 minutes to think this through this part of the challenge. Give yourself time to figure out exactly what you need. I will show you how I approached this, but make sure to try it out on your own first.

Solution – Design a usable API

This is a big design challenge with a lot of moving pieces. When I was thinking this through for myself, I actually did a lot of sketching things on paper first while I tried to figure out these details. The API design that I will show here is just an example. I don't work in e-commerce and so it probably isn't even that great of an example.

In real-world scenarios, there might be things I'm not considering that those who work with APIs like this all the time would notice and consider. The point isn't for you (or me) to have a perfectly designed API; it is to spend some time thinking through how you would design an API. I can tell you different considerations, but when you actually work through something like this on your own, you'll end up noticing a lot of things that I wouldn't be able to teach you explicitly.

Instead of just showing you the end result of what I did, I'll walk you through some of the steps that I took to get there.

Defining the actions

I started with thinking about what actions users would need to perform on the page. Based on the description I shared previously and my experience with purchasing products online, I came up with the following list of actions:

- Get a list of products.

- Get a list of products that is filtered based on a specified category.

- Add a product to the cart.

- View the products in the cart.

- Remove items from the cart

- Pay for the products in the cart.

- View a purchase history.

While creating this list, I thought of some other things that many e-commerce sites have. For example, most sites will let you search the product list. Most sites will also let you modify the quantity of an item in your cart. Those things aren't in the requirements, so I won't include them, but if I was working with a product team on these, I would bring them up as topics to talk about. It probably does make sense to leave them out as part of making the smallest possible viable product, but you would want to make sure that decision was being made deliberately.

There are a couple of other things that came to my mind as well, while I was working through this list. In the first place, there is the question of the categories. In order for users to filter the product list by a category, they are going to need a list of categories that they can choose from. This means that the UI will need to display that list somehow, and so we have another action that our API needs to do where it gets a list of available categories. This highlights an important point in API design. It is great to think of end users when creating it, but don't forget that sometimes the user interface itself is one of your end users.

Another consideration that came to my mind was how to pay for the products. We would need to get a credit card or some other type of payment information from the user and at this point, we don't have a way for them to input that information. We don't need to add that to the API, though. We could just send the users to an external payment processing system such as PayPal or Stripe. This is probably a good design choice for a small e-commerce site, but in real life, this is again a decision that should be noted and discussed with the team.

I started the design process by thinking through the actions, because the whole point of having a website is to allow people to do something, and so I started with the verbs. Now I want to think about the objects users would be doing something with.

Defining the endpoints

I have defined the actions that I think I'll need, but what kind of information is needed for the various actions? I'm going to start thinking about which endpoints I want this API to have. The first thing I need is some endpoints to represent the products:

- I want a `/products` endpoint that will give a full list of the products.
- I also want a `/products/{{productId}}` endpoint that will give the information about any one product item in the catalog.

I need an endpoint that can be used to add a specified product to a cart. I thought of a couple of options for this. I could make one called `/cart/{{cartId}}/{{productId}}`, but that feels a little bit funny to me, the reason being that I would be modifying the cart and so I would want to do a `POST` or `PUT` call. If I include `productId` in the endpoint URL, I would not need to specify a body for the request. This will technically work for a `POST` or `PUT` request, but I really don't like that design pattern, so I will try to avoid it in this case. Instead, I will just add an endpoint called `/cart/{{cartId}}` that can be used to add items to the cart. I also need an endpoint to remove items from the cart, but in that case, I don't need to worry about sending anybody data since I will want to use the `DELETE` method for it. So, after thinking it through, I decide to add the following endpoints to support the cart workflows:

- `/cart/{{cartId}}` for adding items to the cart. This can also be used to view all items in the cart.
- `/cart/{{cartId}}/{{productId}}` for removing items from the cart.

I still have a couple of miscellaneous items that I need to be able to support. I need to support payments, as well as login, history, and viewing by categories. I decide to define the following endpoints to support those needs:

- For the payment step, I won't design an endpoint but will instead plan on sending users to a third-party API that will do the payment processing for me.

- I will also want a `/purchaceHistory/{{userId}}` endpoint where I can view the purchase history of the specified user.

- In order to get the different categories, I will also want an endpoint called `/ categories` that gives a list of available categories.

Each of these endpoints is going to have a different schema and support different methods. I won't define them in detail at this point, but I do want to flesh out a couple of other details, including the parameters and data that the endpoint will need, so we will do that next.

Defining the input schema

At this point, I have a pretty good idea of what most of the endpoints are going to do, but still want to flesh out in a little more detail what the inputs will look like. I won't define the schema or responses at this point but will instead focus on the methods and inputs that I want each endpoint to support. They are as follows:

- `/products` will support the `GET` method and will also need to include support for a query parameter so that users can filter down the results to the categories they are interested in. I will call this parameter `?category`.

- `/products/{{productId}}` will support the `GET` method and will not have any other inputs.

- `/cart/{{cartId}}` will support the `POST` method and the body of it will need to include information about the product that is going to be added to the cart. It will also support the `GET` endpoint and return a list of the items in the cart.

- `/cart/{{cartId}}/{{productId}}` will support the `DELETE` method to remove the specified product from the cart.

- `/purchaseHistory/{{userId}}` will support the `GET` method, which will return a list of purchases that the user has made.

- `/categories` will support a `GET` call and will return a list of the available categories.

There are some relationships between these various endpoints. For example, the `products` endpoint will need to know category information when sending filtered requests, and the `cart` endpoints will need to know something about the products when items are added. I won't explicitly show you those relationships here, but when I was working out a design for this on paper, I drew lines between those parts of the API. Knowing that these relationships are there is helpful because we will want to make sure that we use the same data for those different parts of the API. The next thing I will get you to do is to take this information and encode it into an API specification. Those relationships will show you areas where you can create a shared schema for the different endpoints.

Challenge 2 – Create an API specification file

Now it's time to take all this design work and encode it into a specification file. If you want to refresh your memory on API specifications, you can review *Chapter 3, OpenAPI and Other Ways to Document an API*. I also went through an exercise in *Chapter 11, Designing API Specifications*, where I walked you through a similar (albeit simpler) challenge.

For this challenge, I want you to take the design considerations and encode them into an OpenAPI specification file. There are some more advanced OpenAPI features that might be helpful for this. I haven't explicitly covered them in this book, but that is part of the reason I am giving this to you as a challenge right now. You will need to be able to learn things that go beyond what I am able to cover in this book. I want you to be able to take the grounding that you have received while going through this book and apply it to new things that I did not have the space to cover (or that have changed since this book was written). You may need to do some internet searches and reading through the OpenAPI documentation to figure some of this stuff out. I would strongly encourage you to try that before reading ahead to see what I did. The skill of being able to take what you have learned and leverage it to help you with new things that you have not seen before is a hugely important skill. Take the time to practice it now!

Solution 2 – Create an API specification file

I hope that you have tried this out on your own. If you have a specification file already and you want to just skip ahead to see the end solution of what I came up with, you can find the file that I made on GitHub (`https://github.com/PacktPublishing/API-Testing-and-Development-with-Postman/tree/master/Chapter14`). However, if you aren't quite sure about your solution or if you just want to see my thought process in creating this, I have broken down the way I think about this. I haven't covered every step that I took as that would get repetitive, but I have highlighted some of the more complex things that needed to be done along the way.

The first thing I started with was the boilerplate at the top, and then I defined the paths. At this point, the file looked like this:

```
openapi: 3.0.1
info:
  title: Example Ecommerce API
  description: Provides data for an ecommerce page
  version: '1.0'
servers:
  - url: http://localhost:5000/ecommerce/api/v1
paths:
  /products:
  /products/{{productId}}:
  /cart/{{cartId}}:
  /cart/{{cartId}}/{{productId}}:
  /purchasehistory/{{userId}}:
  /categories:
```

I then filled out the data for each of the endpoints based on the design decisions that I made there. The /products endpoint needed a query parameter. A query parameter can be described like this:

```
parameters:
  - in: query
    name: category
    schema:
      type: string
```

In the parameters section for the path, I specified that I wanted an input parameter and that this parameter was a query parameter. I also specified the name and then made a reference to the schema for it. However, before creating the schema, I remembered that in the design process I had identified a dependency between this parameter and the /categories endpoint. I want to explicitly reference this link between the two endpoints, and I can do that with the links feature in OpenAPI.

This is a new feature in **OpenAPI 3** and it can be difficult to understand. In fact, the complexity and length of the documentation for this feature, which you can read here, https://swagger.io/docs/specification/links/, shows just how challenging this feature can be. I'll work through this example in a bit of detail so that you will be able to understand and use this in the future.

The starting place for using the `links` object is in the response of the endpoint that will provide the data. In our case, we are going to be able to get the list of categories from the `/categories` endpoint, and so that is also where we will need to define the `links` object. I will first fill out some of the basic items for the `/categories` endpoint, and in the `200` response section, I will add a links section at the same level as the `content` section. It should look something like this:

```
/categories:
    get:
        summary: gets a list of available categories
        responses:
            '200':
                description: got a list of categories
                content:
                    application/json:
                        schema:
                            $ref: '/#components/schemas/categories'
            links:
```

Now I can start filling in the `links` section. The first thing to add is a name for this link. You are not required to give this any particular name, so I will choose to name it `ListOfCategories`, as shown here:

```
            links:
                ListOfCategories:
```

The next thing that needs to be specified is where the responses link to. In other words, what request or endpoint is going to use the data that this response gives? In this case, we know that we want to use the list of categories as the list of possible inputs to the category parameter in our `/products` endpoint. There are two different ways we can reference that endpoint. We can either use `operationRef` or `operationId`. With `operationRef`, you can specify the path to the request that you want the data to be linked to. In our case, this would look like this: `operationRef: '#paths/~1products/get'`. However, I will instead use `operationId` since using it is simpler and less error prone. In order to use it, I must first define it on the `/products GET` request, which I can do right under `summary` like this:

```
paths:
    /products:
        get:
```

```
summary: gets the list of products
operationId: GetListOfProducts
```

`operationId` is an optional unique string that you can use to identify an operation in the description file. In this case, I have decided to name the identifier for this operation `GetListOfProducts`, and now I can simply reference that identifier in my link like this:

```
links:
    ListOfCategories:
        operationId: GetListOfProducts
```

Now that I have specified what operation this response is linked to, I still need to specify what data in the response is linked and also what part of the /products request it is linked to. In our case, I need to pass the values of the /categories response body to the category query parameter of the /products request. I can specify this with the parameters keyword under which I can specify key/value pairs where the key is the name of the parameter that is receiving the data and the value is the value that is being sent. In our example, that would look like this:

```
links:
    ListOfCategories:
        operationId: GetListOfProducts
        parameters:
            category: '$response.body'
```

The category key points back to the category parameter in the /products endpoint and the '$response.body' value is a **runtime expression** that will return the body of the /categories response. There are a number of different runtime expressions that you can create to give you the values you want, and you can see the full syntax that is available for them in the documentation here: https://swagger.io/docs/specification/links/.

Now that we have finished filling out the link between these two endpoints, we can fill out the schema for them. This is pretty much the same as in other examples that I've done in this book, so I'm not going to walk through it in detail this time. I'll share a couple of examples here, but if you want to see the rest, you can look at the example file on GitHub to see the full solution.

One example that's worth looking at is the `POST` response of the `/cart/{{cartId}}` endpoint:

```
post:
    summary: add an item to the cartId
    responses:
      '201':
        description: add the specified item to the cart
    requestBody:
      required: true
      content:
        application/json:
          schema:
            $ref: '#/components/schemas/product'
```

As you can see, this one is simple to make since you can directly reference the body as having the same schema as the product. This is an example of how you can use references to share data between different parts of the API. When we were designing it, we realized that there was a relationship between the different parts of the API, and the shared schema is a way that we can enforce that relationship and ensure that the different endpoints are all using the data in the same way.

Setting up the API in Postman

As you can probably anticipate, the next thing I want you to do is to set this API up in Postman. Think of this as a review of the different things that you have learned about setting up APIs with Postman. I think that the best way to check whether you really know something isn't with a test or a quiz, but rather by getting you to do it. In this section, I will once again give you a challenge that I want you to work through on your own and then show you how I went about solving it.

Challenge – Add an API and mock server in Postman

For this challenge, I want you to take the specification file that you've made and import it into Postman. I want you to then set up an environment and a mock server for this API.

This challenge should be straightforward, but if you need to review how it should be done, you can look at *Chapter 12, Creating and Using a Mock Server in Postman*, to see how to do this. I will, of course, also show the solution in the next section, but as always, you will learn the most if you work through this on your own first.

Solution – Add an API and mock server in Postman

The first thing to do here is, of course, to import the specification file. I did this by clicking on the **New** button and then choosing the API option as shown in the following figure:

Figure 14.1 – Adding an API

I then named the API eCommerce and set the version to 1.0.0, and then, under the **Import API schema (optional)** section, I used the **Select File** button to browse to and select the API definition file that I had created earlier. I clicked on **Create API** and Postman made the API for me.

After the API was made, the first thing I did was to check that everything was working OK. I did that with the following steps:

1. I went to the **APIs** tab on the navigation panel on the left and selected the **eCommerce** API that I had just created.

2. I then clicked on the **Define** tab and checked that the specification did not have any syntax errors in it. Postman shows you this by showing a green checkmark and the words **Schema validated** at the bottom of the schema view:

```
35    /cart/{{cartId}}:
36      get:
37        summary: tells you what items are in y
38        responses:
39          '200':
```
✓ Schema validated

Figure 14.2 – Schema validated option

In my case, there were no errors, but if there were, I would fix them at that point.

The next thing I decided to do was to create an environment. It is nice to have an environment to use with mock servers, but the mock server setup wizard does not allow you to create environments directly from it. You need to create an environment ahead of time as it is much easier to associate a mock server with an environment when creating the server than it is to do so after the server has been created.

I added the environment to the server with the following steps:

1. I clicked on the **New** button and selected the **Environment** option.
2. I named the environment `My eCommerce Env`.
3. At this point, I just wanted to have an environment available. I will add variables into it later, so for now, I closed the **Manage Environments** tab and went back to the **eCommerce** API.
4. I navigated to the **Develop** tab and clicked on the **Add Environment** link as shown in the following figure:

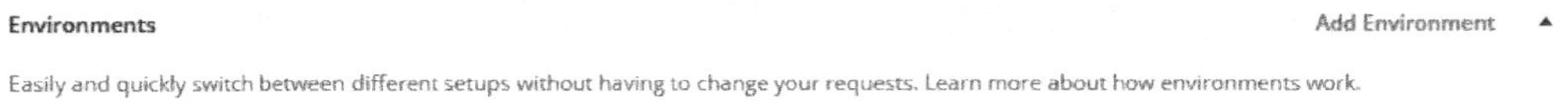
Environments
Add Environment
Easily and quickly switch between different setups without having to change your requests. Learn more about how environments work.

Figure 14.3 – Add Environment

5. On the resulting popup, I selected **My eCommerce Env** from the **Select an Environment** dropdown and then clicked on **Add Environment** to associate that environment with the API.

Now that I had an environment set up and associated with the API, I decided to create a collection that I could use with the mock server. I did that with the following steps:

1. I clicked on the **Generate Collection** button as shown in the following figure:

Watch
0
Reports
Share
Generate Collection

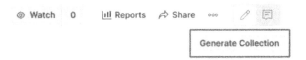

Figure 14.4 – Generate Collection

2. I named the collection eCommerce Mock Collection and selected the **API Mocking** option:

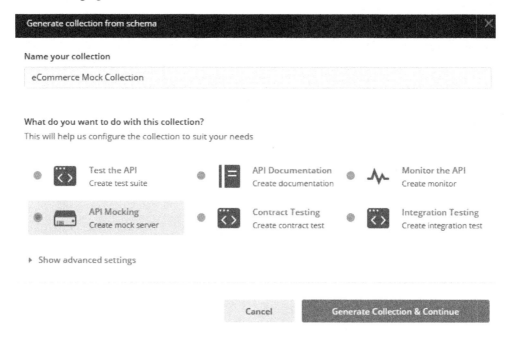

Figure 14.5 – Adding a mock collection

3. I then clicked on the **Generate Collection and Continue** button.

4. I named the mock server eCommerce Mock Server and chose **My eCommerce Env** from the **Use an environment (optional)** dropdown.

5. I then clicked on **Create Mock Server** to create a mock server based on the collection.

6. I clicked on the mock server URL to open it up in a new request.

7. I then added /products to the end of the URL in the request and hit **Send** to test things out.

I got back a response that had a list with a couple of product objects in it, so everything seemed to be working. There was one more thing I wanted to verify, though, so I returned to the eCommerce API and, on the **Develop** tab, clicked the **Click to validate** button beside **ecommerce Mock Server**:

Figure 14.6 – Click to validate button

Once the validation was completed, I clicked on the **Review Issues** button. This opened a tab where Postman highlighted some issues for me. For example, one of the highlighted issues looked like this:

▼ **GET gets the information about the product with the specified productId**

Request doesn't match schema when validated against **GET /products/{{productId}}**

▼ 🔲 GOT BACK PRODUCT INFO

RESPONSE BODY

Response body doesn't match schema:

```
1    1  {
2       -      "productId": "<integer>",
3       -      "description": "<string>",
4       -      "price": "<number>",
5       -      "imageLink": "<uri>"
      2  +  "productId": 10,
      3  +  "description": "<string>",
      4  +  "price": 12.55,
      5  +  "imageLink": "https://www.alink.com"
6    6  }
```

Figure 14.7 – Schema validation issues

This issue is being highlighted because when Postman is doing the schema validation, it is using the example in the schema and comparing that to the example defined in the collection. When it created the collection example, it created the response for it in a generic way. If you look at the request in the collection called *gets the information about the product with the specified productId* and open up the example for it (by clicking on it in the navigation tree as shown in the following figure), you will see that the example is set to return the values shown in red in the preceding figure:

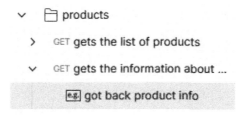

Figure 14.8 – View request example

You can update the example here in Postman, but it is quicker and less error prone to let Postman take care of it for you, and so I went back to the **Review Issues** tab. If you have already closed it, you can easily get back to it by going to the **Develop** tab of the API, clicking on the **Issues found** button beside the mock server, and then selecting the **Review Issues** button as shown in the following figure:

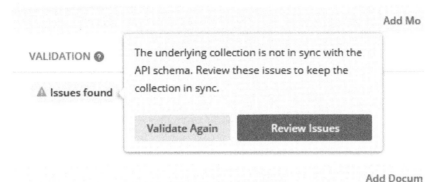

Figure 14.9 – Review Issues

Once you are back on the page for reviewing issues, you can choose the **Make this change to the request for the requests** option that you want to update. In my case, all of the highlighted issues were this same kind of issue where the examples in the specification were not the same as the examples in Postman, and so the Postman examples needed to be updated. Since that was the case, I could choose the **Select all changes** option at the bottom of the page and then click on the **Confirm Changes to Collection** button to update all the requests:

However, I think it is a good idea to review changes more carefully, and so I looked through the list of changes and checked each one to see whether it made sense. If it did, I selected the **Make this change to the request** option beside that change:

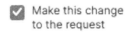

Figure 14.10 – Making request changes

This ended up being really helpful for me, because it turned out that I had made a small mistake in my API definition file. In the schema definition for the cart data, I had said that it was an array of product items. Take a look at this schema, though, and see whether you notice anything wrong:

```
cart:
    type: array
```

```
       items:
          $ref: '#/components/schemas/products'
```

Did you notice it? I missed it too, until I was reviewing the updates. The reference should be to the `product` schema and not the `products` (with an s) schema. What alerted me to this was that the examples that Postman was trying to update were made up of a list of lists instead of a list of objects:

```
+ [
+    {
+       "productId": 10,
+       "description": "<string>",
+       "price": 12.55,
+       "imageLink": "https://www.alink.com"
+    },
+    {
+       "productId": 10,
+       "description": "<string>",
+       "price": 12.55,
+       "imageLink": "https://www.alink.com"
+    }
+  ],
+  [
+    {
+       "productId": 10,
+       "description": "<string>",
+       "price": 12.55,
+       "imageLink": "https://www.alink.com"
+    },
+    {
+       "productId": 10,
+       "description": "<string>",
+       "price": 12.55,
+       "imageLink": "https://www.alink.com"
+    }
+  ]
]
```

Figure 14.11 – List of lists

As you can see in the preceding figure, there is a list (square brackets represent lists) that is made up of a series of lists, which then have the `product` objects inside. I did not intend for that to be the case. I wanted just a list of `product` objects. However, since I had both a `product` and a `products` schema, it was valid to reference the `products` one even though it was not the one I wanted.

I think there are a couple of important lessons to learn from this. In the first place, an API definition file is not a magic bullet. They are helpful, and there are a lot of ways to validate that they are correct, but at the end of the day, you can still make mistakes with them. That leads to the second observation, which is that you should be careful to check through your work. Although Postman has the **Select all changes** option on this page, it is a good idea to be cautious of using it. Check your work.

In this case, the fix was easy. All I had to do was go through the following steps:

1. Go back to the Postman app and in the **Define** tab of the API, update the schema reference to use `product` instead of `products` and save it.

2. Go to the **Develop** tab and click on the **Issues found** button, and this time choose the **Validate Again** option.

3. Click on **Issues found** again and click the **Review Issues** button.

4. Review the issues, choosing the **Make this change to the request** option for each request that it makes sense to update.

   Note that this time when I got to the `/cart/{{cartId}}` request, the suggestion was what I would have expected:

```
+  {
+    "productId": 10,
+    "description": "A Shirt",
+    "price": 12.55,
+    "imageLink": "https://www.alink.com"
+  },
+  {
+    "productId": 10,
+    "description": "A Shirt",
+    "price": 12.55,
+    "imageLink": "https://www.alink.com"
+  }
   ]
```

Figure 14.12 – Correct example

5. Once all the requests are selected, click on **Confirm Changes to Collection** and close the tab.

I then did a couple of quick checks to make sure everything had updated correctly. On the **Develop** tab, I checked that the mock server validation was OK. Postman had nicely updated it for me with a green checkmark to let me know that everything was in order. I then went back to a couple of the examples for a few of the requests and checked that they had the updated values in place. Everything looked good, so there was just one last thing I wanted to check before considering this to be done. I wanted to make sure that I could make calls to the mock server. I went through the following steps in order to check that:

1. I went back to the API **Develop** tab once again and hovered my mouse over **eCommerce Mock Server** and clicked on the **Copy URL** button:

Figure 14.13 – Copy URL

2. I then clicked on the + button beside the currently open request tabs at the top of the app:

Figure 14.14 – Adding a new request

3. I then pasted the mock server URL in the **request URL** field.

4. I then added /products to the end of the request URL and clicked on **Send**.

Everything worked as expected and I successfully created a mock server. Now that we have a mock server in place, we can start adding additional things such as tests and documentation to the API. We will look at that in the next section.

Creating tests and documentation for the API

Now that you have the basic structure of the API in place, the next challenge I want you to do is to set up some tests and documentation in Postman. As with all of these challenges, consider this to be a review of the things that you learned in this book and so try to work through this on your own. You can review the materials in *Chapter 6, Creating Test Validation Scripts*, to see ways to set up tests. You can also look through some sections of *Chapter 2, Principles of API Design*, to review how to document an API within Postman.

Challenge – Add tests to the API

For this challenge, I want you to add some tests to your API. Add some functional tests and some contract tests. You could spend a lot of time doing this, but don't go into excessive detail. Try to create a contract test collection and a test suite for your functional tests. Although you don't need to add a complete suite of tests, make sure to still add a few tests so that you can practice adding test validation scripts. Working through this might take you a half-hour to an hour or so.

Solution – Add tests to the API

While working through this challenge, I started on the **Test** tab of the API and created a test suite with the following steps:

1. I added a test suite by clicking on the **Add Test Suite** button and choosing the **Create new test suite** option.

2. I named the test suite eCommerce Functional Tests and clicked on **Create Test Suite** to create the collection.

Once I had this collection, I could start creating tests in it. I went over to the **Collections** tab on the navigation pane and went to the functional tests collection. I chose the request that gets the list of products. At this point, I want to add a test to this request, but before I do that, I need to set it up so that I can get data for it. Postman has automatically created a baseUrl variable that references the server URL that I specified in the API definition. However, I haven't yet created this API, so that server isn't ready for calls yet. I can, though, tell it to use the mock server instead, with the following steps:

1. Go to the **Develop** tab of **eCommerce API**.

2. Mouse over **eCommerce Mock Server** and click on the **Copy URL** button.

3. Go to the **eCommerce Functional Tests** collection and choose **Edit** from the **view more actions** menu for that collection.

4. On the **Variables** tab, replace the current value of the baseUrl variable with the copied mock server link.

5. Click the **Save** button to save the changes.

With that set up, I can once again go to the request that gets the list of products, and now I can send that request and get back the data from my mock server. I have some data, but in order to create functional tests, I will need a little bit more. For the /products endpoint, I want to be able to check some different categories, so I will create a couple of examples. I can create an example by using the following steps:

1. Modifications to mock responses need to be done in the collection that the mock server is generating its data from. In this setup, I have that in **eCommerce Mock Collection**, so I need to navigate to the collection and then click on the request that gets the list of products.

2. I then click on the **View more actions** menu and choose the **Add example** option:

Figure 14.15 – Add example

3. I will name this first example get list of men's clothes.

4. I'll set **Status** as 200 OK.

5. I will set the example response to have a list of product items, each of which has a **category** value set to "Men's Clothes".

6. I also need to set the response header to have a Content-Type value of application/json, which I can do on the **Headers** tab of the example response:

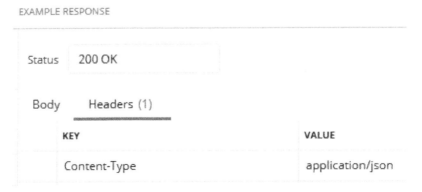

Figure 14.16 – Setting the example response header

7. One other thing that I need to set is the query parameter. I want this example to be returned when the **category** query is set to "Men's Clothes", so in the **Query Params** section, I set the value of **category** to "Men's Clothes":

Figure 14.17 – Setting the category value

8. I then click on **Save** to apply all the changes

Now that I have this example set up, I can try it out in the **eCommerce Functional Tests** collection. I go to the **gets the list of products** request and set the **category** parameter to have a value of "Men's Clothes" and click **Send** to verify that I get back the example I just made. I also try removing the category query from the endpoint so that I can see what I will get back without it, and I notice that I get back the data from the example I just made. I want it to give me back the data from the other example, so need to make some slight modifications using the following steps:

1. I once again open up **eCommerce Mock Collection** and go to the example in the **gets the list of products** request that is called **got back the list of products**.

2. I uncheck the box beside the category query parameter to remove it from the request URL definition before saving the example.

Now, if I return to the functional tests and send the request without a query parameter, I get back the data from the example I expect.

With this additional data set up, I can start to set up some tests. I want to create a test that uses the query parameter, and so I make sure I have it enabled. I then go to the **Tests** tab for the request. I want to check that all the items in the list have the same category as the category specified in the query. In this case, I decide to just hardcode the value, and so I add the following test to the request:

```
pm.test("Check that men's clothes category filter gives back
the correct products", function () {
    var jsonData = pm.response.json();
    var i;
    for (i in jsonData) {
```

```
        pm.expect(jsonData[i].category).
            to.eql("Men's Clothes");
    }
});
```

This test will check that each product item in the list has the correct category. Of course, at this point, we are using data from the mock server so we know this is correct, but once we have a live API to test against, we can modify the `baseUrl` variable to point to the live API and verify that its behavior is correct. We could have set up this test without a mock server, but it is nice to be able to have some real data to look at when creating tests. I could add many more functional tests to the request, but I will leave that as an exercise for you. At this point, I want to move on to looking at adding some documentation.

Documenting an API in Postman is done at the collection and request level, so I will document the `eCommerce Functional Tests` folder. I will first add some documentation to the collection itself with the following steps:

1. Click on the collection in the navigation panel.

2. Click on the **Documentation** icon on the right-hand side, as shown in the following figure:

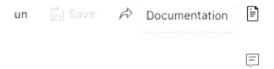

Figure 14.18 – Documentation

3. Click on the **edit** icon on the flyout and enter the documentation that you want:

Figure 14.19 – Editing the documentation

There is some documentation automatically put in there based on the summary that was specified in the specification file, but I add in a little more detail:

```
Provides data for an eCommerce site.
This site is for demonstration purposes only and should not be
used in production.
### Owner
Please contact Dave Westerveld with any questions or concerns
```

You'll notice that I put several # tags before the word **Owner**. Since this is written in Markdown, that will turn the word **Owner** into a title. After you click **Save**, it will look something like this (notice how the word **OWNER** is rendered as a title):

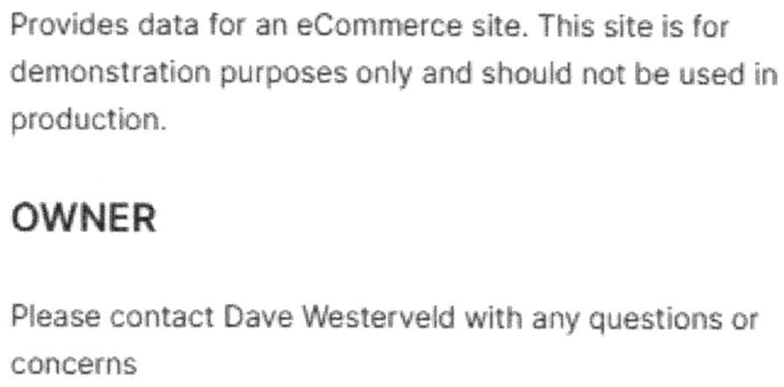

Provides data for an eCommerce site. This site is for demonstration purposes only and should not be used in production.

OWNER

Please contact Dave Westerveld with any questions or concerns

Figure 14.20 – Rendered documentation

Once I've made some changes to the collection documentation, I click on **Save** to apply them and then go to the individual requests and add documentation to them as well. For example, I add the following documentation to the /products request:

```
This request will give back a list of all the products in the
system. If you specify the category query parameter, it will
only return those products that have the given category.
```

In addition, Postman will automatically add examples to the documentation based on the examples that you have saved for the request. This is another reason why it is important to check through your examples and make sure they are accurate and make sense. Often, that is the first thing developers using your API are going to look at when they are trying to understand how the API works.

Sharing what you have done

As we get to the end of this book, I want to make sure that you have the opportunity to showcase what you have learned. You have your own set of reasons for working through this book and trying to understand API testing, but I suspect that you probably want to be able to show others what you have done and learned. Perhaps you want to share your learning with other teammates and colleagues, or perhaps you want to be able to show interviewers that you have been able to acquire skills related to API testing and Postman. Whatever the reason for it, I want you to be able to show others what you have done and learned.

You can use the **Share API** option on the **show more actions** menu beside your API to create a shareable API:

Figure 14.21 – Share API

When you do this, you can select a workspace to share this with. If you share your API with a public workspace, you can let others know where that workspace is so that they can see the work you've done as you have gone through this book. Similarly, you can share collections. You can also, of course, create a GitHub repository and add things such as your OpenAPI definition files to demonstrate what you have done with those. There are a lot of options for sharing what you have done and I would encourage you to look into them. If you have worked through this entire book, or even just this chapter, you have covered a lot of ground related to API testing and you should take a moment to celebrate and share what you have done!

Summary

I wanted this entire chapter to work as a review and summary. Learning new things takes some time and looking at things from a few different angles can help to make the learning stick in the long term. I have taken you through worked examples of many of the concepts that I've covered in this book to help you get a solid understanding of them.

We've covered how to design an API, including how to think about and approach defining the actions and endpoints that an API should have. We also looked at how to think about the kind of inputs that the API might take.

After that, we looked at taking our design thoughts and codifying them into an OpenAPI specification file. In doing this, we went over some material that had already been covered in previous chapters, but we also learned about some additional advanced features of this specification, including things such as how to link together outputs from one part of the API that serve as inputs to other parts of the API.

Once we had a definition file set up, we used it to set up an API in Postman. We also set up a mock server and created examples that the server could use. Along the way, we learned how to validate a schema and how to debug issues that might come up.

The final area we reviewed in this chapter was how to add tests and documentation to an API. While doing this, we also expanded the data in the mock server so that we could test the things we wanted. We reviewed how to use documentation in Postman and also covered ways to share everything that you've learned.

As we come to the end of our API testing journey together, I hope that you have learned a lot along the way. We have come a long way in this book. We started with the basics of what an API is and how to use one. We also learned how to think about API test automation and how to design APIs. We, of course, learned how to do this all in Postman and learned how to use many powerful Postman features, such as data-driven testing and mocking. We covered API authorization and how to create good test validation scripts. We looked at how to run tests in continuous integration build environments and saw how to monitor APIs in production.

Along the way, I have taken you through challenges and examples that have helped you learn and apply these ideas. You really have learned a lot! As you finish this book, I want you to stop and take a moment to reflect on how far you have come. It is a big accomplishment and you should feel confident in your ability to tackle any API testing challenges that come your way.

A learning journey is just that, a journey. Don't let your learning journey end at the end of this book. I have given you a good grounding, and if you have worked through the examples, you have been able to see a lot of the details of how to use Postman, but the more you use it in real-life scenarios, the more you are going to learn. Keep using this tool. Keep reading about API testing. Keep testing and exploring and never stop learning.

Happy testing!

`Packt.com`

Subscribe to our online digital library for full access to over 7,000 books and videos, as well as industry leading tools to help you plan your personal development and advance your career. For more information, please visit our website.

Why subscribe?

- Spend less time learning and more time coding with practical eBooks and Videos from over 4,000 industry professionals

- Improve your learning with Skill Plans built especially for you

- Get a free eBook or video every month

- Fully searchable for easy access to vital information

- Copy and paste, print, and bookmark content

Did you know that Packt offers eBook versions of every book published, with PDF and ePub files available? You can upgrade to the eBook version at `packt.com` and as a print book customer, you are entitled to a discount on the eBook copy. Get in touch with us at `customercare@packtpub.com` for more details.

At `www.packt.com`, you can also read a collection of free technical articles, sign up for a range of free newsletters, and receive exclusive discounts and offers on Packt books and eBooks.

Other Books You May Enjoy

If you enjoyed this book, you may be interested in these other books by Packt:

Enterprise API Management

Luis Augusto Weir

ISBN: 978-1-78728-443-2

- Create API strategies to deliver business value
- Monetize APIs, promoting them through public marketplaces and directories
- Develop API-led architectures, applying best practice architecture patterns
- Choose between REST, GraphQL, and gRPC-style API architectures
- Manage APIs and microservices through the complete life cycle
- Deploy APIs and business products, as well as Target Operating Models
- Lead product-based organizations to embrace DevOps and focus on delivering business capabilities

Building Low-Code Applications with Mendix

Bryan Kenneweg, Imran Kasam, Micah McMullen

ISBN: 978-1-80020-142-2

- Gain a clear understanding of what low-code development is and the factors driving its adoption
- Become familiar with the various features of Mendix for rapid application development
- Discover concrete use cases of Studio Pro
- Build a fully functioning web application that meets your business requirements
- Get to grips with Mendix fundamentals to prepare for the Mendix certification exam
- Understand the key concepts of app development such as data management, APIs, troubleshooting, and debugging

Packt is searching for authors like you

If you're interested in becoming an author for Packt, please visit `authors.packtpub.com` and apply today. We have worked with thousands of developers and tech professionals, just like you, to help them share their insight with the global tech community. You can make a general application, apply for a specific hot topic that we are recruiting an author for, or submit your own idea.

Leave a review - let other readers know what you think

Please share your thoughts on this book with others by leaving a review on the site that you bought it from. If you purchased the book from Amazon, please leave us an honest review on this book's Amazon page. This is vital so that other potential readers can see and use your unbiased opinion to make purchasing decisions, we can understand what our customers think about our products, and our authors can see your feedback on the title that they have worked with Packt to create. It will only take a few minutes of your time, but is valuable to other potential customers, our authors, and Packt. Thank you!

Index

Printed in Great Britain
by Amazon

14829993R00194